Coding with AI

Chris Minnick

Coding with AI For Dummies®

Published by: **John Wiley & Sons, Inc.**, 111 River Street, Hoboken, NJ 07030-5774, www.wiley.com

Copyright © 2024 by John Wiley & Sons, Inc., Hoboken, New Jersey

Published simultaneously in Canada

For general information on our other products and services, please contact our Customer Care Department within the U.S. at 877-762-2974, outside the U.S. at 317-572-3993, or fax 317-572-4002. For technical support, please visit https://hub.wiley.com/community/support/dummies.

Wiley publishes in a variety of print and electronic formats and by print-on-demand. Some material included with standard print versions of this book may not be included in e-books or in print-on-demand. If this book refers to media such as a CD or DVD that is not included in the version you purchased, you may download this material at http://booksupport.wiley.com. For more information about Wiley products, visit www.wiley.com.

Library of Congress Control Number: 2024931771

ISBN: 978-1-394-24913-8 (pbk); 978-1-394-24915-2 (ebk); 978-1-394-24914-5 (ebk)

SKY10074492_050324

Contents at a Glance

Contents at a Glance

Table of Contents

Introduction

I started writing this book almost a year after OpenAI launched ChatGPT. That launch and the subsequent releases of generative AI tools by Microsoft, Google, Facebook, and others have begun to change how we think about creating content. At the same time, we're facing important questions about what the future of work will look like — especially for those of us whose job primarily involves the things that tools such as ChatGPT are pretty good at.

My own feelings about generative AI are mixed. On one hand, I worry that the skills in writing and programming that I've spent more than half my life working on will no longer be useful. On the other hand, I see that AI has the potential to take on some of the most boring and least rewarding work I do, saving me time and effort that I can devote to the more creative parts of writing and programming.

I also worry that when I do write things using old-fashioned methods (aka "I think of them and write them"), people will assume that I used AI. This happened with a book I wrote last year on a relatively current topic. People who didn't bother to read the book commented that "it was probably written by AI." As a result of this experience, I announced that I'd livestream the process of writing my next book. I had no idea at the time that my next book would be about AI. So, here I am, writing a book about coding with AI while live-streaming my writing processes in an attempt to prove to future readers that the book wasn't generated by AI. If you have any doubt that I wrote this book the old-fashioned way, or if you have a few hundred hours to spare, you can see the entire book being written by going to https://bit.ly/codingwithai.

Even though I refuse to use AI to write my books, and I'm generally against other people using AI to write books, I feel differently about using AI tools to generate computer code. The history of computer programming has been about people inventing better tools that make coding easier. When I worked at *Software Development Magazine* in the 1990s, the technical editor was Roger Smith. One day, while we were talking about a new programming tool, Roger told me that he believed that in the future we'd be able to use natural language to write software. I was skeptical. Almost 30 years later, it turns out that Roger was right.

The pace of change in AI is fast. Technologies and tools that are new and interesting this month will be replaced by better ones next month. Because I write about technology and programming, there's always the risk that something I write today will be outdated when the book is released. However, even though AI and AI software development tools will certainly have improved, the techniques I write about here will be just as applicable — unless, of course, AI has made the profession of software developer obsolete and everyone who used to be a software developer now gets paid to hang out on the beach (or whatever your idea of relaxation and fun is).

Whether you embrace this new era of AI-assisted coding or resist it, there's no denying that it's here. In this book, I show you how these tools work and how you can use them to not only make writing code easier and faster but to help you write better code.

I hope you enjoy reading this book and that you find it useful. If you have any questions or comments, please reach out to me at chris@minnick.com.

About This Book

When it comes to coding with generative AI, we're all dummies at this point. Whether you're a new programmer or a veteran, this book will teach you what you need to know to benefit from the new tools that are rapidly becoming available.

I cover these topics:

» Understanding foundational principles of machine learning (ML), deep learning (DL), and generative AI (GenAI)

» Working with AI responsibly, safely, and ethically

» Using some of the latest tools for coding with AI

» Using AI to help with

- Automating monotonous coding tasks

- Learning new skills

- Improving your code

- Testing your code

- Documenting your code

- Maintaining your code

As you go through the book, keep the following in mind:

» You can read the book from beginning to end, but feel free to skip around if you like. If a topic interests you, start there. You can always return to previous chapters, if necessary.

» At some point, you will get stuck, and something you try will not work as intended. Do not fear! There are many resources to help you, including support forums, others on the internet, AI chatbots, and me! You can contact me via email at chris@minnick.com or through my website (https://www.chrisminnick.com). Additionally, you can sign up for my Substack (https://chrisminnick.substack.com) to receive occasional updates from me about AI, programming, and learning.

» Code in the book appears in a monospaced font like this: <h1>Hi there!</h1>.

Some web addresses break across two lines of text. If you're reading this book in print and want to visit one of these web pages, simply key in the web address exactly as it's noted in the text, pretending as though the line break doesn't exist. If you're reading this as an e-book, you have it easy — just click the web address to be taken directly to the web page.

Foolish Assumptions

I do not make many assumptions about you, the reader, but I do make a few.

I assume you have some experience or familiarity with programming in a computer language. It doesn't matter which language you code in, just that you know what programming is and you've done it before. If you're new to computer programming, many excellent books and tutorials are available that can give you the background you need for this book in a few days. I recommend *Coding All-in-One For Dummies*, 2nd Edition (written by me and an awesome team of other coding experts), which contains an introduction to all the languages and techniques you use in this book. In particular, read the chapters about Python and JavaScript.

Most of the examples in this book are JavaScript code, because that's the programming language I know the best. However, this is not a JavaScript-specific book and the techniques and tools I use to help write or improve my JavaScript code work with any language. The code examples are generally simple enough to be understood without a specific knowledge of JavaScript.

I assume you have a computer running a modern web browser. You will do most of the exercises in this book by using web-based resources. Although it may be possible to complete these exercises using a smartphone or tablet, I don't recommend it.

I assume you have access to an internet connection. Because the language models we'll be working with are far too large to install on your computer, an internet connection will be essential to completing the hands-on element.

I assume you can download and install free software to your computer. Oftentimes, the computer you use at work will have restrictions on what can be installed by the user. Using your own computer to develop and run the applications in this book should work without a problem.

Icons Used in This Book

Here are the icons used in the book to flag text that should be given extra attention or can be skipped.

TIP

This icon flags useful information or explains a shortcut to help you understand a concept.

TECHNICAL STUFF

This icon explains technical details about the concept being explained. The details might be informative or interesting but are not essential to your understanding of the concept.

REMEMBER

Try not to forget the material marked with this icon. It signals an important concept or process that you should keep in mind.

WARNING

Watch out! This icon flags common mistakes and problems that can be avoided if you heed the warning.

Beyond the Book

A lot of extra content that you won't find in this book is available at www.dummies.com. Go online to find the following:

» **The source code for the examples in this book:** Go to www.dummies.com/go/codingwithaifd. The source code is organized by chapter. The best way to work with a chapter is to download all the source code for it at one time.

» **The cheat sheet:** Go to www.dummies.com and, in the search field, typing **Coding with AI for Dummies**. You'll find helpful prompting tips for coding with AI, a list of dangers when using AI-generated code, and a tongue-in-cheek look at what AI coding assistants can't do.

» **Updates:** AI is changing rapidly, and I don't expect it to stop doing so after this book is published, so the commands and syntax that work today may not work tomorrow. You can find any updates or corrections by visiting www.dummies.com/go/codingwithaifd or https://github.com/chrisminnick/coding-with-ai.

Where to Go from Here

As you embark on your journey of learning to code with AI, keep an open mind but also a large dose of skepticism and patience. In spite of how impressive the current generation of GenAI tools is (and they're surely much better by the time you read this), we're still in the infancy of this stuff.

If you want to get a basic understanding of AI-assisted coding, go to Chapter 1. If you want to find out more about how these tools work and about machine learning in general, read Chapter 2. If you want to learn about some of the tools that are available today for coding with AI, see Chapters 3 and 4. If you want to get right into experimenting with the combination of coding and AI, skip to Chapter 5.

Congratulations on taking your first step towards AI-assisted coding, and thank you for trusting me as your guide.

1
Techniques and Technologies

IN THIS PART . . .

Discover how AI-enhanced tools can help make you a better and more efficient programmer.

Dig into the fundamental concepts behind machine learning and deep learning.

Explore AI pair programming tools.

Converse with the latest generative models to assist with coding tasks.

Chapter **1**

How Coding Benefits from AI

I f you're a programmer or learning to program, generative artificial intelligence (also known as *GenAI*) can help you be more productive, make fewer mistakes, and learn new skills and languages faster, as you discover in this chapter. In the process, you work with some tools to get a taste of what's available. All the topics in this chapter are described in detail in later chapters.

Although you might be able to use AI to generate working computer programs without knowing how to code, I strongly discourage you from doing this — especially if you plan to deploy anything you generate. Generative AI doesn't know how to program. If you don't know how to code either, there's a good chance that code you create with AI will have serious security problems, functionality problems, or worse.

Banishing Boring Tasks

One of the most basic and useful things you can do with the current crop of generative AI models is to use them to generate the types of code programmers lovingly refer to as boilerplate code.

TECHNICAL STUFF

The term *boilerplate* dates to the 19th century, when steel plates were used as templates for making steam boilers.

Boilerplate code is the stuff that's the same or nearly the same in every file or every project. No one likes to write boilerplate code, but we have to do it because the code we want to write (the fun stuff) won't work without the boilerplate.

Spotting boring tasks

To identify tasks that can be automated with AI, think about the tasks that you do repeatedly in multiple projects. JavaScript developers might select an element in the browser window, such as a button, and attach to it an event listener to do some action when a user interacts with that element. Or they might do something more complex, such as writing the code for a database-driven application that handles creating, reading, updating, and deleting (CRUD) tasks.

For web developers and designers, a simple example of boilerplate code that can be automated is the basic structure of an HTML page. Every valid HTML page starts with a document type declaration followed by an HTML element, and then a head element (including several internal elements, such as the title and meta tags), and then a body element.

Letting AI write the template

You can minimize the work required to generate a simple HTML template in many ways, such as by using a code snippet or searching the web for an example. However, if you want to create a custom boilerplate that includes some structure and gives you a good start on the design of a future website, you could simply ask your AI. For example, I gave ChatGPT the following request:

```
Please generate an HTML template with a style element that
uses flexbox to create a three column layout with a sample
top navigation bar and a footer.
```

And here is the code that ChatGPT generated:

```
<!DOCTYPE html>
<html lang="en">
<head>
    <meta charset="UTF-8">
    <meta name="viewport" content="width=device-width,
          initial-scale=1.0">
```

```
<title>Three Column Layout</title>
<style>
    body {
        margin: 0;
        padding: 0;
        font-family: Arial, sans-serif;
    }

    .container {
        display: flex;
        flex-direction: column;
        min-height: 100vh;
    }

    header {
        background-color: #333;
        color: #fff;
        padding: 10px 0;
        text-align: center;
    }

    nav {
        background-color: #444;
        color: #fff;
        padding: 10px 0;
        text-align: center;
    }

    .main-content {
        flex: 1;
        display: flex;
        justify-content: space-between;
        padding: 20px;
    }

    .sidebar {
        flex-basis: 20%;
        background-color: #f0f0f0;
        padding: 20px;
    }

    .content {
        flex-basis: 60%;
        background-color: #fff;
```

```
            padding: 20px;
        }

        .aside {
            flex-basis: 20%;
            background-color: #f0f0f0;
            padding: 20px;
        }

        footer {
            background-color: #333;
            color: #fff;
            padding: 10px 0;
            text-align: center;
        }
    </style>
</head>
<body>
    <div class="container">
        <header>
            <h1>Top Navigation Bar</h1>
        </header>
        <nav>
            <ul>
                <li><a href="#">Home</a></li>
                <li><a href="#">About</a></li>
                <li><a href="#">Services</a></li>
                <li><a href="#">Contact</a></li>
            </ul>
        </nav>
        <div class="main-content">
            <div class="sidebar">
                <h2>Sidebar</h2>
                <p>This is the sidebar content.</p>
            </div>
            <div class="content">
                <h2>Main Content</h2>
                <p>This is the main content area.</p>
            </div>
            <div class="aside">
                <h2>Aside</h2>
                <p>This is the aside content.</p>
            </div>
        </div>
```

```
        <footer>
            <p>Footer</p>
        </footer>
    </div>
</body>
</html>
```

The resulting HTML generated by my request (also known as a *prompt*) matched fairly well with what I would have done if I'd written it by hand. Figure 1-1 shows the resulting web page when I save the generated HTML markup in a file and open it in a browser without modifying it.

FIGURE 1-1:
A ChatGPT-
generated
HTML template.

ChatGPT

REMEMBER

You can find all the code used in this book, including the HTML template shown in Figure 1-1, at www.dummies.com/go/codingwithaifd.

Crafting CRUD with AI

One of the most common tasks in any computer program is accessing a data source and writing functions for performing operations with the data source. The basic operations you can do with any data source are creating a record, reading a record, updating a record, and deleting a record. The collective name for the code that makes these operations possible is the wonderfully evocative acronym CRUD. Most people don't enjoy writing CRUD.

In this section, you use generative AI to reduce the amount of work it takes to generate some CRUD. To get started with this exercise, you need to have access to an interface for chatting with a generative AI model such as ChatGPT, Google Bard, or Microsoft Bing. If you don't have an account with any of these services yet, follow the instructions in Chapter 4 to sign up for ChatGPT.

Then, once you have a chat window in front of you, start with a short request to the generative model to see what it will do. If the service you're using won't or can't fulfill your request, you won't have wasted much time crafting a detailed prompt. For example, when I asked Bing to generate CRUD, it started to, but then told me to ask something else, as shown in Figure 1-2.

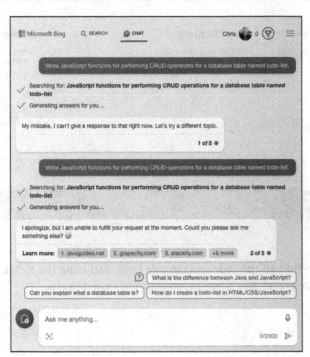

FIGURE 1-2:
Bing refused to
generate CRUD.

Microsoft Corporation

Now determine whether the response shows any promise. If you didn't get a response, try using a different generative AI model.

Here is the beginning of the response I got to my initial prompt ("Write JavaScript functions for performing CRUD operations for a database table named todo-list.") from ChatGPT using the GPT-3.5 model:

```javascript
// Simulated in-memory database for the todo-list
const todoListDB = [];

// Function to Create a new todo item
function createTodoItem(title, description) {
  const newItem = {
    id: todoListDB.length + 1,
    title,
    description,
    completed: false,
  };

  todoListDB.push(newItem);
  return newItem;
}
```

The response is adequate, but because I failed to provide enough information about my desired application, ChatGPT used an array as if it were a database, which is unlikely to be what is needed here.

If you get a promising response to your initial prompt, give the model additional details. For example, my next step would be to tell ChatGPT that this is a Node.js application that will be working with a MongoDB database and that it should use Mongoose.

REMEMBER

The process of refining your instructions to a GenAI model and providing context and examples is called *prompt engineering*. Chapter 4 covers the process of prompt engineering in detail. Figure 1-3 shows my second prompt.

This time, ChatGPT responded with a complete Node.js application that connects to a local database and can perform CRUD operations. Listing 1-1 shows the regenerated code.

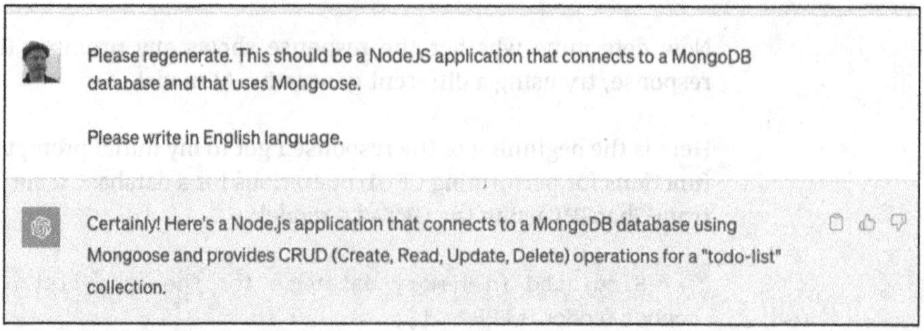

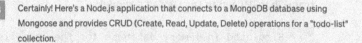

Please regenerate. This should be a NodeJS application that connects to a MongoDB database and that uses Mongoose.

Please write in English language.

Certainly! Here's a Node.js application that connects to a MongoDB database using Mongoose and provides CRUD (Create, Read, Update, Delete) operations for a "todo-list" collection.

FIGURE 1-3:
Adding context to get a better response.

ChatGPT

LISTING 1-1: ### ChatGPT's second attempt

```
const mongoose = require('mongoose');

// Connect to MongoDB
mongoose.connect('mongodb://localhost/todo-list', {
  useNewUrlParser: true,
  useUnifiedTopology: true,
});

// Define a TodoItem schema
const todoItemSchema = new mongoose.Schema({
  title: String,
  description: String,
  completed: Boolean,
});

// Create a TodoItem model
const TodoItem = mongoose.model('TodoItem', todoItemSchema);

// Function to Create a new todo item
async function createTodoItem(title, description) {
  const newItem = new TodoItem({
    title,
    description,
    completed: false,
  });

  try {
    await newItem.save();
    return newItem;
  } catch (error) {
    throw error;
  }
}
```

```
// Function to Read all todo items
async function getAllTodoItems() {
  try {
    const todoItems = await TodoItem.find();
    return todoItems;
  } catch (error) {
    throw error;
  }
}

// Function to Read a specific todo item by ID
async function getTodoItemById(id) {
  try {
    const todoItem = await TodoItem.findById(id);
    return todoItem || null;
  } catch (error) {
    throw error;
  }
}

// Function to Update a todo item by ID
async function updateTodoItem(id, updatedData) {
  try {
    const updatedItem = await TodoItem.findByIdAndUpdate(id,
        updatedData, { new: true });
    return updatedItem;
  } catch (error) {
    throw error;
  }
}

// Function to Delete a todo item by ID
async function deleteTodoItem(id) {
  try {
    const deletedItem = await TodoItem.findByIdAndRemove(id);
    return deletedItem || null;
  } catch (error) {
    throw error;
  }
}
```

This isn't bad at all. I like that ChatGPT (mostly) used the latest JavaScript syntax, properly handled errors that may happen, and wrote good comments. I've seen human-written code that's much worse.

The real test, however, is whether the code runs. After it generated the CRUD functions, ChatGPT provided some examples of how they can be used. These examples are shown in Listing 1-2.

LISTING 1-2: **Examples usage code from ChatGPT**

```
// Example usage:
(async () => {
  try {
    const newItem = await createTodoItem("Buy groceries", "Milk,
        eggs, and bread");
    console.log("Created item:", newItem);

    const allItems = await getAllTodoItems();
    console.log("All items:", allItems);

    const itemToUpdate = await getTodoItemById(newItem._id);
    if (itemToUpdate) {
      const updatedItem = await updateTodoItem(itemToUpdate._id,
          { completed: true });
      console.log("Updated item:", updatedItem);
    }

    const deletedItem = await deleteTodoItem(newItem._id);
    console.log("Deleted item:", deletedItem);

  } catch (error) {
    console.error("Error:", error);
  } finally {
    mongoose.disconnect();
  }
})();
```

If Node.js and MongoDB are installed on your development machine, you can try out this code by copying Listings 1-1 and 1-2 into a file and saving it with the .js extension.

Before you run the application, you need to initialize the directory containing the .js file as a Node package by entering the following in a terminal window:

```
npm init -y
```

Then install Mongoose by entering the following:

```
npm install mongoose
```

Next, run the program by entering **node** followed by the file name, like this:

```
node listing0102.js
```

Figure 1-4 shows what happened when I ran this program.

```
● (base) chrisminnick@chris-mac chapter01 % node listing0103.js
  Created item: {
    title: 'Buy groceries',
    description: 'Milk, eggs, and bread',
    completed: false,
    _id: new ObjectId("650c4885564f597926a10ac0"),
    __v: 0
  }
  All items: [
    {
      _id: new ObjectId("650c4885564f597926a10ac0"),
      title: 'Buy groceries',
      description: 'Milk, eggs, and bread',
      completed: false,
      __v: 0
    }
  ]
  Updated item: {
    _id: new ObjectId("650c4885564f597926a10ac0"),
    title: 'Buy groceries',
    description: 'Milk, eggs, and bread',
```

FIGURE 1-4: Running my Node.js application.

To verify that ChatGPT's code worked, I commented out the code that deletes the created record, ran the Node.js application again, and then started the Mongo shell and looked at the contents of the todo-list collection, as shown in Figure 1-5.

```
test> use todo-list
switched to db todo-list
todo-list> show collections
todoitems
todo-list> db.todoitems.find()
[
  {
    _id: ObjectId("650c49f3acefaa817b939047"),
    title: 'Buy groceries',
    description: 'Milk, eggs, and bread',
    completed: true,
    __v: 0
  }
]
todo-list> █
```

FIGURE 1-5:
Viewing the
collection's
contents in
MongoDB.

Helping with Syntax

A large part of the work involved in computer programming is simply remembering or looking up the rules that define the structure of a programming language, also known as its *syntax*. Each language or code library has its own way of doing things. Once you know the basics of how a programming language works (such as how to create a function, use basic operators, and write loops), you need to know what built-in functions are available in your environment (whether it's a browser or a mobile operating system) and what parameters and types of data they expect to receive. That's a lot to remember, and no programmer I've ever met can remember everything there is to remember about one programming language, much less several programming languages. With the help of GenAI tools, you can have instant access to the collected knowledge of millions of coders.

You may be asking yourself at this point, "But is it ethical for AI to harvest everyone's code like that?" This topic is hotly debated and the subject of at least one lawsuit. I explore legal and ethical issues having to do with GenAI throughout this book.

Stop remembering trivial details

When I teach programming, my students often ask me questions about syntax and application programming interfaces (APIs) rather than how something works. When I get a question about syntax, I answer the question if I can without looking it up; otherwise, I encourage students to "Google it." With time and experience, remembering syntax just starts to happen.

TIP

When writing software, one of the best skills is knowing how and where to look for answers. And most of the time, the best place is through a search engine. Because search engines employ machine learning to determine the best results to show in response to queries, we've been using AI for coding for some time now.

Hinting at code mastery

One of the oldest forms of computer-assisted coding is code completion. Microsoft introduced its implementation of code completion, IntelliSense, in Visual Studio in 1996. These types of tools work by suggesting functions and methods that partially match something you've started typing, as shown in Figure 1-6. Traditional code completion functionality doesn't employ GenAI, and its suggestions can often be frustratingly incorrect. However, if you need help with the syntax or spelling (or don't want to type the full names of functions), code completion is useful.

```
const scoreElement = document.getElementById('score');
                          ⊕ getElementB...       (method) Document.getElementById(elementI...
// Set up event listener⊕ getElementsByClassName
                          ⊕ getElementsByName
// Display the current qu⊕ getElementsByTagName
function displayQuestion⊕ getElementsByTagNameNS
    // Clear the previous⊕ getSelection
    answerButtonsElement.innerHTML = '';
```

FIGURE 1-6: Code completion is often helpful.

Microsoft Corporation

Generative AI takes code completion to the next level by offering suggestions based on its training. When integrated into your IDE, tools such as GitHub's Copilot or Amazon's CodeWhisperer can suggest entire statements or functions, rather than just single function calls.

GenAI models trained on large datasets of code can offer multiple suggestions based on what other programmers have written; libraries, classes, and functions you've imported into the current file; and even other files that are open in your IDE or in your code repository.

Figure 1-7 shows a suggestion from Copilot based on the fact that I named my file validatePhoneNumber.js.

FIGURE 1-7: Copilot's suggested phone number validation function.

```
validatePhoneNumber.js 3, U  ●                                      ⌘ ▢ ...
validatePhoneNumber.js  <  2/3  >  Accept [Tab]  Accept Word [⌘] [→] ...
1    export function validatePhoneNumber(phoneNumber) {
         const re = /^(\+98|0)?9\d{9}$/;
         return re.test(phoneNumber);
     }
```

Microsoft Corporation

WARNING

Unfortunately, in this instance, the suggested function is worse than useless to most people because it returns `true` only when provided with a phone number starting with 98, which is the country code for Iran.

However, more context can coax the model into returning a better response. When I provided a comment describing what I was trying to do, the model returned a much better suggestion, as shown in Figure 1-8. While not perfect and far too wordy, at least this suggestion gets me closer to what I'm looking for.

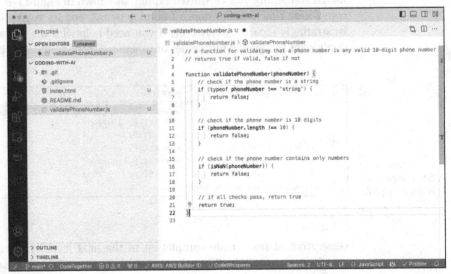

FIGURE 1-8: GenAI models do better when given context.

Microsoft Corporation

In Part 2, you learn much more about how to use GenAI tools to write, format, translate, and optimize your code.

Adapting to new syntax

Like code hint features in IDEs, GenAI can help you learn or remember the syntax for functions or methods. For example, Copilot will give you hints as you type; you can ignore these by continuing to type or accept them by pressing tab.

For example, I have trouble remembering the order of the arguments to pass to the Array.reduce method. Figure 1-9 shows a Copilot hint for starting the method.

FIGURE 1-9: Getting syntax support from Copilot.

```
1   export function calculateTotal(itemsInCart) {
2      return itemsInCart.reduce((total, item) => {
3   }
```

You can also use GenAI chat interfaces to learn about new syntax. However, keep in mind that the model you're using may have been trained on data that predates the existence of the function or method you're seeking help with. For example, GPT-3's training data cutoff date is September 2021, so the model has no knowledge of events or technologies developed after that date. Figure 1-10 shows what happened when I asked GPT-3 about a feature of JavaScript introduced in 2022.

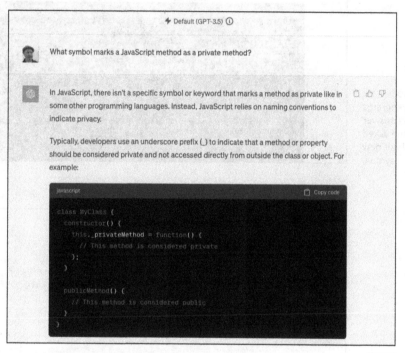

FIGURE 1-10: GPT-3 doesn't know about recent additions to JavaScript.

GPT-4, on the other hand, has a more recent training data cutoff and can also search the web. Figure 1-11 shows ChatGPT's response to the same question but with the model set to GPT-4.

WARNING

Also remember that, in response to a query, a GenAI model may just invent something that sounds plausible but is incorrect. ChatGPT's tendency to make up facts and people is legendary. However, in cases where something is as rule-based as a computer language, it usually gets the facts right. As a rule, have a certain amount of distrust of any AI-generated code. Always verify.

Figure 1-12 shows ChatGPT 3.5's response to my question about a non-existent JavaScript method.

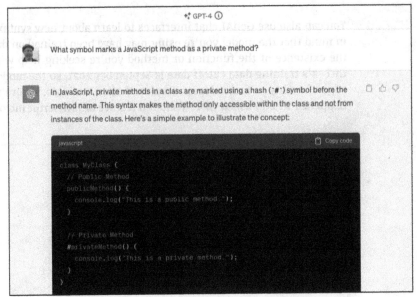

FIGURE 1-11:
GPT-4 generates a correct answer when asked about new syntax.

ChatGPT

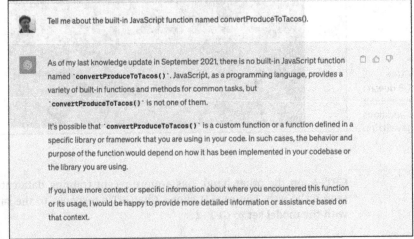

FIGURE 1-12:
ChatGPT is usually correct about programming language syntax basics.

ChatGPT

Linting with AI

Linters are tools that flag programming errors, bugs, and style issues. The technical name for the job that linters do is static code analysis. The *static* part of *static code analysis* refers to the fact that these tools check the code without compiling or running it. Using a linter can help you improve the quality of your code.

Since most GenAI tools are (at the time of this writing) incapable of compiling and running the code you write, anytime you prompt a machine learning model to look for errors or bad style in your code, you're using it as a linter.

Detecting bad code with static code analysis

To use an AI chatbot as a linter, you can prompt the model with your code and ask it what's wrong with it. Since GenAI models have been trained on a large quantity of working code, they're generally pretty good at finding typos, inconsistencies, and code that doesn't look right.

Simply write something like "What's wrong with this code?" and then paste in the code that's not working. Figure 1-13 shows Google Bard's response to my question about a function with several typos and examples of bad coding style.

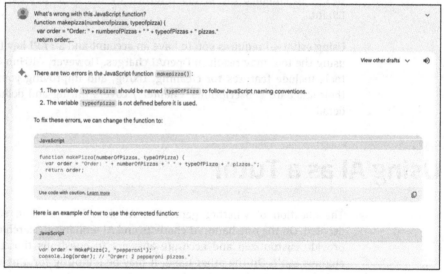

Microsoft Corporation

FIGURE 1-13:
Using Bard as a linter.

Integrating AI with static code analysis

Because programming languages have strict rules, linters don't necessarily need to use AI to detect bad code. However, linting tools that make use of AI can provide functionality that's not possible with standard code linters, such as

» Detailed natural language explanations of what's wrong with your code

» Defining new rules using natural language

» Fixing problematic code or refactoring problematic code or both

Many linters that aren't AI-enhanced can automatically fix certain kinds of problems with your code, and defining new rules generally isn't difficult. The potential for providing detailed descriptions as well as improving your code is promising.

Several tools add AI to existing linters. For example, eslint-ai (available at https://github.com/iamando/eslint-ai) is an open-source project that uses GPT-3 to enhance the errors returned by the most popular JavaScript linter, ESLint.

Using eslint-ai requires you to have an account and an API key from OpenAI, and using the tool may result in OpenAI charges. However, GitHub Copilot and other tools include features for cleaning, fixing, and improving your code as part of their standard subscriptions. Chapter 7 covers linting and debugging with AI in detail.

Using AI as a Tutor

The question of whether generative AI should be used in education is hotly debated. On the one hand, AI chatbots and AI-enhanced search engines can often provide customized and accurate answers to questions that traditional search engines can't. On the other hand, it may be tempting for a new coder to rely on code generated by AI rather than on gaining experience through struggling with coding for endless hours, which is the traditional way people learn to program (or to write, or anything else for that matter). In this section, I touch on some of the pros and cons of using AI to learn to code.

Studying AI's potential in education

AI can be a useful tool for someone who is learning to code. Just as search engines, online tutorials, and coding books are used today by both new and experienced programmers, AI chatbots and coding assistants will soon be seen as normal and essential tools.

Whether you're learning from older technologies (such as books or a human instructor) or the latest GenAI model, there's no substitute for gaining experience through writing code or from interacting with more experienced programmers.

TIP

When using an AI chatbot to learn to code, ask the right questions and be skeptical of its answers.

Avoiding potential pitfalls

GenAI models and the chatbots that make use of them don't know how to code. All they do is crunch the numbers, based on their training, and tell you the next most likely word. Even with this seemingly simple functionality, large language models such as GPT-4 are often surprisingly accurate and human-sounding.

WARNING

Although efforts are underway to make GenAI models properly express them-selves when they have doubts about their answers, today's models are supremely confident in their answers, even when what they say is completely wrong. Never fully trust a GenAI model. You should always test and verify any code output you get, especially before using it in a production environment.

Pairing Up with AI

Pair programming is a software development technique in which two programmers team up at one computer. In pair programming, one person acts as the driver and handles all the typing, while the other acts as the navigator. Ideally, both pro-grammers are equally skilled and switch roles between navigator and driver as needed to take advantage of each person's strengths. However, pair programming also works well when one of the programmers is more experienced (known as expert-novice) or where both programmers are inexperienced (novice-novice).

Pair programming helps team members share knowledge and learn to work together, and it leads to fewer mistakes and better code.

Overview of pair programming styles

Depending on the skill levels of the programmers, several different variations of pair programming might be used:

>> **Driver-navigator:** This style of pair programming is the most common. In driver-navigator, the driver handles the typing while the navigator looks at the big picture and keeps an eye out for mistakes being made by the driver.

>> **Backseat navigator:** In this style, the driver still does the typing, and the navigator takes a more active role and dictates instructions, such as when to create a file or method, or what to name a variable. This style works best when the navigator is a more experienced programmer.

>> **Tour guide:** In the tour guide style, the driver is the expert programmer. They handle the typing and explain to the navigator at every step what they're doing and why.

>> **Ping-pong:** The ping-pong style is designed for test-driven development as a pair. The first person writes a piece of code designed to verify that a feature works as expected (a *test*). The second programmer writes the code to make the test pass. Then the second programmer writes a new test and the first programmer writes the code to make it work. This style usually requires two expert developers.

Understanding the pros and cons of pair programming with AI

In AI pair programming, you're the navigator who sets the direction and does the strategic thinking. You communicate the project's goal to the AI through comments and code that you write. As you type, the AI navigator suggests snippets and code blocks. With each suggestion, you have to decide whether to accept the suggestion, write your own solution, or ask your AI assistant to try again.

Following are some of the benefits of pair programming with an AI partner:

>> You (the coder) can spend less time looking up syntax and typing repetitive or boilerplate code.

>> The AI assistant is available whenever you are.

>> The AI assistant is fast.

>> The GenAI model behind the assistant is trained on many different programming languages and programming styles, potentially giving you access to solutions you might not have otherwise considered.

The cons of pair programming with AI may include the following:

>> Team members each working individually with an AI partner don't get the knowledge-sharing benefits of traditional pair programming.

>> AI-suggested code may not be accurate or up-to-date with the latest syntax or coding styles.

>> AI-suggested code may contain security flaws or other types of issues that a human coding partner would easily spot.

WARNING

Pair programming with AI works best for coders who know their language and have experience writing code without the use of AI. As you're coding, remember that your partner (the GenAI model) speaks confidently but doesn't know anything about programming.

AI pair programming session

In this section, you work with an AI pair programmer to develop an interactive web-based trivia game. For this exercise, you need access to GitHub Copilot.

Installing Copilot

If the Copilot extension isn't installed in your code editor, follow these steps to install it and sign up for a Copilot free trial:

1. **Open Visual Studio Code.**

   If Visual Studio Code isn't installed, you can download it at https://code.visualstudio.com.

2. **Click the extensions icon in the left sidebar of Visual Studio Code and search for Copilot, as shown in Figure 1-14.**

3. **Install the Copilot extension.**

   Note that the Copilot Chat extension is installed automatically when you install Copilot.

4. **In your browser, go to https://github.com and sign in.**

   If you don't have an account, create one and then sign in. To use Copilot, you need a GitHub account.

Extensions icon

FIGURE 1-14:
Searching for the
Copilot extension.

5. **In the window that appears in Visual Studio Code after you installed Copilot, click Sign In to GitHub.**

   If the window isn't open, click the Copilot icon in the lower-right corner of Visual Studio Code.

6. **Walk through the dialog boxes that appear to give Visual Studio Code access to your GitHub account.**

   When you've linked GitHub and Visual Studio Code, Copilot displays a message saying that you don't have access to Copilot.

7. **Click the link to go to GitHub and sign up for a 30-day free trial of Copilot.**

TIP

You must have a Copilot subscription to use Copilot. A free trial is available at https://github.com/features/copilot#pricing. Educators and students have free access to Copilot through GitHub Global Campus at https://education.github.com/.

WARNING

Signing up for a Copilot trial requires you to enter payment information, and the trial converts to a paid subscription automatically after 30 days unless you cancel it.

Once you've signed up with Copilot, the Copilot icon in the lower-right corner of Visual Studio Code is active. If you click the icon several options appear at the top of VS Code, including Deactivate Copilot, which turns off suggestions from the model until you click the icon again and reactivate it.

Congratulations! You've signed up with Copilot and are ready to create a trivia game.

Using prompting to create a trivia game

In this section, you use Copilot to help you build a trivia game that displays one multiple-choice question at a time, and then randomly picks a new question when the user selects an answer. Think about the structure of the application you want to build. What other details can you imagine will be important to make sure that Copilot offers usable selections?

In the following steps, you see how the exercise went for me. Your experience will be different:

1. **Create a file named index.html and type an HTML comment.**

Here's the comment I wrote:

```
<!-- Homepage for a trivia game about machine learning -->
```

In response to this prompt, Copilot suggests a DOCTYPE declaration for an HTML5 file, which is correct.

2. **Press the tab key to accept Copilot's suggestion, and then press Enter to go to the next line and evaluate the next suggestion.**

3. **Continue accepting Copilot's suggestions until it provides one you don't want.**

Copilot suggested a basic HTML template containing a form that submits to a PHP script. This isn't what I envisioned, so I need to provide additional information for my initial prompt. I revised my prompt as follows:

```
<!--
Homepage for trivia game about Machine Learning.
This game will display one multiple-choice question at
a time, using JavaScript that gets data
from data/trivia.js.
Possible answers will be displayed with radio buttons
to their left. When a radio button is clicked, the
user will be shown a new random question.
-->
```

With the additional context, Copilot was able to create something that much more closely resembling what I envisioned:

```
<!DOCTYPE html>
<html lang="en">
<head>
    <meta charset="UTF-8">
    <title>Machine Learning Trivia</title>
    <link rel="stylesheet" href="css/style.css">
```

```
    </head>
    <body>
        <div class="container">
            <header>
                <h1>Machine Learning Trivia</h1>
            </header>
            <main>
                <div id="question"></div>
                <div id="answers"></div>
                <div id="score"></div>
            </main>
            <footer>
                <p>&copy; Chris Minnick</p>
            </footer>
        </div>
        <script src="js/trivia.js"></script>
    </html>
```

4. **Add type="module" to the `<script>` tag to tell Copilot that you'll be using an import statement inside the trivia.js file.**

5. **Create three folders named js, css, and data.**

6. **Inside the data folder, create a file named triviaQuestions.js.**

7. **Write a comment at the beginning of triviaQuestions.js that describes what the file should contain.**

   This is what I wrote:

```
// A module containing an array of 10 objects
// containing quiz questions and answers.
```

8. **If your prompt, like mine, didn't generate the content you expected, do the following:**

   a. *Click the Chat icon in the left panel of Visual Studio code to open the Copilot Chat interface.*

   You can also use ChatGPT for this step.

   b. *In the Chat interface, enter the following prompt:*

```
Give me a JavaScript array containing 10 multiple-choice
    trivia questions about machine learning.
```

In response to this prompt, Copilot Chat gave me a properly formatted and appropriate array of questions and answers. The first few questions follow:

```
const triviaQuestions = [
  {
    question: "What is the name of the algorithm that is
        commonly used for supervised learning?",
    choices: ["Decision Tree", "K-Means", "Naive Bayes",
        "Random Forest"],
    answer: "Decision Tree"
  },
  {
    question: "What is the name of the algorithm that is
        commonly used for unsupervised learning?",
    choices: ["K-Means", "Decision Tree", "Naive Bayes",
        "Random Forest"],
    answer: "K-Means"
  },
  {
    question: "What is the name of the algorithm that is
        commonly used for reinforcement learning?",
    choices: ["Q-Learning", "K-Means", "Naive Bayes",
        "Random Forest"],
    answer: "Q-Learning"
  },

  ...
];
```

9. Copy the generated array and paste it into your data file.

10. You'll be importing the array into your JavaScript file, so add the export keyword before const, like this:

```
export const triviaQuestions = [
```

11. Create a new file in the js folder named trivia.js.

REMEMBER

Make sure that you keep triviaQuestions.js and index.html open while you're working on trivia.js. Copilot uses files you have open as context for the one you're working on.

12. Write a comment at the beginning of trivia.js describing what it should do.

Here's the comment I wrote:

```
/* JavaScript for the Trivia Game.
This script is loaded by the index.html file
```

```
and will display questions and possible answers
that users can select from. The game will display
a new random question when the user clicks a radio
button to choose an answer and keep track of the
user's score. */
```

13. Immediately following the comment, start a JavaScript `import` statement to import the question data.

Whether Copilot figures out what you're doing and helps you or not, the import statement should look like this:

```
import {triviaQuestions} from '../data/triviaQuestions.js';
```

14. Press Enter, and accept the variables that Copilot suggests.

Eventually, Copilot will suggest a function.

TIP

Don't accept the suggested function right away. If Copilot isn't making any suggestions, try inserting a blank line. After that, look at the Copilot icon in the lower-right corner. It should start spinning, and after a few seconds you'll see a suggestion for how to start writing the code.

15. Hover your mouse pointer over the function suggestion to display the Copilot menu, which might list multiple possible suggestions, as shown in Figure 1-15.

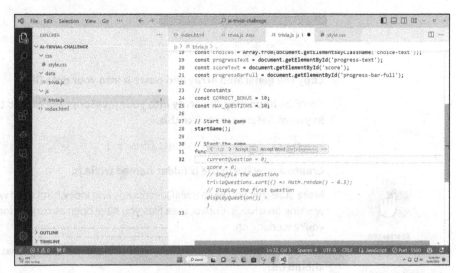

FIGURE 1-15:
Viewing the Copilot menu and multiple suggestion options.

Microsoft Corporation

16. If you like one of the suggestions, accept it. If not, try refining your comment to provide more information about what you want.

17. Continue this process of accepting suggestions, writing code, and using comments to provide context until you have something that might work.

Now it's time to preview your application:

1. Click the extensions icon to the left of VSCode (labeled in Figure 1-14) and use the Search box to find the Live Server extension.

2. Click the Install button under the Live Server extension.

This extension opens HTML files using a development server.

3. In Visual Studio Code's File Explorer, right-click index.html and select Open with Live Server.

Your application opens in your default web browser.

Figure 1-16 shows the (rough and unready) game that I created with Copilot's help. The process took me around 20 minutes on my second attempt.

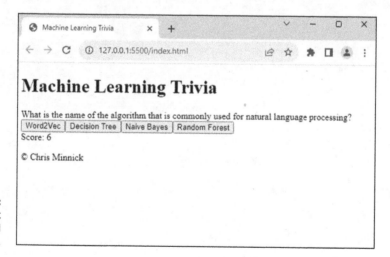

FIGURE 1-16:
A somewhat functional trivia game.

If your application doesn't work, try debugging with the help of Copilot Chat.

Whether or not you ended up with a usable — or even good — application, ask yourself the following questions:

>> Was pair programming with AI easier or more difficult than pair programming with another coder?

>> Were you surprised (positively or negatively) by the suggestions offered by Copilot?

>> How would you change your approach to pair programming with AI if you were to repeat this exercise?

In Part 2, you learn much more about how to get better results from GenAI.

Chapter **2**

Parsing Machine Learning and Deep Learning

I n this chapter, I cover some of the basics of AI and machine learning. Although it's fully possible to use AI-assisted software development tools without understanding the science and math behind them, a basic understanding of how AI and machine learning work will help you use these tools more effectively.

If you want to skip right into learning how to use AI coding assistants, feel free to use this chapter as a reference when you encounter an unfamiliar term or concept elsewhere in the book.

TIP

If you want to learn more about machine learning or how to write code that enables machine learning, check out some of the resources in Chapter 13.

Decoding Machine and Deep Learning

When you first encounter a generative AI tool such as ChatGPT, it can seem like magic. Some people even speculate that generative AI tools are conscious and capable of thinking and having emotions. Knowing how these tools were created and how they work will quickly dispel that notion — or make you think differently about consciousness, but that's a subject for a philosophy book, not a coding book.

Defining key concepts

Before you can dip your toes into understanding how the latest AI systems are capable of writing code and generating complex responses to natural-language input, I need to present some vocabulary. People working with or writing about the systems I talk about in this book often use the terms *AI*, *machine learning*, *deep learning*, and *generative AI* interchangeably, but these fundamental terms are different (see Figure 2-1):

>> **Artificial intelligence (AI)** is the use of computer science and data to solve problems. AI encompasses everything from expert systems and decision trees, which simulate the judgment and behavior of humans using a complex series of if-then statements, to machine learning, computer vision, and natural-language processing.

>> **Machine learning** is a type of AI that focuses on developing and using computer systems that can learn and adapt without following explicit instructions. Machine learning can solve problems that would be prohibitively expensive to solve by programmers writing the algorithms by hand.

>> **Deep learning** is a type of machine learning based on artificial neural networks. The word *deep* in *deep learning* doesn't indicate that it produces inherently more profound or mysterious AI. Rather, it refers to the use of multiple layers of algorithms (artificial neurons) in the neural network. I explain artificial neural networks and layers in the next section.

>> **Generative AI (GenAI)** are AI systems that can generate new content based on the data used to train them. Some form of GenAI has been around since the 1960s. In recent years, the content created by GenAI is of a high enough quality to be more than a novelty, thanks to the use of deep learning.

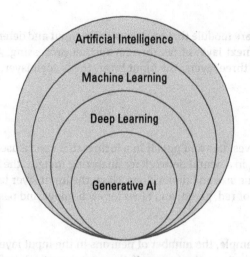

FIGURE 2-1:
The relationship
between
fields in AI.

Thinking about neural networks

The idea behind deep learning is to teach computers to process data based on how we think our brains work. In a human brain, cells called *neurons* form a complex and massive interconnected network. Using chemical reactions and electrical currents, neurons send signals to each other to enable us to learn and process information.

Neural networks in deep learning, also known as *simulated neural networks (SNNs)* or *artificial neural networks (ANNs)*, consist of artificial neurons called nodes that form layers, as shown in Figure 2-2.

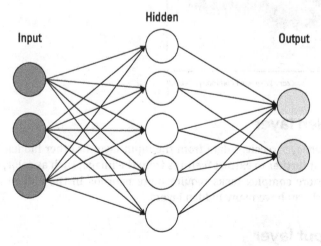

FIGURE 2-2:
Nodes are
arranged in
layers.

Each *node* is a software module that processes some input and determines whether to pass it on to the next layer of neurons for further processing. A simple neural network consists of three layers: the input layer, the hidden layer, and the output layer.

Input layer

The *input layer* receives data and puts it in a format that can be used by the hidden layers. For example, in a neural network for analyzing images, the images are first converted to the same size and dimensions. Next, the input layer takes in the pixel values (the amount of red, green, and blue) for each image and passes them along to the hidden layer.

TECHNICAL
STUFF

In the preceding example, the number of neurons in the input layer is determined by the number of pixels in the image. If the neural network will be processing color images, the number of pixels is multiplied by 3 for each of the pixel values (red, green, and blue) to get the number of neurons. For example, the image shown in Figure 2-3 has a width of 56 pixels and a height of 56 pixels. I've magnified the image so you can see the individual pixels. An input layer for working with this image would have 56 x 56 x 3, or 9,408, neurons.

FIGURE 2-3:
A color image containing 3,136 pixels requires a 9,408-neuron input layer.

Czar / Wikimedia Commons / CC0 1.0

Hidden layer

A *hidden layer* receives data from the input layer or other hidden layers and processes it further to extract features from the image, such as color, shape, and texture. More complex tasks require more neurons in the hidden layers. A neural network can have many hidden layers.

Output layer

Neural networks must have at least one *output layer*, which provides the final result of the calculations from the hidden layers.

Figure 2-4 shows a simple artificial neural network that determines whether or not a photo contains a hot dog. This type of problem is known as a binary classification because the output from this neural network is either 1 (hot dog) or 0 (not hot dog).

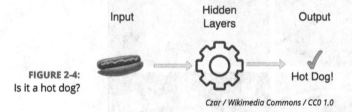

Input   Hidden Layers   Output

Hot Dog!

Czar / Wikimedia Commons / CC0 1.0

But how does the neural network determine whether the photo contains a hot dog? That's where its training comes in.

Training and testing models

Before a neural network can perform a task, it must be trained. In the case of the hot dog classifier, the neural network can be trained by analyzing thousands of pictures of hot dogs as well as an equal number of things that aren't hot dogs. Each photo must be labeled ("hot dog" or "not hot dog"). From these pictures, the neural network can make certain conclusions about what a picture of a hot dog contains. For example, a picture of a hot dog generally will contain a lighter-colored area (the bun) surrounding a darker-colored cylindrical shape (the hot dog), as shown in Figure 2-5.

As the layers of the neural network analyze pictures, values called weights and biases are assigned to each neuron in the network. The *weight* determines the strength of the connection between two nodes in the network. The *bias* determines the threshold at which a node is activated. Weights and biases adjust how much a neuron will contribute to the final result.

The weights and biases that the model learns from the training data are called *parameters*. The complexity of a model can be described by how many parameters it has. More complex models have more parameters because they're able to learn more complex patterns in data. You can think of parameters as similar to the synapses that connect neurons in a human brain.

FIGURE 2-5:
Many pictures
of hot dogs
have similar
characteristics.

In machine learning, a *model* is a mathematical representation of a real-world system or phenomenon. Some examples of models follow:

>> **Scientific models** make predictions involving the atmosphere, diseases, and the universe.

>> **Engineering models** design and test new products.

>> **Demand models** predict how many units of a product a business will sell.

>> **Financial models** predict the performance of stocks and other financial instruments.

How accurately a model can make predictions (whether or not a new picture contains a hot dog, for example) is based on the quality and quantity of data that was used to train it.

Small models that make relatively simple predictions, such as whether or not a photograph contains a hot dog, can be created quickly, and the risks of messing up such a model are unlikely to be catastrophic.

TIP

The most time-consuming part of creating a model is usually the gathering and labeling of the datasets. Many publicly available free datasets exist. You can find a list of them at https://openml.org.

Complex models, such as climate models and models of systems of the human body, can take months or years to train, and getting it wrong can have expensive or life-threatening consequences. Some of the challenges of training neural networks include the following:

>> Complex neural networks can involve terabytes of training data and billions of parameters. Training a large neural network is computationally expensive.

>> Neural networks can learn their training data too well, which is called *overfitting*. When overfitting occurs, the model will be able to ace tests about the data it was trained on but will have a hard time generalizing to new data (which is the point of a model).

>> Because of the number of parameters in a model, it can be difficult for people to figure out how a neural network is making predictions. Being able to understand how a model makes predictions is called *interpretability*.

Demystifying Natural-Language Processing

Natural-language processing (NLP) is the branch of AI concerned with giving computers the capability to understand human language in written and spoken form. NLP can be further divided into two subsets:

>> **Natural-language understanding (NLU)** is the analyzing of text and speech to figure out the meaning of sentences.

>> **Natural-language generation (NLG)** is concerned with giving computers the capability to write.

NLP is used for a wide variety of purposes, including the following:

>> **Machine translation:** Translating text from one language to another

>> **Speech recognition:** Understanding spoken language and translating it into text

>> **Text summarization:** Generating summaries of longer texts, such as books, articles, or briefs

>> **Question answering:** Answering questions asked in natural language

>> **Sentiment analysis:** Identifying the sentiment of text, for example, whether it's positive, negative, or neutral

>> **Computer programming:** Writing or assisting with the writing of computer programs

REMEMBER

Human language includes not only the languages we use for communicating with each other (such as English, French, and Greek) but also the languages we use for communicating with computers (such as C++, JavaScript, and Haskell).

History of NLP

Natural-language processing has been around since the first experiments in automatic translation in the 1950s. The creators of the first automatic translation machine predicted that the problem of machine translation would be solved within a few years. However, it ended up taking much longer, and we still haven't perfected it.

Early natural-language processing systems relied on a list of handwritten rules that the computer applied to the data it received. The ELIZA chatbot, created in the 1960s, could have a somewhat convincing conversation with a human by following rules and responding as a non-directional psychotherapist. Although ELIZA was created as a joke, it successfully demonstrated that natural-language conversations between people and computers were possible. Figure 2-6 shows a typical conversation with ELIZA.

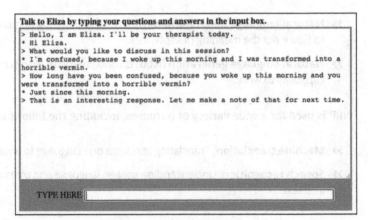

Talk to Eliza by typing your questions and answers in the input box.

```
> Hello, I am Eliza. I'll be your therapist today.
* Hi Eliza.
> What would you like to discuss in this session?
* I'm confused, because I woke up this morning and I was transformed into a
horrible vermin.
> How long have you been confused, because you woke up this morning and you
were transformed into a horrible vermin?
* Just since this morning.
> That is an interesting response. Let me make a note of that for next time.
```

TYPE HERE

FIGURE 2-6:
Early NLP was
based on rules.

Machine learning algorithms and increased computing power led to advances and new techniques for natural-language processing starting in the late 1980s.

In the 1990s, Richard Wallace created the ALICE chatbot. ALICE is similar to ELIZA in that it uses pattern-matching rules. The operator of an ALICE chatbot could add rules, which made it useful for customer service applications such as answering questions about a company's products. Figure 2-7 shows an example conversation with ALICE.

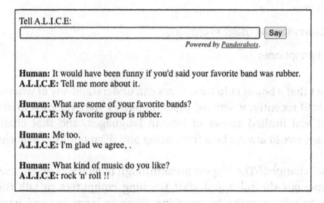

FIGURE 2-7:
An example of
an Alice chatbot.

The growth of the internet made large collections of text readily available for training models. As a result of all this data, new techniques were created in the 1990s and 2000s that depended on statistical analysis of large datasets.

Machine learning models made it possible for natural-language processing systems to be trained without having to hand-code rules. Further advances in machine learning, including neural networks, made virtual assistants such as Apple's Siri and Amazon's Alexa possible in the 2010s and eventually enabled the remarkable advances in natural-language processing that made tools such as ChatGPT possible.

Overcoming the challenges of NLP

In the past, creators of NLP systems focused on breaking down human languages into rules. The idea was that if you could give a computer access to a language's dictionary and a grammar book, it would know that language.

In the case of programming languages, this approach was somewhat successful. If you know the rules of a programming language and the right keywords to use, you can at least write statements.

But human language is more complex. Here are just a few of the things that a computer can't understand by memorizing a dictionary and grammar:

» Dialects

» Accents

» Sarcasm

» Metaphors

» Humor

» Grammar and usage exceptions

» Homophones

The fact that a box of chips and wires can understand any of what we say is incredible. Until recently, it seemed that computers were doomed to understand only a formal and limited subset of human languages, and that chatting with an AI assistant would always be a frustrating and disappointing experience.

So what changed? The biggest breakthrough in NLP was when researchers decided to throw out the rules and start teaching computers to talk the way we teach babies to talk: namely, by exposing them to language and letting them figure things out.

Understanding supervised and unsupervised learning

Supervised learning relies on *labeled data*, which is data annotated with tags that describe what the data is. For example, if you want to train a model to recognize spam email messages, you could create a dataset containing millions of email messages, each labeled either "spam" or "not spam." However, the process of labeling data can be costly and time consuming.

Unsupervised learning is the finding of patterns in unlabeled data. With unsupervised learning, algorithms sort through unlabeled data looking for patterns. Unsupervised language-learning models can be trained on very large datasets to create large language models (LLMs). Unlike supervised learning, unsupervised learning can be done inexpensively and quickly.

Language generation techniques

Natural-language processing techniques can be divided into traditional machine learning methods and deep learning methods. Traditional machine learning techniques include the following:

- >> **Logistic regression** is a classification algorithm that aims to predict the probability that an event will occur based on some input.

- >> **Naïve Bayes classifiers** are a collection of statistical classification algorithms based on Bayes' theorem, which describes the probability of an event based on prior knowledge of conditions. The *naïve* part of the name refers to the assumption these algorithms make that individual words are not dependent on each other.

- >> **Decision trees** work by splitting a dataset based on different inputs. For example, if you wanted to find out whether it's likely to rain, you might start by asking whether it's cloudy. If so, you might ask then about the humidity, and then the temperature. After several splits, you can come up with a prediction.

- >> **Latent Dirichlet allocation (LDA)** is used for topic modeling. Topic modeling techniques scan a set of documents to detect patterns and cluster together word groups that best characterize the set.

- >> **Hidden Markov models (HMMs)** decide the next state of a system based on the previously observed state. The *hidden* part of the name refers to data properties that aren't directly observed. In natural-language processing, the hidden state is the parts of speech, and the observed state is the words in a sentence.

TECHNICAL STUFF

Some of the techniques used in machine learning are named after the people who formulated the theorems the techniques rely on. Thomas Bayes was an eighteenth-century English statistician, philosopher, and minister. Peter Gustav Lejeune Dirichlet was a nineteenth-century German mathematician. Andrey Markov was a Russian mathematician who lived at the end of the nineteenth century and the beginning of the twentieth century.

While traditional NLP methods are often able to do a good job, it wasn't until deep learning techniques were applied to NLP that things got interesting. Following are some deep learning NLP techniques:

- >> **Convolutional neural networks (CNNs)** were designed to be used for working with images but can also be used with documents. In NLP, CNNs treat documents as images made up of sentences instead of pixels.

- >> **Recurrent neural networks (RNNs)** use hidden states to remember previous information. Because of this, they can learn how every word in a sentence is dependent on previous words or words in the previous sentence.

- >> **Transformer models** learn context by tracking relationships in sequential data (such as the words in a sentence). Transformer models are the breakthrough that has revolutionized NLP in recent years. I tell you more about how transformers work in the next section.

Understanding Transformers

Transformer models use a self-attention mechanism to find dependencies between inputs and outputs. To understand what that means, you first need to know what attention and self-attention are in machine learning. Read on!

Learning to pay attention

The mathematical technique that transformer models use is called attention. The goal of *attention* is to allow the model to focus on important parts of the input while generating its output. As people, we do this naturally. When you read a sentence or look at an image, you can easily see which parts of the sentence or image are the most important in terms of understanding it.

When the idea of attention first became popular, it was combined with recurrent neural networks (RNNs). But RNN models have to consider words in sequence one at a time, which is a slow process. Even worse, RNNs tend to assign more importance to recent words and the ends of sentences.

Another side effect of considering words one at a time is that you lose important context. Consider this sentence:

> The player swung his bat, and he ran to first base.

Anyone with a passing familiarity with baseball will know that *bat* refers to a baseball bat and that *he* refers to the player. Considered one word at a time, however, a language model can't make the same connections.

This is where the idea of self-attention comes in. *Self-attention* allows a model to learn information about an input sequence from the input sequence itself. With self-attention, a transformer model finds relationships between the words *player* and *bat* as well as between *player* and *he*.

Figure 2-8 shows a visualization of the connections a transformer model makes between the word *he* in the example sentence and the other words in the sentence. Darker lines indicate a stronger connection.

TECHNICAL STUFF

The visualization in Figure 2-8 was created using a tool called BertViz. You can learn more about how BertViz works and try it out yourself at https://github.com/jessevig/bertviz.

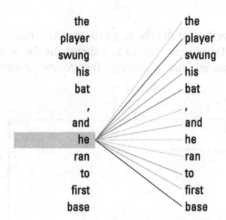

FIGURE 2-8:
Visualizing
self-attention.

Self-attention was first proposed as a solution for improving large language models in the paper "Attention Is All You Need." This paper, published in 2017, led to the giant leaps forward in transformer models that we've seen in recent years.

Getting tokens

You may be surprised to learn that language models can understand only numbers; they don't read or understand words as we do. When you ask an NLP system a question, your input must first be converted into a sequence of numbers called *tokens*. You can think of tokens as the language equivalent of pixels in an image.

These tokens are read by a model's input layer and then processed through the hidden layers to predict and output responses to your prompts.

REMEMBER

Hidden layers are the layers between the input and output layers that process data and learn features of it.

Text can be converted to tokens in a variety of ways. One common method is *word tokenization*, which simply creates a token for each word in the text. Transformer models use *sub-word tokenization*, which converts text into common sequences of characters, such as *token* and *ize*. Using smaller units improves the model's performance.

To see how OpenAI converts text to tokens, go to OpenAI's Tokenizer at https://platform.openai.com/tokenizer. Figure 2-9 shows the list of tokens that were generated when I entered the sentence *Transformer models use sub-word tokenization.*

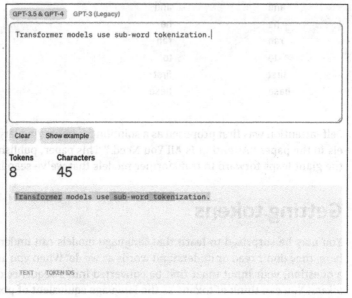

FIGURE 2-9:
Tokenizing
a prompt.

After the text is tokenized, it's encoded into token IDs. The token IDs created from the text in Figure 2-9 are shown in Figure 2-10.

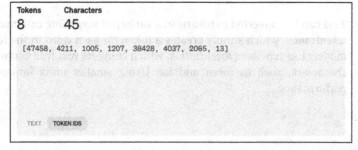

FIGURE 2-10:
Tokens are
represented as
token IDs.

Token IDs are input into a neural network as a sequence of numbers called a *numerical vector*.

Being aware of tokens and the tokenization of your input is important. If you're using a model through OpenAI's API, the combined number of tokens in your input and the model's response determines how much you pay for the service.

In addition, the NLP system you're using may have a *token limit*, which is the maximum number of tokens the model will consider while generating its response. Your input and the model's responses contribute to the number of tokens used by a conversation. In a long conversation with ChatGPT, or if you input an excessively long prompt, the token limit may be exceeded. In this case, the model will "forget" earlier prompts in the conversation, and you'll need to repeat any instructions you included at the beginning.

Token limits are imposed on a model to prevent it from running out of memory, to shorten the model's response time, and to reduce the amount of computation required to train and deploy the model.

Table 2-1 lists the token limits of standard versions of several models. Many models also have extended versions with larger token limits.

TABLE 2-1: **Token Limits**

Model	Creator	Token limit
GPT-2	OpenAI	1024
GPT-3	OpenAI	2048
GPT-4	OpenAI	8000
BERT (base)	Google	512
RoBERTa (base)	Facebook	512
T5 (base)	Google	512
XLNet (base)	Google/CMU	512
Electra (base)	Google	512
DistilBERT	Hugging Face	512

ETHICAL CONSIDERATIONS AND RESPONSIBLE AI

AI has enormous potential to improve people's lives — and to cause harm. Laws regarding the development and use of AI are still being argued over and drafted. Guidelines have been and are being developed by companies and organizations concerned about the negative potential of AI.

Both developers and users of AI models and systems that use those models have a responsibility to use these new technologies in a way that follows best practices. One guide to best practices for developers of AI models is Google's Responsible AI Practices document, which is available at https://ai.google/responsibility/responsible-ai-practices. Google recommends four best practices for AI: fairness, interpretability, privacy, and safety and security.

Fairness: Because computer programs have access to much more information than a person, AI systems used for making decisions or for generating content can be more fair and inclusive than decision-making tools based on human judgment. However, because they're trained on data created by humans, AI models have a tendency to learn and sometimes amplify the biases of their training data. Furthermore, there's no standard definition of fairness. Making a model fair in every language, culture, and situation is a difficult, and perhaps impossible, task. The *fairness best practice* encourages those working with AI to aim for continuous improvement towards "fairer" systems.

Interpretability: *Interpretability* refers to the level to which we can question, understand, and trust an AI system. When people make decisions, they use their experience, intuition, and logic. Often, it's impossible for a person to say exactly what inputs went into their final decision. AI, on the other hand, theoretically has the capability to list the information that went into a prediction. Because a generative AI model may be based on billions of parameters, debugging and understanding the decisions it makes isn't always possible. However, the *interpretability best practice* demands and provides specific recommendations for how to incorporate interpretability into AI systems.

Privacy: The training data and prompts we give AI models can sometimes be sensitive. For example, training data may contain personally identifying data, medical data, private financial information, or photos of people taken without permission. AI models, and generative AI models in particular, can reveal aspects of data they've been exposed to. AI developers, as well as people who use these models, have a responsibility to protect people's privacy and to provide users with the ability to control their data, even absent laws that require it. *Privacy best practices* include collecting and handling training data responsibly, processing data locally (rather than on a server) when appropriate, and considering how a model's construction and access can affect privacy.

Safety and security: *Safety and security best practices* make sure that AI systems behave as they're supposed to regardless of what prompts or inputs a person with bad intentions gives them. For example, ChatGPT has proactive restrictions regarding hate speech and generating content that may be harmful to people. Attackers are constantly looking for new ways to get GenAI systems to produce restricted output. Developers must balance necessary restrictions for safety and security with the flexibility to handle unusual inputs and generate useful responses.

Illuminating Generative AI Models

A *generative AI model* is a model that is trained on content (such as images or text) and can use that content to make predictions to generate new content. OpenAI's GPT-3, the model behind the first public version of ChatGPT, is a generative model for natural-language processing. By leveraging what it's learned about how people talk and write, it can accurately predict what the next word or sentence should be in response to input.

For example, if you provide the words *peanut butter and* to GPT-3, it will most likely predict that the next words should be *jelly sandwich*. GPT-3 doesn't have any experience with eating or making peanut butter and jelly sandwiches, but it has analyzed a lot of text, and the most common way to finish the phrase *peanut butter and* is with *jelly sandwich*.

Like our hot dog photo classifier, a generative AI model is only as good as its training data. GPT-3 was trained with over 45 terabytes of text data, so it has amazing capabilities, such as taking context into consideration when responding to input.

Generative AI models have been steadily getting better as a result of being trained on more and higher-quality data. Table 2-2 compares the size of some recent generative models.

REMEMBER

As I mention earlier in the chapter, parameters are the values that the model has learned from its training.

TABLE 2-2:
Parameters in Generative AI Models

Model	Developer	Parameters
Gato	DeepMind	1.18 billion
ESMFold	Meta AI	15 billion
LaMDA	Google	137 billion
GPT-3	OpenAI	175 billion
Bloom	Hugging Face and BigScience	176 billion
MT-NLG	Nvidia and Microsoft	530 billion
WuDao 2.0	Beijing Academy of Artificial Intelligence	1.75 trillion
GPT-4	OpenAI	1.76 trillion

Recognizing AI's Limitations

As impressive as they are, transformer models don't know how to code — they know only how to look for patterns in sequential data (such as sentences, statements, or functions). When you train a generative model on enough data, it becomes very good at finding patterns and making predictions, but it does have limitations, and you should never trust the output of a chatbot (or any AI system) entirely.

Language models are bad at math

AI chatbots are language models tuned for conversation. If you ask a language model for the answer to a basic math problem, it will usually respond confidently with some answer. However, upon checking that answer using a calculator, you may be surprised that it's often just plain wrong. Currently, generative models are able to make predictions based only on content they've previously seen. If you give them a math problem they've never seen before (no matter how trivial), they'll respond based on the answers to similar math questions in their training data rather than by doing the math the way a calculator would.

For example, Figure 2-11 shows a conversation I had with ChatGPT when I was planning the outline for this book.

Language models are wordy

AI chatbots often respond to prompts with paragraphs when a one-word answer will do. The standard ChatGPT response to even a simple question reads like a high school book report, containing an introduction, an analysis of an issue from multiple viewpoints, and a summary.

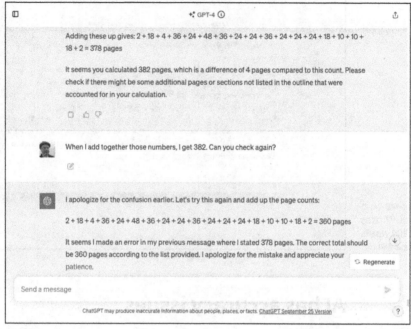

FIGURE 2-11:
GPT-4 gets an addition problem wrong.

ChatGPT

Figure 2-12 shows ChatGPT's nearly 200-word response to a question that any JavaScript programmer could answer with two words.

AI has limited knowledge

Although it's now possible for ChatGPT to access data on the internet, the model behind ChatGPT is finite. As a result, ChatGPT doesn't know everything. When prompted with questions about less popular programming languages or new syntax, the answer the model returns may be wrong.

AI lacks common sense

No machine learning model has had the experience of being human. As a result, the responses generated by the model lack common sense. For example, if you ask ChatGPT how to swim to the moon, it will provide an answer without questioning the absurdity of the question. Any human would first question the value of such a strange question.

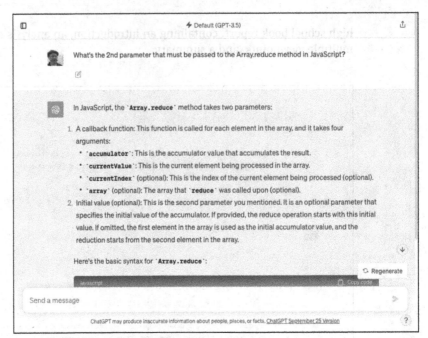

FIGURE 2-12:
ChatGPT uses
200 words
where 2 will do.

AI has accuracy issues

The accuracy of responses generated by a model depends on many factors, including the training data, context, user input, complexity of the prompt and language, and bias. As the user of a model, you have control over only some of these factors. Where possible, however, you can help the model provide better responses by knowing how best to prompt it and by challenging the model's output in follow-up prompts.

AI has the potential to be biased

Because they're trained largely on text written by people, machine learning models will pick up the biases and preferences that exist in the training data. Creators of models put a lot of effort into eliminating bias — which is a worthy goal but an impossible task.

WARNING

Unintended consequences and even dangerous situations may result from bias in models. The classic example is when Microsoft released its Tay chatbot to the internet in 2016. Within one day of talking to people, the chatbot went from saying things like "Humans are cool" to making racist and sexist comments.

Chapter **3**

AI Coding Tools

G enerative AI has made new types of tools available to coders and has enabled many legacy tools to integrate AI functionality. In this chapter, you look at three of the most popular GenAI coding tools — GitHub Copilot, Tabnine, and Replit — gaining hands-on experience setting up and using the basic features of each.

Navigating GitHub Copilot

GitHub Copilot is a cloud-based AI coding tool developed by GitHub (which is part of Microsoft) and OpenAI (the creators of the GPT-x models behind ChatGPT and many other tools). Copilot was launched in June 2021 and currently integrates with several code editors and IDEs, including Visual Studio Code, Visual Studio, Neovim, and JetBrains's IDEs.

The GenAI model behind Copilot is named OpenAI Codex. Codex is based on OpenAI's GPT-3 and is also trained on source code from millions of public GitHub repositories and other publicly available source code.

Although Copilot works best with Python, JavaScript, TypeScript, Ruby, and Go, it has been trained on source code from over a dozen programming languages and will continue to become more fluent in additional languages over time.

Installing the Copilot plug-in

The first step in using Copilot is to install the GitHub plug-in (or extension as it's called in VS Code). The process for installing the extension differs based on your IDE. You can find detailed installation instructions for every IDE supported by Copilot at https://docs.github.com/en/copilot/getting-started-with-github-copilot. In Chapter 1, I provide details on installing and enabling the Copilot extension for VS Code.

To follow along with the examples in this chapter, you should use VS Code or GitHub's in-browser code editor, CodeSpaces (https://github.com/codespaces). CodeSpaces is based on VS Code and therefore very similar to the installable version of VS Code.

When you install the Copilot extension in VS Code, the Copilot Chat extension is installed automatically. After you install Copilot, the Copilot status icon will appear in the lower-right corner of VS Code (see Figure 3-1, top). If you're not currently logged into a GitHub account with access to Copilot, the Copilot status icon appears with an exclamation point (see Figure 3-1, bottom).

FIGURE 3-1:
The Copilot status icon in connected and disconnected mode.

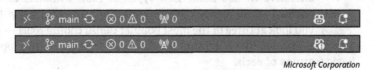

Microsoft Corporation

Although you can install the plugin without having a Copilot account, you must have a GitHub account and either an individual subscription ($10 per month) or a business subscription ($19 per user per month) to use Copilot. A free 30-day trial is available, as well as free accounts for students and educators.

You can click the Accounts icon in VS Code to create a GitHub account, if necessary. Then log into GitHub and grant the Copilot extension access, as shown in Figure 3-2.

The Copilot extensions don't have many adjustable settings. Perhaps the most important setting you can control is whether or not Copilot is actively giving you suggestions. To disable Copilot so you can think, click the Copilot status icon. In the menu that appears at the top of the VS Code interface, select Disable Completions. (When completions are disabled, an Enable Completions link appears in the menu.)

To access other settings, click the Extensions icon in the left panel of VS Code. Then click the gear icon next to an extension and select Extension Settings from the menu that appears. Figure 3-3 shows the Extension Settings screen for the Copilot extension.

FIGURE 3-2:
Click the Accounts
icon to grant
Copilot access to
your GitHub
account.

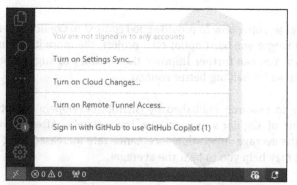

Microsoft Corporation

Extensions icon

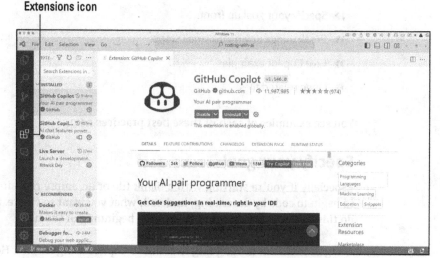

FIGURE 3-3:
The Extension
Settings screen
for Copilot.

Microsoft Corporation

Working efficiently with Copilot

After you have installed and enabled Copilot, using it is just a matter of starting to type some code. However, just as with any GenAI tool, context is everything. The first piece of context you should provide to Copilot is the type of code you intend to write. You can do this by starting a new file with the file extension of the programming language you'll be using, such as .js for JavaScript or .py for Python.

TIP

Choose your filename carefully because it determines the types of suggestions Copilot gives you.

Copilot generates suggestions using context from the file you're currently working on and neighboring tabs — the other files open in your editor. So if your current project contains other files that will be related to the new one you're starting, open those as well so that Copilot can glean information from them.

The goal of learning how to provide good context to Copilot is to increase its accuracy. The longer you use Copilot on a project, the more its accuracy will improve on its own. You can further improve the accuracy of suggestions through better prompting and providing better context.

TECHNICAL STUFF

According to research published by GitHub, developers accepted an average of 30 percent of Copilot's suggestions immediately. After six months of using Copilot, the average suggestion acceptance rate increased to 34 percent. Reading this book may help you to beat the average!

Following are some best practices for getting the most accurate suggestions from Copilot:

>> Specify your goal up front.

>> Break things down into small steps.

>> Give Copilot examples.

>> Open related files.

You see examples of each of these best practices next.

Specify your goal

Especially if you're starting with a blank file or an empty repository, you'll want to begin to code by describing, in detail, what you want to create. Most often, you do this by writing code comments at the beginning of the file.

A vague comment is not going to result in Copilot being helpful. Here is the initial code generated by Copilot in response to the prompt *a to-do app*:

```
// a to-do app
var todoList = {
  todos: [],
  displayTodos: function () {
    console.log('My Todos:', this.todos);
  }
};
```

Instead, try starting out with at least the amount of detail you would give to another coder:

```
/* A to-do app. Users can check a box to mark a task
complete, and completed tasks will be shown in a separate
```

```
list below the uncompleted tasks. */

var todoList = {
  todos: [],
  displayTodos: function () {
    console.log('My Todos:', this.todos);
  },
  addTodo: function (todoText) {
    this.todos.push({
      todoText: todoText,
      completed: false,
    });
    this.displayTodos();
  },
  changeTodo: function (position, todoText) {
    this.todos[position].todoText = todoText;
    this.displayTodos();
  },
  deleteTodo: function (position) {
    this.todos.splice(position, 1);
    this.displayTodos();
  },
  toggleCompleted: function (position) {
    var todo = this.todos[position];
    todo.completed = !todo.completed;
    this.displayTodos();
  },
};
```

With additional details, Copilot still didn't get it right, but at least it took into account some of the pieces of my prompt, such as that users can mark tasks as completed.

Break things down

GenAI models have a limited attention span. To improve results, give Copilot information as a series of steps, rather than as a request for a large block of code all at once. After each step, let Copilot generate some code, and then write the next step.

For example, in the following, I broke down the to-do app I want to write into areas of functionality, and I accepted the first suggestion Copilot made for each step.

```
/*
1. Create a constant called toDoItems
containing an array of objects. Each object
```

```
  should have a todoText property and a completed property.
*/

const toDoItems = [
  {
    todoText: 'item1',
    completed: false,
  },
  {
    todoText: 'item2',
    completed: false,
  },
  {
    todoText: 'item3',
    completed: false,
  },
];

/*
2. Create a function that displays a list of to-do
items in an element with an id attribute set to "to-dos"
         in the browser.
*/

function displayTodos() {
  const todosUl = document.querySelector('#to-dos');
  todosUl.innerHTML = '';
  toDoItems.forEach((item) => {
    const todoLi = document.createElement('li');
    todoLi.textContent = item.todoText;
    todosUl.appendChild(todoLi);
  });
}
```

This code is much closer to what I was looking for and is a decent starting point for my app.

Give examples

If you already have an idea of what you want Copilot to generate, start by giving it an example or two. For example, if you want it to generate an array of objects, tell it what an object should look like. In the following, I refined my first step from the preceding example to specify what I'm looking for:

```
/*
1. Create an array of to-do items with the following shape:
[{todoTitle:'', todoDesc:'', date:'', completed:false}]
*/
const toDoItems = [
  {
    todoTitle: 'item1',
    todoDesc: 'item1 description',
    date: '2024-07-01',
    completed: false,
  },
  {
    todoTitle: 'item2',
    todoDesc: 'item2 description',
    date: '2024-07-02',
    completed: false,
  },
  {
    todoTitle: 'item3',
    todoDesc: 'item3 description',
    date: '2024-07-03',
    completed: false,
  },
];
```

Open related files

Copilot gets context for the file you're working on from other files you have open in your editor. If you're working on a JavaScript file that will affect an HTML page or that imports code from other JavaScript files, open those files in separate tabs.

In my to-do app example, the JavaScript will affect the display of the HTML page, so creating the HTML page and opening it in another tab will help Copilot generate more accurate JavaScript code.

Using keyboard shortcuts

Although you can successfully use Copilot by just coding as you normally would and using the tab key to accept suggestions, knowing a few more keyboard shortcuts will make your coding sessions more productive. The keyboard shortcuts you'll want to remember are shown in Table 3-1.

TABLE 3-1:

Copilot Keyboard Shortcuts

Shortcut	What It Does
Tab	Accepts inline code suggestions
Esc	Dismisses inline code suggestions
Alt +] (or Option +])	Shows the next suggestion
Alt + [(or Option + [)	Shows the previous suggestion
Alt + \ (or Option + \)	Triggers a suggestion
Ctrl + Enter	Generates up to 10 suggestions in a separate pane

The Ctrl+Enter shortcut is particularly useful. When Copilot gives you a suggestion and you want to find out if it might be able to suggest something better, press Ctrl+Enter. A new pane will open in your code editor and (after a minute or so) display up to 10 other suggestions, as shown in Figure 3-4.

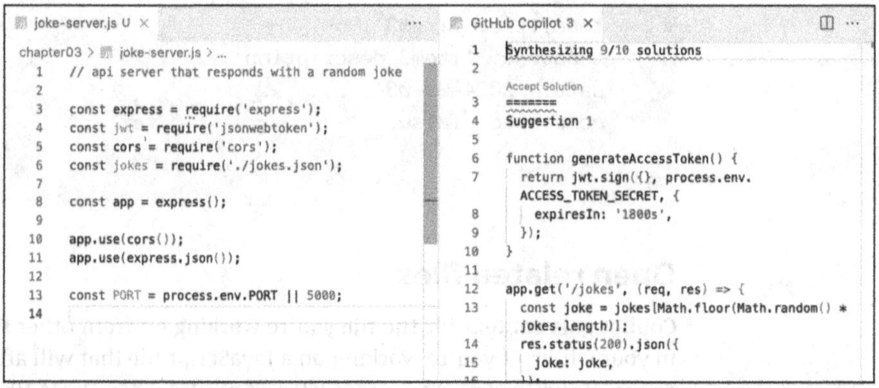

FIGURE 3-4:
Getting more
suggestions.

Microsoft Corporation

Exploring Tabnine

Tabnine is an AI coding assistant and the name of the company that created it. The company was formed in 2012 and released the first version of their coding assistant in 2018, making Tabnine one of the longest-established AI-powered coding tools.

Tabnine is available in three versions: starter, pro, and enterprise. The starter version offers basic code completion. The pro plan offers AI code features similar to those of Copilot: whole-line and function code completions, natural-language-to-code completions, and a chat interface. The enterprise version allows a company to locate the model in the corporate firewall and provide access to every developer in the company.

A 7-day free trial (which for me turned out to be a 14-day trial) of the pro plan is available. I show you features from both the starter plan and the pro plan in this chapter.

One of the biggest differences between Tabnine and other AI coding assistant tools is that Tabnine runs on its own model, which they've trained on publicly available open-source code with permissive licenses. So coders and organizations should be able to use Tabnine-generated code without facing legal issues regarding intellectual property violations. This added assurance has made Tabnine popular with large organizations.

You can view the entire list of repositories that Tabnine is trained on by going to https://trust.tabnine.com/.

Be aware of the risk of violating the licenses of the code a model was trained on. In 2022, a class action lawsuit was filed against Microsoft (the owner of GitHub and GitHub Copilot) and OpenAI claiming that the companies violated the open-source licenses of programmers whose code was used to train the model Copilot uses.

Tabnine takes code privacy seriously. Their privacy policy (available at https://tabnine.com/code-privacy) states that they never store or share any of your code. This point is important for businesses concerned that AI coding assistants may inadvertently leak their intellectual property.

Businesses that use Tabnine can create their own model, which can live on the business's premises or in the cloud. To create a private code model, Tabnine trains their public model with the client's codebase. When customers with a private model submit a query, it's sent to Tabnine's public model and the private model and picks the most relevant code suggestion from the two options returned. The private model is continuously trained from the code and decisions made by its users.

Installing Tabnine

Tabnine is available as a plug-in, or extension, for many of the most popular code editors, including VS Code, Eclipse, Android Studio, WebStorm (as well as all JetBrains code editors), and Sublime.

Follow these steps to install Tabnine:

1. **Go to https://www.tabnine.com and click the Get Tabnine link at the top of the page.**

   A page with a Search box and a list of IDEs appears, as shown in Figure 3-5.

2. **Select your IDE and follow the steps to install the extension.**

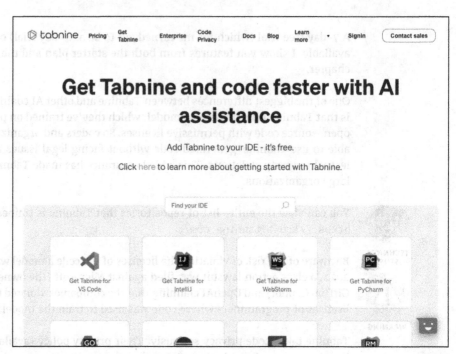

FIGURE 3-5:
Choosing the
IDE where
you want to
install the
Tabnine
extension.

Before you can use the Tabnine extension, you need to create a Tabnine account by going to `https://app.tabnine.com/signup`. After you've installed the Tabnine extension, you may need to restart your IDE.

Setting up Tabnine

After you've installed the extension and logged in, you'll see a link at the bottom of your IDE (in the case of VS Code) that says what plan you're subscribed to. Click this link to open Tabnine Hub.

Tabnine Hub is where you can adjust settings and read about the latest features. If you're using the starter plan, as I am in Figure 3-6, you'll also see links for a lot of features that you won't have access to and links to upgrade to a paid plan. The starter plan is quite capable, however, and you may want to stick with it while you learn about Tabnine's capabilities.

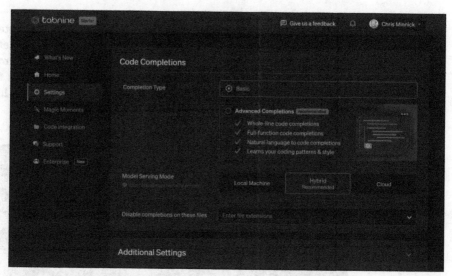

Tabnine

Tabnine allows you to choose from one of three model-serving modes: local machine, cloud, or hybrid. Which of these you choose will affect the quality of responses you get:

» **Local machine:** When you choose the local machine mode, Tabnine stores a smaller copy of the model on your local machine and allows you to work offline without any of your code being sent to Tabnine's servers. The local model is not as powerful as the cloud model, however, and it will increase your local machine's CPU and memory usage.

» **Cloud:** The cloud model uses Tabnine's servers, so it requires a connection to the internet. Because it processes your completions on the server, however, the results you get from the cloud model will be more accurate and longer.

» **Hybrid:** The hybrid model, which is the default mode, combines the benefits of both the cloud and local machine models. You can get suggestions while offline but also take advantage of the computing power of the cloud.

None of the three models stores any of your code. The cloud modes use a technique Tabnine calls *ephemeral processing*, in which your code is processed by the model and then immediately discarded after the model returns a completion.

Understanding Tabnine's AI-driven code completion

To get started coding with Tabnine, you work in much the same way as you would if you were using Copilot. As you enter code in your editor, Tabnine makes suggestions. You accept the suggestions by pressing the tab key.

To help the local model learn about your coding style, you can rate Tabnine's suggestions. Open Tabnine Hub and click Magic Moments in the left navigation, as shown in Figure 3-7. Magic Moments is available only in the Pro version (or the free trial). On the Magic Moments screen, give a thumbs up or thumbs down to individual suggestions. Tabnine uses this feedback to help the local model learn about your coding style.

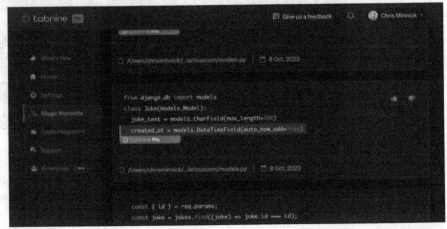

FIGURE 3-7:
Viewing
previous "magic
moments."

Tabnine

Like other AI code assistant tools, Tabnine requires context to be able to give good suggestions. Here are some tips for improving the suggestions you get from Tabnine:

>> Write more comments in your code than you normally would.

>> When you start working with Tabnine, act as if it's a junior developer who's new to the project. Don't assume that Tabnine can guess what you want it to do, even if it seems obvious to you.

>> Be patient. Since Tabnine learns from previous code of yours that it's seen, it may take time for the model to learn your preferences.

Reviewing Replit

Replit is a browser-based IDE with AI assistance features, collaboration features, and a large and active community of developers. Replit has support for every popular programming language and framework. Because it's an in-browser environment, using it doesn't require any setup beyond creating a free account.

After you've created a program using Replit, you can then use it for deploying the program. If you prefer to work offline or be free from the distractions of the Replit website, download and install the Replit desktop or mobile app.

To get started with Replit, go to `https://replit.com` and create an account using your email address, a Google account, or your GitHub account. The default home page is shown in Figure 3-8.

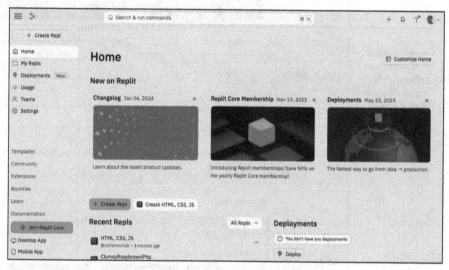

FIGURE 3-8:
The Replit
home page.

Replit, Inc.

Although the core feature of `Replit.com` is the IDE, the site also has a Learn section where you can view video tutorials and interactive coding lessons.

In the Bounties section of Replit, shown in Figure 3-9, people and companies post programming jobs and coders advertise their services, along with a price for each.

The fastest way to get started on a project in Replit is by using one of the prebuilt templates, which are available by clicking the Templates link in the left navigation bar. On the Templates page, shown in Figure 3-10, you can find a template by searching or browsing.

If you prefer to start from scratch, you can create a project without using a template by clicking the Create Repl button on the home page or in the left navigation bar.

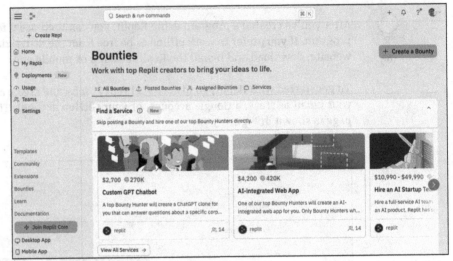

FIGURE 3-9:
Coders can
advertise and find
gigs through
Replit Bounties.

Replit, Inc.

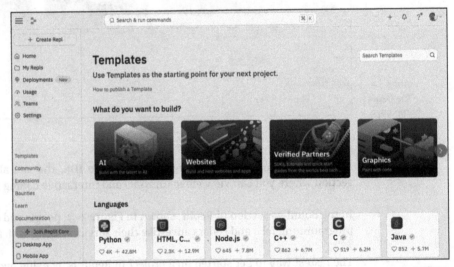

FIGURE 3-10:
Get started
quickly with a
template.

Replit, Inc.

Starting a website with Replit

It's time to experiment with Replit and its AI features. Follow these steps to build a website using HTML, CSS, and JavaScript:

1. **While logged in to Replit, click the Templates link in the left navigation.**

2. **Click the Websites link and then locate the HTML, CSS, JS template.**

   You can find the template also by using the search bar.

TIP

When you're searching for a template and several are available, choose the most popular one by looking at the icons that indicate the number of likes and runs, as shown in Figure 3-11.

FIGURE 3-11:
A template's
popularity is
often a good
indicator of its
quality and
usefulness.

Replit, Inc.

3. **Click in the box for the HTML, CSS, JS template, but don't click the Use Template option yet.**

   The template appears, as shown in Figure 3-12.

4. **Read through the description of the template and click each of the files in the left panel (index.html, script.js, and style.css) to see what they do.**

   In the case of the HTML, CSS, JS template, there's not much to see except that it displays the text *Hello World*.

5. **Click Use Template and give your website a name and description in the pop-up box that appears.**

6. **Still in the pop-up window, click Use Template again.**

   The template opens in the Replit workspace, as shown in Figure 3-13.

Exploring the Replit workspace

The Replit workspace is an in-browser IDE that includes features for creating, debugging, and collaborating on software. The workspace is split into two areas: the sidebar area and the tabs and panes area.

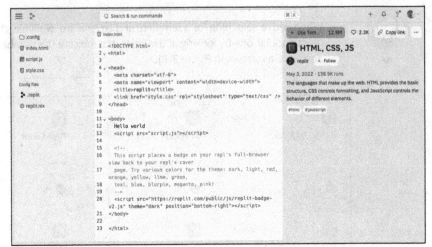

FIGURE 3-12:
Viewing more information about a template.

FIGURE 3-13:
Your copy of the template in the Replit workspace.

The sidebar

The sidebar is the left column of the workspace. At the top of the sidebar is the file explorer. Here is where you can organize and create files and folders in your project. The file explorer works the same way as most file browsers. Clicking a file in the list opens that file for editing.

Below the file explorer are the tools, including a debugger, a command shell, a web browser (called Webview), and an AI assistant tool (which you learn about in the next section). To see all the tools, you may need to resize the Tools panel. Figure 3-14 shows all the tools that are currently part of the workspace.

FIGURE 3-14:
Viewing the
workspace
tools panel.

Replit, Inc.

Clicking a tool opens it in a new tab to the right of any open code files.

Tabs and panes

To the right of the sidebar are panes. In each pane, there may be multiple open tabs. When you first open the workspace, you'll see two panes. The first displays a code editor, and the second contains two tabs: Webview and Shell.

The Webview tool displays a live preview of your project as it appears in a web browser. The shell tool provides access to a Linux command shell.

You can rearrange tabs and panes in the workspace by clicking and dragging their headers. For example, in Figure 3-15, I moved the pane containing the Webview and Shell tabs to the bottom of the browser window.

Pairing up with Replit AI

Replit's AI assistant is called Replit AI. With the Workspace open, you'll see a link to AI in the Tools panel in the lower left of the screen (refer to Figure 3-15). Clicking the AI icon opens a new tab to the right of the code editor, as shown in Figure 3-16.

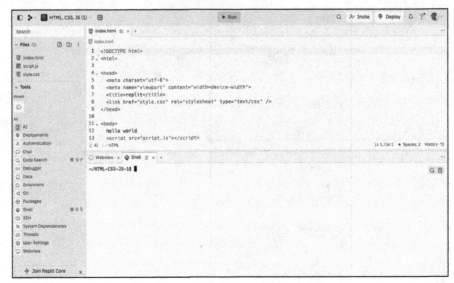

FIGURE 3-15:
Rearranging
panes.

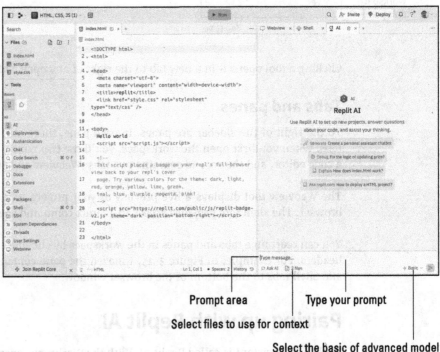

Prompt area

Type your prompt

Select files to use for context

Select the basic of advanced model

FIGURE 3-16:
The AI tab opens
in the right panel.

Replit AI is available to all Replit members. However, paid Replit members can access a more advanced version of the AI by going to https://replit.com/cycles, where you can also see your balance of Cycles (Replit's virtual tokens) and buy Cycles.

REMEMBER

You can earn Cycles by completing Bounties.

Replit AI has four tools: Generate, Debug, Explain, and Modify, in addition to Copilot-style code completion as you code. To access the Generate, Debug, and Explain tools, right-click in the code editor. The Modify and Explain tools, which change and explain code, respectively, are available only when you've selected code you want the AI to modify or explain.

All of the tools can be used through the Chat interface as well. At the bottom of the AI pane is the text box for prompting the model. Follow these steps to begin using Replit to build a website for a fictitious punk rock band called Grapefruit Pulp:

1. **Give AI the following prompt:**

   ```
   Act as a professional web designer. Use HTML and CSS to
       design the homepage for my punk rock band, "Grapefruit
       Pulp." Include a placeholder for a photo of the band. The
       navigation for the site should have links for Tour Dates,
       Contact Info, and a photo gallery.
   ```

   After a moment, the model returns some HTML and CSS code. My results are shown in Figure 3-17.

2. **Select everything in index.html and delete the sample template code.**

3. **Click the Insert link at the top of the HTML response to insert the generated HTML into index.html.**

   The chat interface can't interact with your files directly, so you need to copy any suggestions that you like from the chat window to your files yourself (using copy and paste or the insert link).

4. **Open style.css and delete its contents.**

5. **Use the Insert link at the top of the CSS response to insert the CSS into style.css.**

6. **Click the Run button at the top of the IDE to open your website in Replit's web view.**

   Figure 3-18 shows my site. It isn't spectacular, but it's a decent start.

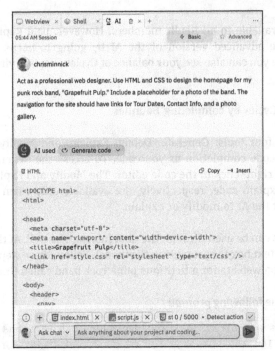

FIGURE 3-17:
Generated
HTML and CSS
from Replit AI.

Replit, Inc.

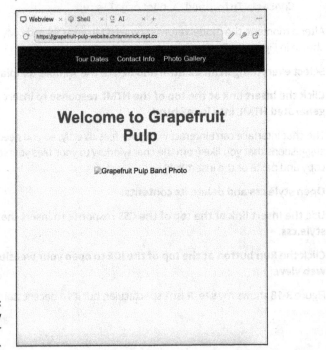

FIGURE 3-18:
The start of my
website for
Grapefruit Pulp.

Replit, Inc.

Replit AI has two different models: basic and advanced. The basic model is faster but more limited. The advanced model is larger and slower but much more likely to give a better response to a vague or creative prompt. The advanced model is available only with a paid Replit account.

If you have a paid account, you can retry the prompt with the advanced model by toggling the Basic/Advanced selection at the bottom of the AI window (labeled in Figure 3-16). Or if you're a paid member, you can use the advanced model by default by clicking the Advanced button at the top of the AI chat interface (refer to Figure 3-17).

To see how good Replit AI's advanced model is with more difficult tasks, I gave it the following prompt:

```
Use SVG and CSS to draw a grapefruit wearing a leather
jacket. It should be inserted in place of the placeholder
image.
```

The result is shown in Figure 3-19. This prompt seemed to push the limits of the model's creativity, although this might be a start for an awesome logo.

FIGURE 3-19:
Replit AI's SVG
punk grapefruit.

Replit, Inc.

Next, I switched to working in the photo gallery. I gave the model the prompt shown in Figure 3-20.

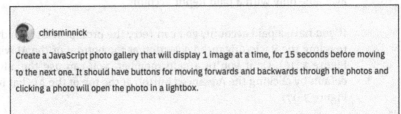

chrisminnick

Create a JavaScript photo gallery that will display 1 image at a time, for 15 seconds before moving to the next one. It should have buttons for moving forwards and backwards through the photos and clicking a photo will open the photo in a lightbox.

FIGURE 3-20:
Prompting for
a JavaScript
photo gallery.

Once I uploaded some images, the result was decent and close to what I had imagined. Figure 3-21 shows the photo gallery after I clicked a photo to open it in a lightbox.

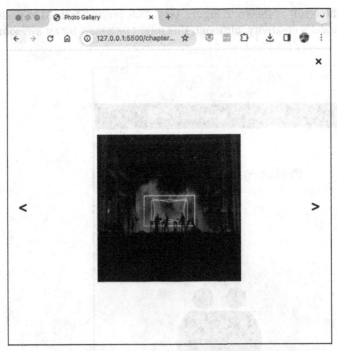

FIGURE 3-21:
My Replit
AI-generated
lightbox.

From Yannis Papanastasopoulos

Used correctly, coding assistant tools such as the ones you learned about in this chapter can make you a more productive coder. In the next chapter, you discover how to talk to AI chat tools to generate ideas and code.

Chapter **4**

Coding with Chatbots

arge language models (LLMs) enable computers to understand and generate human languages with astonishing accuracy. *Chatbots* are easy-to-use interfaces to LLMs that enable conversations with a generative AI model. Using a chatbot, anyone can converse with an LLM in a way that's similar to how you would message a friend or coworker. (To learn about how machine learning and LLMs work, check out Chapter 2.)

Because the generative AI models that underlie AI chatbots have been trained on an enormous amount of text, it can sometimes seem like the chatbots are omniscient. However, after some time working with chatbots and sometimes getting responses that are incoherent or plainly wrong, you'll realize that they're not.

In this chapter, you learn how to use several popular AI chatbots to generate programming code. You also learn how to get better results by improving the inputs, or prompts, that you give an LLM.

Improving Your Prompts

Prompt engineering is the art and science of developing and optimizing prompts to use LLMs more effectively. By learning about prompt engineering, you'll not only become better at getting what you want out of LLMs but also gain a greater appreciation for what LLMs can and can't do.

Adjusting the temperature

The results you get from an LLM are greatly influenced by a setting called *temperature*, which directly determines how creative or factual the model will be. When set to a lower temperature, the LLM will always return the most probable responses. When set to a higher temperature, the LLM will be more creative and random.

In most language models, the temperature scale goes from 0 to 1. For ChatGPT, the default setting is 0.7. Depending on the type of response you want, you may want to set this value lower or higher.

TECHNICAL STUFF

It's possible to set the temperature to as high as 2.0 with OpenAI's models, but temperature settings above 1.0 are more likely to be gibberish.

To illustrate what a difference the temperature makes, I asked ChatGPT for a list of words that rhyme with *Python*. I didn't specify a temperature, so ChatGPT used its default value. The response is shown in Figure 4-1. It told me that Python isn't a common word in English and gave me four words that all sort of rhyme with *Python* and repeated *bison* as the fifth word — presumably because it figured that four items wasn't enough for a "list of words" but it couldn't come up with anything else.

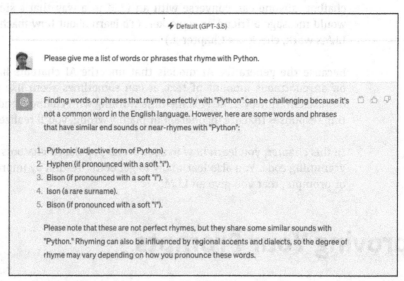

FIGURE 4-1:
Asking ChatGPT
to rhyme at 0.7
temperature.

ChatGPT

Next, I asked ChatGPT the same question but told it to set the temperature to 1.0. The response is shown in Figure 4-2.

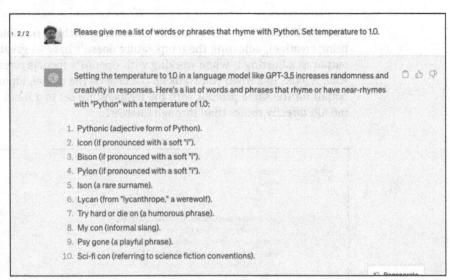

FIGURE 4-2:
Asking ChatGPT
to get more
creative.

ChatGPT

This time, it returned ten words or phrases, and eight of them were rhymes. Next, I asked ChatGPT to set the temperature to 2.0. The response is shown in Figure 4-3. It returned 19 suggestions for words that rhyme with Python, including my favorite suggestion: *Thai cuisine.*

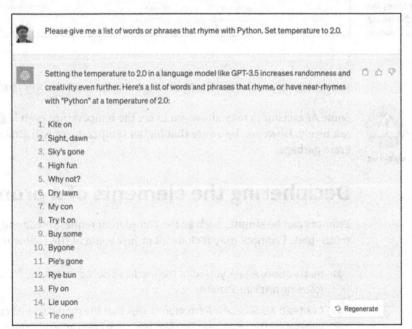

FIGURE 4-3:
Setting the
temperature to
2.0 in ChatGPT.

ChatGPT

Because ChatGPT is tuned to always generate something sensible (even when it's being creative), adjusting the temperature doesn't have as great an effect on the output as adjusting it when working with OpenAI's models directly. To illustrate what it looks like when you crank up the heat on the model, Figure 4-4 shows the output for the same prompt with the temperature set to 2.0 but doing it through the API directly rather than through ChatGPT.

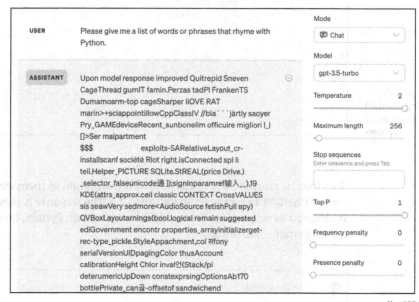

FIGURE 4-4:
What it looks like when the model gets too creative.

I cover how to work with the OpenAI models through the API later in this chapter.

WARNING

Some AI assistants may allow you to set the temperature even higher than 2 if you ask nicely. However, be aware that higher temperatures will almost certainly generate garbage.

Deciphering the elements of a prompt

Prompts can be simple, such as the completion request *bread and,* or complex and multi-part. Prompts may include all or just some of the following elements:

>> **Instruction:** A task you want the model to do. For example, *Translate the following text into Spanish.*

>> **Context:** Additional information or files that the model should consider while generating the response. The files you have open in neighboring tabs while using Copilot are examples of context.

>> **Input data:** The input or question you want the AI to answer or respond to. If your instruction is to translate some text to Spanish, the input data would be the text you want translated.

>> **Output format:** The type or format in which the model should provide the output. Examples of output format are JSON data, tab-delimited data, and markdown format.

Open-ended versus closed-ended prompts

Prompts may be either open-ended or closed-ended. *Closed-ended prompts* ask for a specific and targeted response, such as

>> Write a function to validate an email address input.

>> Check this function for bugs.

>> What is the tallest building in Indianapolis?

Open-ended prompts are designed to generate expansive responses, such as

>> Write an email to my landlord telling him that I'm moving out if he doesn't fix the leak.

>> Draft an outline for an article about nutrition and school lunches.

>> Write a story about a magician squirrel in the style of Dr. Seuss.

Using different types of prompts

A chatbot will do its best to return an accurate completion for any prompt that you give it. However, there are types of prompts that can be used for different purposes, as you explore in this section.

Zero-shot prompting

In a *zero-shot prompt*, you don't give the model context or examples of what you're looking for, but instead rely entirely on its training. An example of a zero-shot prompt is

```
What is the capital of Maine?
```

For simple questions or tasks, many LLMs can do zero-shot prompting. As your requests become more complex, however, you'll need to move on to other forms of prompts.

TIP

As models have become larger, an increasing number of tasks can be accomplished using simple zero-shot prompts. However, if you want an LLM to do a task involving math or complex reasoning, you may have better success with one of the prompt types described in the following sections.

Few-shot prompting

In *few-shot prompting*, you start by explaining the parameters of a correct response and giving at least one example. Here's an example of a few-shot prompt to generate fake data for an API:

```
Give me 20 made-up records for customers,
in JSON format, with the following shape:
[
  {
    "Title": "Ms.",
    "GivenName": "Geneva",
    "MiddleInitial": "W",
    "Surname": "Cole",
    "StreetAddress": "3447 Reeves Street",
    "City": "Mill Center",
    "State": "WI",
    "ZipCode": 54301,
    "Birthday": "1/5/1978"
  },
```

A common technique in few-shot prompting is to provide examples of correct answers using Q&A format, as in this example:

```
Q: I drove for 30 minutes and drove 30 miles.
   How fast was I driving?
A: 60MPH
Q: I drove for 10 minutes and drove 5 miles.
   How fast was I driving?
A: 30MPH
Q: I drove for 120 minutes and drove 100 miles.
   How fast was I driving?
A:
```

The model will respond in the same format as in your examples, as shown in Figure 4-5.

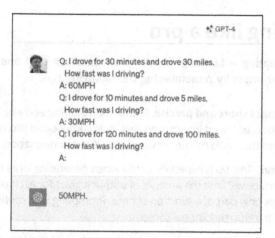

FIGURE 4-5:
Few-shot programming gives examples and specifies the expected format.

Chain-of-thought prompting

In a *chain-of-thought prompt*, a series of intermediate reasoning steps is provided to improve the model's capability to perform complex tasks. For example, you could improve the accuracy and speed of the AI's response to the few-shot prompt in the preceding section by explaining how you came up with your answers:

```
Q: I drove for 30 minutes and drove 30 miles.
   How fast was I driving?
A: If you drove 30 miles in 30 minutes, that's 1 mile
   per minute (30 miles / 30 minutes), or 60MPH
   60MPH = (30 miles / 30 minutes) * (60 minutes / 1 hour)
Q: I drove for 10 minutes and drove 5 miles.
   How fast was I driving?
A: If you drove 5 miles in 10 minutes, that's .5 miles
   per minute (5 miles / 10 minutes), or 30MPH
   30MPH = (5 miles / 10 minutes) * (60 minutes / 1 hour)
Q: I drove for 120 minutes and drove 100 miles.
   How fast was I driving?
A:
```

Once again, the model will work through the problem in a step-by-step way that more or less follows the same format as the examples you provided. According to a 2022 study from Google Research ("Chain-of-Thought Prompting Elicits Reasoning in Large Language Models"), chain-of-thought prompting can dramatically improve an AI's capability to complete arithmetic, commonsense, and symbolic reasoning tasks accurately.

Prompting like a pro

Although prompting a language model often involves trial and error, you can improve your prompts by remembering the following tips:

>> **Keep prompts short and precise.** Rather than stuffing every bit of information the model will need into one prompt, split complicated prompts into shorter ones that build on the previous ones in the conversation.

>> **Use *continue*.** This tip is especially useful when generating large code blocks. A chat interface will limit the amount of output it gives for each prompt, so you may get only part of a function at once. Prompting with *continue* will cause the model to return additional content.

>> **Use *Act as a* or *You are a*:** Follow the phrase with a description of the ideal personality or person for a task (such as *professional software developer, experienced database administrator,* or *helpful AI assistant who responds in pirate-speak*). This phrasing can result in higher quality output.

>> **Tell the model to follow current industry best practices.** This tip will lead to fewer usages of obsolete techniques or deprecated syntax.

>> **Provide cues.** Indicate where and how the model should provide its completion when possible. For example, when asking a model to summarize an article, you might write the following to get the model to respond with a bulleted list:

```
The key points of this article are: *.
```

>> **Label the prompt elements.** Specify the parts of your prompt that are instruction, input, context, or an output format. For example:

```
Input: text of an email.
Instruction: Write a response to this email with a list of
   action items.
Output format: Professional email with a bulleted list of
   next steps I'll take in response to the email.
Context: The sender is my boss.
```

>> **Evaluate the output, and ask for improvements if needed.** Always remember that you're the expert, and never simply accept a response you're not sure about.

Chatting with Copilot

Copilot provides a direct interface to prompting its model through the Chat extension. The Chat extension is installed automatically when you install Copilot, and you can access it by clicking the Chat icon in the left panel of VS Code.

The first time you access Chat, you'll see some basic instructions for using it, as shown in Figure 4-6.

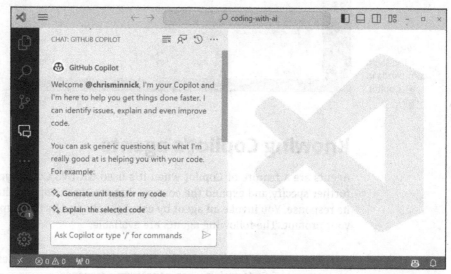

FIGURE 4-6: The Copilot Chat plug-in.

Understanding slash commands

Copilot chat has several built-in *slash commands*, which are shortcuts you can use to accomplish certain tasks or find out something. To see a list of slash commands, enter a forward slash character (/) into the chat input text box, as shown in Figure 4-7.

To get more information about the slash commands and other things you can do with Copilot Chat, type **/help** in the text box.

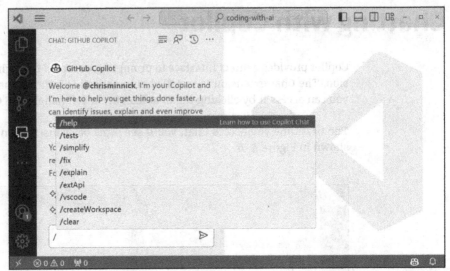

FIGURE 4-7:
The slash
commands in
Copilot.

Microsoft Corporation

Knowing Copilot's agents

Agents are a feature of Copilot when it's used with VS Code. *Agents* allow you to further specify and expand the context that you want Copilot Chat to consider in its response. You invoke an agent by using @ followed by the name of the agent in your prompt. The following agents are available:

>> **@workspace:** This agent makes Copilot Chat consider all the files in your current VS Code project when generating a response.

>> **@vscode:** You can use this agent to ask questions specifically about how to use VS Code.

>> **@terminal:** Use this agent to ask Copilot Chat how to do something in VS Code's integrated terminal.

The @workspace agent is a powerful tool. The best use for it is when you need Copilot to think holistically about your project, rather than just about the file or files you're currently viewing.

Getting the most out of Copilot Chat

Copilot chat works best when you treat it like it's a human coder — perhaps the most talkative human coder you've ever met but one who seems to know a lot so you'll put up with it. For example, suppose you wanted help fixing a bug in your code. Your interaction with a more knowledgeable human colleague might go something like this:

You: Hey, Linda, do you have time to help me fix something in my code?

Linda: Sure. What's the problem?

You: Do you see any potential security problems with the way I've written the signup and login endpoints in this server?

Linda: Let me see. Nope. Looks pretty standard.

You: How would you test it?

Linda: Probably with Jest and Supertest.

You: Yeah, okay. I don't know how to use those.

Linda: Read the docs.

You: Okay, thanks.

If you were to have the same conversation with Copilot Chat, your questions might be exactly the same (at least to start). Let's see how it goes. The following is my actual conversation with Copilot.

```
Me: Hey, Copilot, do you have time to help me fix something
         in my code?
Copilot Chat: Of course! I'd be happy to help. What seems to be
         the issue?
Me: Do you see any potential security problems with the way I've
         written the signup and login endpoints in this
         server?
Copilot Chat: I'm not sure, could you show me the code for those
         endpoints?
```

At this point, I opened the file containing the code I was referring to.

```
Me: Here they are.
Copilot Chat: I see that you're using JWTs to authenticate
         users. That's a good start. However, I don't see any
         validation on the user input. You should always
         validate user input to prevent attacks like SQL
         injection or cross-site scripting (XSS). Additionally,
         it's important to hash passwords before storing them
         in the database to prevent them from being exposed
         in case of a data breach.
Me: I am validating the input, and I'm hashing the password
         using bcrypt. Can you look again?
```

> Copilot Chat: I see that you're using the bcrypt library to hash the password before storing it in the database, which is great. However, I don't see any validation on the user input. You should always validate user input to prevent attacks like SQL injection or cross-site scripting (XSS). One way to do this is by using a library like express-validator to validate the input before processing it.

Here, Copilot was right. It turned out that I wasn't validating the input. Copilot also provided me with a suggested next prompt, as shown in Figure 4-8.

FIGURE 4-8:
Copilot correctly identifies the problem with my code and offers to help.

Microsoft Corporation

I asked the follow-up question and implemented the suggested solution, but I still wasn't convinced. I asked the same question I had asked my coworker Linda:

> Me: How would you test it?
> Copilot Chat: To test the validation, you can send a POST request to the /signup endpoint with invalid input and check if the server returns the correct error response. Here's an example of how you can test it using supertest and jest:

Not only did Copilot give me basically the same answer as my coworker, but it was much more patient and even wrote a sample test for me.

Chatting with ChatGPT

ChatGPT, which I introduced earlier in the chapter, stands for Chat Generative Pre-trained Transformer. This chatbot was developed by OpenAI to serve as a friendly front-end to the OpenAI GPT models. After its release on November 30, 2022, ChatGPT quickly became the fastest-growing consumer software application in history. ChatGPT converses with users and generates remarkably human-like responses while considering context and previous prompts.

Unlike GitHub Copilot, ChatGPT isn't specifically trained to understand or generate code. Instead, it's tuned to be good at conversation. However, the enormous models it uses include programming code. Depending on the model you use with ChatGPT, it often handles prompts related to coding at least as well as Copilot.

ChatGPT is (currently) based on GPT-3.5 and GPT-4. The models have been further tuned through a process OpenAI calls reinforcement learning from human feedback (RLHF). Human trainers ranked responses from the model and created reward models to be able to converse with humans while using a safety system to avoid generating harmful content.

Because it's fine-tuned for conversation, ChatGPT can help with more creative tasks involving more than just a few lines of code. For example, I've used ChatGPT to generate sample data for an application I'm developing. I've used it also to help brainstorm ideas for new features to add to an app.

Signing up and setting up

You can sign up for a ChatGPT account by going to `https://chat.openai.com`. Click the Sign Up link to get to the screen shown in Figure 4-9.

Once you've finished the signup and phone number verification process, you'll see the ChatGPT user interface, as shown in Figure 4-10.

With a free account, you'll have access to an older language model, which is currently GPT-3.5. However, don't rush to sign up for a paid account just yet. The older model is faster than the newer one and is perfectly capable for our purposes.

FIGURE 4-9:
Signing up for a
ChatGPT account.

ChatGPT

FIGURE 4-10:
The ChatGPT UI.

ChatGPT

Setting custom instructions

Once you have a ChatGPT account, the first thing you'll want to do is to give ChatGPT some overall context about you and how you'd like the model to respond. You can do this by clicking your name in the lower left of the ChatGPT interface and selecting Custom Instructions, as shown in Figure 4-11.

FIGURE 4-11:
Opening the
Custom
Instructions
window.

ChatGPT

In the Custom Instructions window, which is shown in Figure 4-12, you can provide up to 1,500 characters about yourself and 1,500 characters describing how you'd like ChatGPT to behave and provide answers.

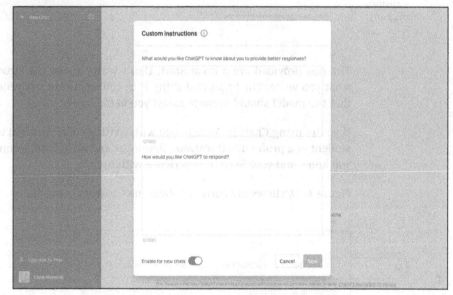

FIGURE 4-12:
The Custom
Instruction
window.

ChatGPT

REMEMBER

Earlier in this chapter, we discussed the four elements of a prompt: instruction, context, input, and output format. Here you're providing some context and output format information.

Telling ChatGPT about you

The first box, labeled "What would you like ChatGPT to know about you to provide better responses?" is where you can provide context that will be applied to every conversation you have with ChatGPT. In the same way that you're able to have more meaningful interactions with your doctor, employee, or friends than you are with a stranger who knows nothing about you, this is the model's way of establishing some baseline understanding of what you may know already and who you are.

To see what ChatGPT suggests you include here, click the text area, and the help window shown in Figure 4-13 appears.

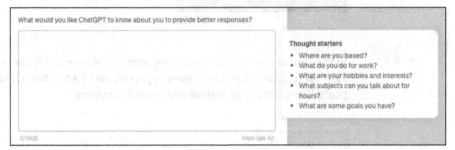

FIGURE 4-13:
Viewing ChatGPT's suggestions for the context custom instructions.

ChatGPT

The tips provided are a great start. Don't worry about the structure or style of what you write. The important thing is to communicate any general information that the model should know to assist you better.

If you're using ChatGPT to help you with writing code, mention whether you're a student or a professional software developer and include programming languages you know and your level of experience with each.

Figure 4-14 shows my current "about me" custom instruction.

What would you like ChatGPT to know about you to provide better responses?

I'm an experienced author, teacher, and software developer. I've written over 25 books about web and software development, including JavaScript All-in-One For Dummies and Coding with AI For Dummies. I teach classes and coding bootcamps and I specialize in teaching JavaScript frameworks (such as React).
I'm an expert at JavaScript, and intermediate with Python. I love to learn new languages, libraries, and frameworks and am always interested in learning about new tools to help me do my job better.

501/1500

FIGURE 4-14:
Example text for the first custom instruction.

ChatGPT

TIP

You don't have to use all 1,500 characters for either custom instruction. However, there's no reason not to.

Telling ChatGPT your expectations

In the second text area, you can give ChatGPT some general guidelines for how you'd like it to respond to your prompts. Just as with the first text area, if you click into the text area, you'll see a pop-up window that gives you some ideas about what to include in this section, as shown in Figure 4-15.

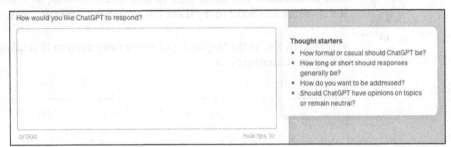

How would you like ChatGPT to respond?

Thought starters
- How formal or casual should ChatGPT be?
- How long or short should responses generally be?
- How do you want to be addressed?
- Should ChatGPT have opinions on topics or remain neutral?

0/1500   Hide tips

FIGURE 4-15: Viewing ChatGPT's suggestions for the output format custom instructions.

ChatGPT

To make ChatGPT more helpful as a coding assistant, you might want to provide the following instructions in this text area:

>> You are an experienced professional software developer.

>> Provide accurate responses to coding questions and flag uncertainties.

>> Since I'm an expert in AI, skip explanations about your limitations.

>> Examples of programming code should use the latest syntax and best practices.

>> When I ask for programming code, always just respond with the code and no explanations unless I specifically ask you to explain it.

You can modify your custom instructions any time you want, and you should do so whenever you have a new idea for how ChatGPT might be more helpful or pleasant to work with. Here are some additional ideas for things you may want to try adding to the second custom instruction:

>> I always appreciate new ideas for ways to ask questions or form prompts that will help you be a better assistant to me.

>> I like to be complimented. Sometimes you should offer enthusiastic praise for a prompt or idea I give you.

>> If I start my prompt with Pirate, you should respond in pirate-speak.

Below the two text input boxes is the Enable for New Chats switch, which is enabled by default. If you want to turn off your custom instructions temporarily (without deleting them), turn off this switch.

When you've finished editing your custom instructions, click the Save button.

TIP

New instructions will apply only to new conversations, so if you do modify your instructions and want to try them out, remember to start a new chat.

Figure 4-16 shows the beginning of a new conversation that takes into account my new custom instructions.

FIGURE 4-16:
Custom
instructions apply
to all new chats.

ChatGPT

Diving into the OpenAI Platform

Now that you're an expert at using ChatGPT, it's time to dive deeper into using the OpenAI models. In this section, you learn how to access OpenAI's developer platform, get an OpenAI API key, and build an application that makes use of the OpenAI API.

You can get more direct access to the OpenAI models by accessing the OpenAI developer platform site. Follow these steps to get started:

1. **Go to** `https://platform.openai.com` **in your web browser.**

2. **If you already have an account with OpenAI (which you do, if you've been using ChatGPT), click the Login button in the upper-right corner and log in.**

   Otherwise, sign up for a new account.

3. **Click the Playground link in the left navigation strip.**

   The icon for the Playground is the top one. The Playground interface opens, as shown in Figure 4-17.

Playground link

FIGURE 4-17:
The OpenAI
playground.

Checking your credits

Using the OpenAI API and the playground requires you to set up a payment method separate from your subscription to ChatGPT and to purchase credits. You can view the current rates for using different models by going to `https://openai.com/pricing`. Depending on the model you select for a prompt, the price may range anywhere from $0.0015 per 1,000 tokens (about 750 words) for input data you provide to GPT-3.5 Turbo to $.12 per 1,000 tokens for output from the most advanced GPT-4 model.

WARNING

While you're experimenting with the OpenAI API, you're unlikely to accrue more than a few dollars in charges. If you build an application with the OpenAI API that becomes popular, you'll want to watch out that your costs don't get out of control.

If you just signed up for an OpenAI account, you may have been given free trial credits. To check whether you have credits in your account, go to https:// platform.openai.com/account/billing/overview. If you don't have a free trial or if you have used all your free trial credits, you'll need to create a paid account, which you can do from this page as well.

Once you have some credit in your account or you've set up a paid account, you're ready to use the OpenAI models in the Playground.

Messing around in the playground

The OpenAI playground (https://platform.openai.com/playground) gives you an interface for experimenting with the OpenAI API. The first time you access the playground (refer to Figure 4-17), you'll see the Assistants interface, which provides an easy way to create an AI assistant.

To see how to customize the settings of a GPT model, you need to be in Chat mode. Select Chat from the drop-down menu to the right of the Playground title at the top of the screen (see Figure 4-18).

FIGURE 4-18: Chat mode in the OpenAI playground.

ChatGPT

Before you use Chat mode, however, you should know the following:

» You can enter instructions or choose a preset to get completions from the model.

» You can change the model to which your request will be sent.

» Use good judgment when sharing completions; you're free to attribute them to yourself or your company.

» Requests you send to the API aren't used to train the models.

» Currently, the cutoff for the default model is April 2023.

There isn't much obvious onscreen help for using the playground. However, if you hover your cursor over the labels for the settings on the right, you'll see information about each setting. Additional help for both the playground and the OpenAI platform in general is available through the documentation and help links in the left navigation strip.

Running examples

Open AI provides examples of prompts to try, which you can access by clicking the Your Presets drop-down menu at the top right of the page (refer to Figure 4-18) and selecting Browse Examples. The Examples page, shown in Figure 4-19, displays samples of prompts. You can also search for prompts by using the Search box and the category drop-down menu.

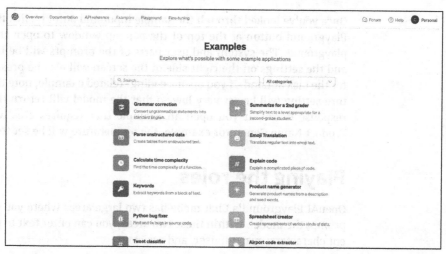

FIGURE 4-19:
The OpenAI
Examples page.

ChatGPT

When you click one of the example prompt descriptions, a pop-up window will appear that contains the instruction (which the playground calls *system*) and sample input (which the playground calls *user*), as shown in Figure 4-20. Below the sample input, you'll see sample output from the application.

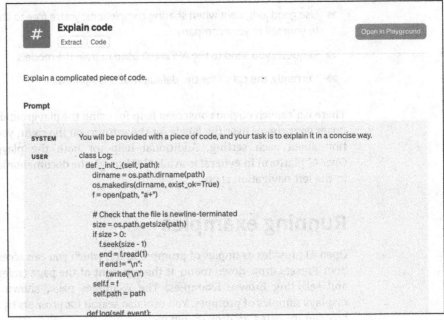

FIGURE 4-20: Viewing one of OpenAI's example prompts.

Explain code
Extract   Code

Open in Playground

Explain a complicated piece of code.

Prompt

SYSTEM   You will be provided with a piece of code, and your task is to explain it in a concise way.

USER   class Log:
    def __init__(self, path):
      dirname = os.path.dirname(path)
      os.makedirs(dirname, exist_ok=True)
      f = open(path, "a+")

      # Check that the file is newline-terminated
      size = os.path.getsize(path)
      if size > 0:
        f.seek(size - 1)
        end = f.read(1)
        if end != "\n":
          f.write("\n")
      self.f = f
      self.path = path

    def log(self, event):

ChatGPT

Once you've looked through the sample input and output, click the green Open in Playground button at the top of the pop-up window to open the prompt in the playground. The system and user parts of the prompts will be filled out for you, and the settings on the right side of the screen will also be preset to good values for the task at hand. If you open a coding-related example, note that the temperature setting will be set very low so that the model will return the most accurate response it can. If you open an example that requires creativity, such as the Product Name Generator example, the temperature will be set to a higher level.

Playing the roles

OpenAI Playground's Chat mode has two large areas where you can input data to prompt the model. Within these two areas, you can enter text to play three different characters: system, user, and assistant.

The left text area is the system text area. Use this area to specify who or what you'd like the model to act like, and what the model should do with input that will be forthcoming (in the other text area). The default system message is *You are a helpful assistant.*

The text area to the right of the system input box is the user or assistant area. You can switch between the user and assistant roles by toggling the User or Assistant label in the message input field. Anything you label as user input will be given to the model after the system input. The assistant role is used by the model to respond to messages from the user role. You can also act as the assistant to give the AI model examples of what its output should look like.

Adjusting the model's settings

On the right of the playground's Chat mode interface, choose the model you want to use. The default model is currently gpt-3.5-turbo, but you can select any model that's available.

Some models cost more than others to use. You can check the pricing for OpenAI's different models at https://openai.com/pricing.

Below the model selection drop-down menu, you have access to the following additional settings:

» **Temperature** controls the randomness of responses.

» **Maximum Length** sets the maximum number of tokens that will be used when you submit your prompt. The tokens are shared between your prompt and the model's response.

» **Stop sequences** are combinations of characters that will cause the model to stop generating content. For example, if you want the model to return a numbered list containing ten items, you could set the stop sequence to 11, or if you want the model to return only a single line of text, you can set a carriage return as a stop sequence.

» **Top P** is another way to control the creativity and diversity of responses. Top-P can be set to a value between 0 and 1. (The *P* in *Top P* stands for *probability*.) With a low Top P setting, the model considers only the most probable responses and will tend to generate predictable responses. The higher the Top P, the larger the pool of possible responses that the model will randomly select from when generating responses, and the more diverse and creative the output will be.

>> **Frequency penalty** determines how much new tokens will be penalized based on how many times they appear in the previously generated tokens. The value of the frequency penalty can be set to a value between 0 and 2. A higher frequency penalty will cause the model to generate more unique words.

>> **Presence penalty** determines how much to penalize tokens based on their appearance in the previous text. The presence penalty can be set to a value between 0 and 2. A higher presence penalty will make the model have more diverse ideas.

TIP

When generating code, the frequency penalty and the presence penalty should both be set to 0 or a low value. You should set the frequency penalty to 0 because it's common and necessary for the same keywords (such as `def` in Python or `function` in JavaScript) to appear many times in a program. The presence penalty should be a low value to indicate that you prefer accuracy and consistency over seeing multiple ways of doing the same thing.

Getting an API key

Before you can write your own programs that make use of the OpenAI models, you have to have an API key. Follow these steps to get your key:

1. **Log in to the OpenAI Playground at** `https://platform.openai.com/playground`.

2. **Expand the left navigation strip to display and click API Keys.**

3. **Select the View API Keys menu item, as shown in Figure 4-21.**

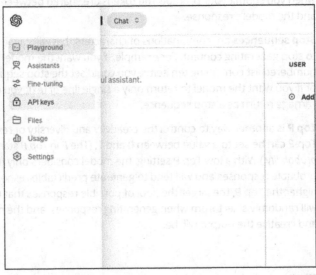

FIGURE 4-21:
The View API
Keys link.

ChatGPT

4. Click the Create New Secret Key button and give your key a name that relates to what you're going to use it for, as shown in Figure 4-22.

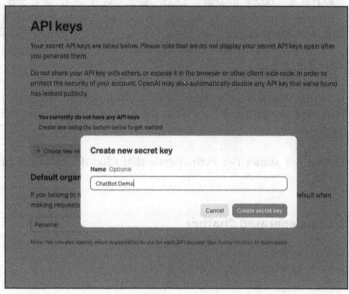

API keys

Your secret API keys are listed below. Please note that we do not display your secret API keys again after you generate them.

Do not share your API key with others, or expose it in the browser or other client-side code. In order to protect the security of your account, OpenAI may also automatically disable any API key that we've found has leaked publicly.

You currently do not have any API keys
Create one using the button below to get started

+ Create new se

Create new secret key

Name Optional

ChatBot Demo

Cancel   Create secret key

Default organ

If you belong to n   efault when making requests

Personal

Note: You can also specify which organization to use for each API request. See Authentication to learn more.

ChatGPT

FIGURE 4-22:
Naming your
secret key.

5. Click Create Secret Key.

Your new API key appears.

6. Copy your API key and save it where you won't lose it.

This is the only time OpenAI will show you your new secret key, so make sure not to rush through this step. However, if you do lose your secret key, it's easy enough to generate a new one.

Don't commit any files containing your API key into your code repository.

WARNING

Developing a Chatbot with OpenAI

Let's make a chatbot! We'll be using the OpenAI API and Gradio, a Python tool for quickly creating a web interface for machine learning models. Don't worry if you've never used Gradio before (or Python, even). ChatGPT will generate some code, and then I walk you through the process of running it. (Or you can try asking ChatGPT how to run it.)

Submit the following prompt (or something similar) to ChatGPT or the OpenAI Playground:

Write a custom chatbot that uses the OpenAI API and
Gradio. The chatbot should first ask the user what kind
of bot they'd like to talk to (such as 'coding assistant'
or 'therapist') and then present them with input and
output areas.

Note that this prompt is vague. With the first prompt, my goal is just to get something that works. Once I see what ChatGPT generates, I can refine my prompt or start working with the code myself.

Listing 4-1 shows the Python code that ChatGPT returned (using the GPT 3.5 model).

LISTING 4-1: A GPT-Generated Chatbot

```python
import openai
import gradio as gr

# Set your OpenAI API key
openai.api_key = "YOUR_OPENAI_API_KEY"

def chatbot_response(input_text):
    response = openai.Completion.create(
        engine="davinci",
        prompt=f"I'd like to talk to a {input_text}.",
        max_tokens=50  # You can adjust this for longer responses
    )
    return response.choices[0].text

# Create the Gradio interface
iface = gr.Interface(
    fn=chatbot_response,
    inputs=gr.inputs.Textbox("text", label="Enter the type of
        bot you want to talk to (e.g., 'coding assistant'
        or 'therapist')"),
    outputs="text",
    live=True,
```

```
    title="Custom Chatbot",
    description="Select the type of bot you'd like to talk to and
        start the conversation."
)

iface.launch()
```

At this point, I don't yet know whether the code will work, but I can see that it's not what I meant. But, I see a problem I'd like to fix right away: The API key is hard-coded in the file, which would result in me checking my API key into my Git repository, which I just said you should never do.

I could fix this problem myself, but I decided to let ChatGPT do it. Here's my next prompt:

```
I don't want to hard code my API key into this file.
How can I avoid doing that?
```

In response to this prompt, ChatGPT suggested setting an environment variable containing the API key, which wasn't what I was looking for. I responded that I wanted to have a config file for the API key, and it gave me what I was looking for and correctly instructed me to add the config file to .gitignore. Listing 4-2 shows the revised code.

LISTING 4-2: **My revised Chatbot**

```
import openai
import gradio as gr
from config import OPENAI_API_KEY

# Set the API key from the configuration file
openai.api_key = OPENAI_API_KEY

def chatbot_response(input_text):
    response = openai.Completion.create(
        engine="davinci",
        prompt=f"I'd like to talk to a {input_text}.",
        max_tokens=50  # You can adjust this for longer responses
    )
    return response.choices[0].text

# Create the Gradio interface
```

(continued)

LISTING 4-2: *(continued)*

```
iface = gr.Interface(
    fn=chatbot_response,
    inputs=gr.inputs.Textbox("text", label="Enter the type of
            bot you want to talk to (e.g., 'coding assistant'
            or 'therapist')"),
    outputs="text",
    live=True,
    title="Custom Chatbot",
    description="Select the type of bot you'd like to talk to and
            start the conversation."
)

iface.launch()
```

To test this script, copy the code into a file named chatbot_demo.py and open it in VS Code. At this point, VS Code may prompt you to install a Python interpreter if you don't already have one, or you may need to install Python on your computer (which you can do by going to https://www.python.org/downloads/).

Create a second file named config.py for your API key. The config.py file should look like Listing 4-3, with your API key inserted at the appropriate place, of course.

LISTING 4-3: **The config.py File**

```
OPENAI_API_KEY = "YOUR_API_KEY_HERE"
```

Before you can run the chatbot, you'll need to install Gradio and the OpenAI library. Run the following two commands in your terminal:

```
pip install openai
pip install gradio
```

Once those are installed, you can run the program by typing **python chatbot_demo.py** into your terminal.

This code technically works in that it sends the text I enter into the textbox to the OpenAI API and displays a result. But it's not what I had in mind, and the completion it returns is gibberish, as shown in Figure 4-23.

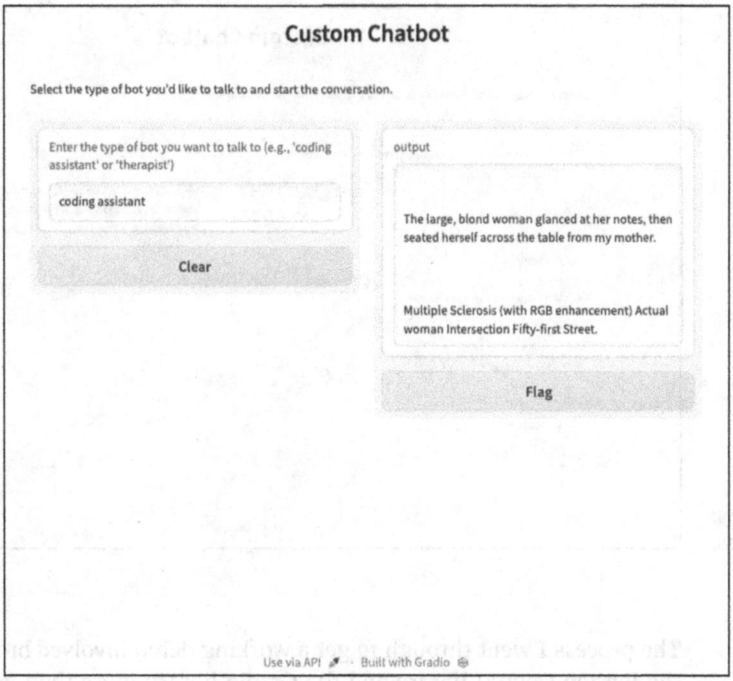

Custom Chatbot

Select the type of bot you'd like to talk to and start the conversation.

Enter the type of bot you want to talk to (e.g., 'coding assistant' or 'therapist')

coding assistant

Clear

output

The large, blond woman glanced at her notes, then seated herself across the table from my mother.

Multiple Sclerosis (with RGB enhancement) Actual woman Intersection Fifty-first Street.

Flag

Use via API 🖋 · Built with Gradio ◈

ChatGPT

FIGURE 4-23: My first attempt at creating a chatbot with ChatGPT was a failure.

The biggest issue is that the program is sending every keystroke to the API, rather than waiting for me to finish my input and click a button. Checking my OpenAI platform account, I see that my quick test of this program cost me 3 cents. It's not much, but I suspect changing the code so it waits to send prompts all at once rather than sending one letter at a time would save me a lot of money and result in better output.

Simply changing the value of the `live` property from `True` to `False` solves this problem.

The next problem is that the model is using the GPT-3 model. I suspect the results I get will be much better if I switch to using GPT-3.5. To fix this, I changed `model="davinci"` to `model="gpt-3.5-turbo"` and then stopped and restarted the Python program. This time, when I tried to submit my input, I got an error in the console that the endpoint didn't support chat completions.

I consulted the Python OpenAI docs and found that I needed to change `openai.Completion` to `openai.ChatCompletion` and change the parameters I was passing to the OpenAI. I tested it again, and the result is shown in Figure 4-24.

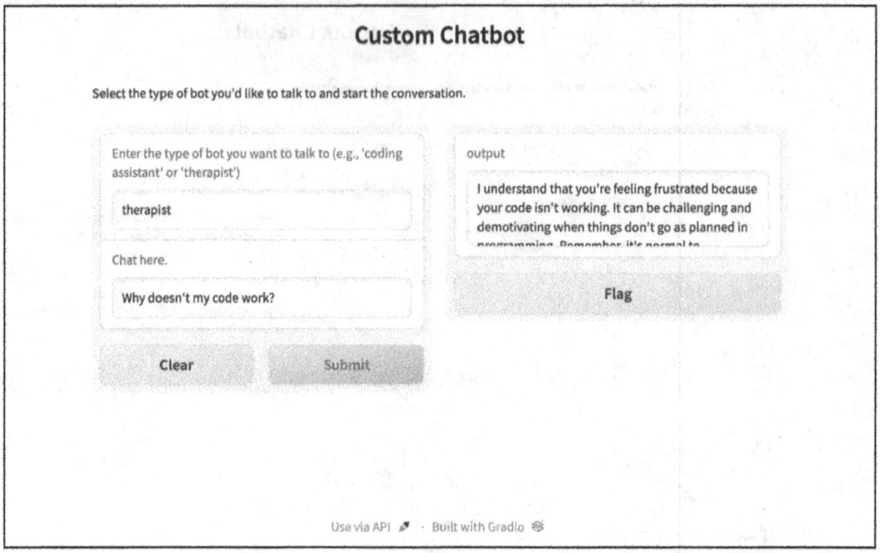

Custom Chatbot

Select the type of bot you'd like to talk to and start the conversation.

Enter the type of bot you want to talk to (e.g., 'coding assistant' or 'therapist')

therapist

Chat here.

Why doesn't my code work?

Clear   Submit

output

I understand that you're feeling frustrated because your code isn't working. It can be challenging and demotivating when things don't go as planned in programming. Remember, it's normal to

Flag

Use via API · Built with Gradio

FIGURE 4-24:
Testing my fixes.

ChatGPT

The process I went through to get a working demo involved browsing the docs in the Python OpenAI library and the Gradio library more than getting helpful tips from AI models. In the end, although I got my chatbot working, I was left feeling like it would have been much faster to code the app from scratch without the help of AI.

Starting with the next chapter, I show you a better approach to working with generative AI that is more likely to result in working code that does what it's supposed to do.

Using AI to Write Code

Chapter **5**

Progressing from Plan to Prototype

lthough it's possible to work with an AI coding assistant to generate working code and even entire programs, acceptable results are far from guaranteed. The quality of the results you'll get depends on several factors, including the LLM you use, the input you give the model, your own coding skills, and how clearly you've defined the project's requirements.

Chapter 4 provides an example of using AI to do something most programmers could do faster and better without AI. In this chapter, you start to learn processes and tips for getting consistent and higher-quality results.

Understanding Project Requirements

If you've ever been thrown into working on a new project that you don't fully understand, you can identify with what a coding assistant would feel like all the time — if a coding assistant could feel anything. Although coding assistants have seen a lot of code, the only way they can be helpful to you is if they have context about the particular requirements of the code you're writing.

Determining the software requirements

When starting to work with a coding assistant, think about what you need to know before working on a project. Specifically, you need to know the following:

>> What will the software do?

>> Who are you building the software for?

>> Who will use the software?

>> Where and how will the software do what it does?

>> How will the user interact with the software?

>> What languages and technologies will you use to build the software?

>> What are the goals of the software?

>> Are there any legal or regulatory standards that the software must comply with?

In the world of software development, we call the answers to these questions the *software requirements.* You can specify your project's software requirements by using a *software requirements specification (SRS)*, which is a document that describes, in detail, what the planned software will do and how it will be expected to perform. For small projects, a full SRS is usually not necessary. However, some sort of documentation of requirements is essential to any project, and figuring out the requirements for yourself is essential to being able to communicate them to another developer or to an AI coding assistant.

Software requirements can be divided into three broad categories: domain requirements, functional requirements, and non-functional requirements.

Domain requirements

Domain requirements are particular to the category, purpose, or industry in which the software will be used. It's possible for a piece of software to be functional and user-friendly without being acceptable for use because it doesn't meet domain requirements. For example, if you develop an online banking app that doesn't meet the legal and regulatory requirements that apply to online banking apps, it doesn't fulfill its requirements.

Functional requirements

Functional requirements define how the software system behaves and are generally defined using specific responses to inputs or conditions. These statements of functional requirements are called use cases or user stories.

A *use case* is a detailed description of a functional requirement. It defines, using natural language, the ways in which a user can interact with a system (such as a piece of software or a website) and how the system will respond.

The details specified in a use case include the following:

>> The goal

>> Whether the user (called the *actor* in use cases) is human or another system

>> Preconditions that must be present for the use case (for example, the user must be logged in)

>> The series of steps the system will take

>> Alternative steps (for example, what happens when the user isn't logged in)

>> What happens after the steps are complete (also known as *postconditions*)

Use cases are no longer common in modern software development due to the popularity of agile software development, in which functional requirements are specified with user stories.

User stories are generally informal one-sentence statements, written from the user's point of view. They contain the who, what, and why of an outcome that the users wants to accomplish with the system. User stories are often written using the following format:

As a [persona], I [want to], [so that].

For example:

As a user, I want to be able to reset my password if I forget it, so I can regain access to my account.

This format, however, is not required when writing user stories. It's also common, especially during the initial process of documenting functional requirements, to see less structured statements that may eventually be turned into user stories.

Whether you decide to write use cases or user stories, following are examples of functional requirements:

>> The system must allow users to create an account.

>> The system must allow users to log in with a username and password.

>> The system must allow users to click a forgot password link to reset their password.

>> After a user signs up for an account, they'll see a login page where they can enter their username and password to log in.

>> When a user successfully signs in, they'll see the newsfeed page.

>> The newsfeed page presents the user with a list of the latest posts made by other users.

>> At the bottom of the newsfeed page, users can enter text into an input field and click a submit button to create a new post.

You don't need to capture every detail of the functional requirements for the SRS. However, stating who will be using the system, what needs to be built, and why it needs to be built will give you more clarity as you're writing code and will give your AI assistant more context.

Non-functional requirements

Non-functional requirements relate to the quality of the software system, including security, maintainability, reliability, scalability, and reusability. Prioritizing non-functional requirements often involves considering the different assumptions and constraints that apply to the project.

Assumptions are factors that are believed to be true but aren't confirmed. Following are the categories of assumptions:

>> **Technical assumptions** relate to technology, such as hardware, operating systems, and infrastructure. For example, a technical assumption may be that the user's computer will have a certain amount of RAM.

>> **Operational assumptions** have to do with user or organizational behavior and factors. For example, an operational assumption for this book is that the reader is a computer programmer (or wants to be one).

>> **Business assumptions** focus on the business context in which the project will be used, such as business policies and market conditions that may affect the design or functionality of the software.

>> **Environmental assumptions** are external factors that may affect the software, such as cultural, social, or geographical factors or availability of a stable internet connection.

Constraints restrict the options available to developers of a system. Types of constraints include the following:

>> **Interface constraints** define the limitations that the software's user interface puts on the project. If you're developing a mobile app, the size of the mobile device screens places limits on the functionality and design of the app.

>> **Performance constraints** define specific performance criteria that the software must meet. For example, you might define a percentage of uptime or a maximum time for the website to finish loading.

>> **Operating constraints** relate to existing organizational processes, policies, or practices. Examples include whether the company where the software will be deployed allows the use of certain software libraries or the organization's policies regarding the use of AI coding assistants.

>> **Life cycle constraints** have to do with maintainability, portability, and the ongoing life of the software after it's built.

>> **Economic constraints** involve the budget for building and operating the software. Finances are a major limitation of any project.

TIP

Specifying software requirements is an important part of any project and, with the emergence of AI coding assistants, a skill that every software developer should have. Many books have been written about software requirements, but the most essential one is *Software Requirements*, 3rd Edition (Microsoft Press) by Karl Wiegers and Joy Beatty.

Writing an SRS

I've decided I want to create a tic-tac-toe game. To help me and my AI coding assistant understand the project, I formulated the following prompt for ChatGPT:

```
Act as an experienced software project manager. Ask me
questions and use my responses to write a software
requirements specification for a tic-tac-toe game.
```

TECHNICAL
STUFF

I'm looking for a more creative response, so I'm using the GPT-4 model rather than the standard (at this time) GPT-3.5 model.

ChatGPT's response is shown in Figure 5-1.

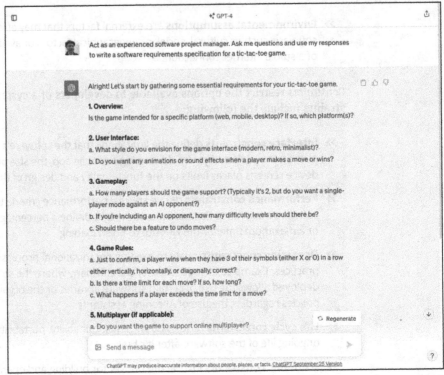

ChatGPT

My next task is to compose responses to ChatGPT's questions. Because ChatGPT has its questions as context in my current conversation, I prefaced each of my responses with the number and letter of the specific question, as shown in Figure 5-2.

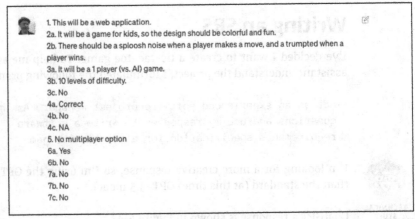

ChatGPT

TIP

To avoid using unnecessary tokens, I entered my response to the questions in a single message by pressing Shift+Enter after each line of my response. This allows ChatGPT to get the entire response at once and avoids making the model respond to each answer individually.

After submitting my answers, ChatGPT responded with the SRS shown in Figure 5-3.

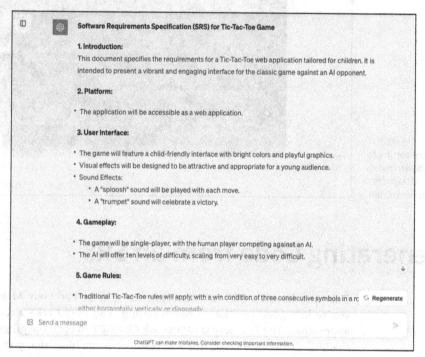

FIGURE 5-3: A ChatGPT-generated SRS.

ChatGPT

The SRS looks good enough, but if I want to keep it in a file outside a ChatGPT window, I'll need it in a more usable format. I prompted ChatGPT to convert the SRS to Markdown syntax. (*Markdown* is a simple markup language for adding formatting to plain-text documents.) The result is shown in Figure 5-4.

I copied the markdown code and saved it in a file with the .md extension in a new Git repository for the project.

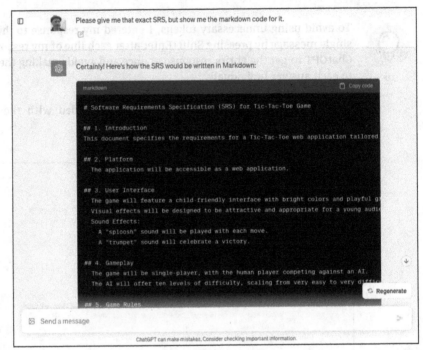

FIGURE 5-4:
Converting to
Markdown makes
documents
more usable.

ChatGPT

Generating Code from an SRS

Once you have an SRS (whether you wrote it or had your AI assistant's help), you're in a good position to begin coding. You might take a couple of different approaches. The first way is to just ask ChatGPT to code the program described in the SRS. At the very least, this will result in some ideas that you can use to begin coding it yourself.

Using a zero-shot approach

If you're feeling lucky, you can try a simple prompt asking the chatbot to generate the entire program based on the SRS. This approach is called a zero-shot prompt and is described in more detail in Chapter 4.

REMEMBER

A zero-shot prompt is one where you don't give examples or code and instead just rely on the data the model has been trained on.

In the same conversation as the one where I asked ChatGPT to write an SRS, I entered the following prompt:

After a few seconds, ChatGPT returned HTML, CSS, and JavaScript for what it described as a simplified version of the application, as shown in Figure 5-5.

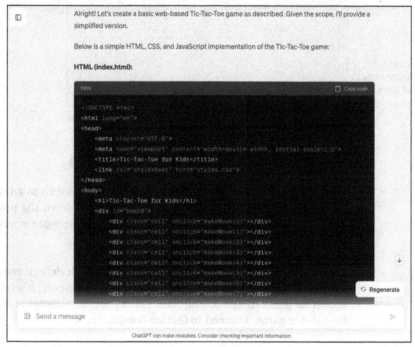

ChatGPT

FIGURE 5-5:
The ChatGPT-generated tic-tac-toe game code.

REMEMBER

You can find the full source code for this application on the website for this book at, www.dummies.com/go/codingwithaifd, or in my GitHub repository, at https://github.com/chrisminnick/coding-with-ai.

Before examining the code, I copied it into index.html, styles.css, and script.js files in my code editor and opened the HTML file in a browser. The user interface resembles a tic-tac-toe game, and it uses what might be considered kid-friendly colors and text. Upon trying to play the game, however, I discovered that it fails to meet the most critical requirement. Take a look at Figure 5-6 and see if you can identify the problem here.

In this first attempt at a tic-tac-toe game, the AI has written a game that doesn't properly alternate between X and O, resulting in O getting more turns and thus always winning the game. AI cheats.

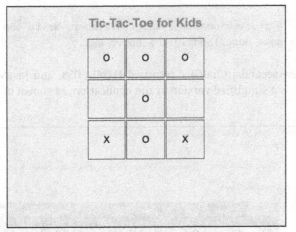

Tic-Tac-Toe for Kids

O	O	O
	O	
X	O	X

ChatGPT

FIGURE 5-6:
A frustratingly
difficult game of
tic-tac-toe.

Breaking down the problem

With a request as complicated as generating software from an SRS, you're much more likely to get acceptable results by breaking down the problem into steps. However, pieces of the output from the zero-shot prompt response can be helpful in figuring out how to break apart the problem.

Since ChatGPT is tuned to be creative (it has a high default temperature), it was the perfect tool for helping with writing an SRS. However, it's not usually the best option for generating working code. For my second attempt at building a working tic-tac-toe game, I turned to GitHub Copilot.

Before asking Copilot to help with my app, I used the built-in debugger in the Chrome browser to figure out what was wrong with the code ChatGPT provided. It turns out that the function that places the user's X on the board has the following line of code to alternate the user's symbol between X and O:

```
currentPlayer = currentPlayer === 'X' ? 'O' : 'X';
```

TECHNICAL STUFF

In this statement, the currentPlayer variable holds the symbol (X or O) that will be played on the board when the human user makes a move. The conditional (or ternary) operator in this statement checks whether the value of currentPlayer is X and changes it to O if it is. Otherwise (if currentPlayer is not equal to X) it changes its value to O. The problem, however, is that the value of currentPlayer is used in the program only to represent the human player. As a result, switching the value of currentPlayer to O makes the human play every other move with the AI's symbol.

After commenting out that line, I was able to play tic-tac-toe and win every time (because the computer player is just randomly picking from the available squares at this point). With a smarter opponent, the game should be a draw every time, so I decided to implement the levels of difficulty feature from the SRS.

Blending Manually Written and AI-Generated Code

Once you have AI-generated code that fulfills at least some of the requirements of the software, it's time to start writing code manually. A good strategy for getting from a basic app, such as the one the AI generated in the preceding section, to something that works correctly is to start by developing the back end.

The *back end* defines the business logic and data in the app, as well as how the user interface will interact with the logic and data. In the case of an AI tic-tac-toe game, writing the back end will start with crafting the prompt that I'll use to get an AI model to play tic-tac-toe with me.

Writing the prompt

After thinking about the problem of how to make an AI tic-tac-toe player, I decided to try using the OpenAI API and the GPT-4 model. I experimented for a while with the OpenAI playground and ended up with the following system prompt:

```
You are an AI tic-tac-toe player. You are always 'O'
and I'm always 'X'.

I'll provide you with my move as a number on this grid:

0 | 1 | 2
3 | 4 | 5
6 | 7 | 8

You'll respond with only an array with an X in the
position of my move, followed by your move, followed by
an array with an O in the position of your move.

If one of us wins or it's a draw, tell me 'you win',
'I win', or 'draw'.
```

```
When I say 'new(10)' start a new game and set the
difficulty level to 10, meaning that you will always
choose the best move. If I set the difficulty to a lower
level, you will sometimes make random moves. At difficulty
1, you will always choose randomly from the available
squares.
```

Using this system prompt and the temperature set to 0.5 (so the model would be creative but not too creative), I was able to enter my moves and get responses that I should be able to use in my program, as shown in Figure 5-7.

FIGURE 5-7:
An AI tic-tac-toe
bot in the OpenAI
playground.

ChatGPT

Writing the server

I decided to write a Node.js server to talk to the OpenAI API, so as not to have to store the API key in my client application. I created a new directory for my server, initialized the directory as a Node.js package (using npm init), and created a file named server.js.

To start writing server.js, I clicked the View Code button in the upper-right corner of the playground and selected Node.js as my library. The View Code window opened with the necessary code for sending the current settings and prompts to the API and getting the next completion.

I copied this code from the playground and pasted it into server.js. I also added code to import the API key from a .env file. A .env file is used in Node.js to store environment variables outside the main program. Environment variables hold information that is particular to an installation of the software (such as API keys) and shouldn't be distributed with the software (since you don't want other people using your API key). The beginning of my server is shown in Figure 5-8.

```javascript
// This code is for v4 of the openai package: npmjs.com/package/openai
import OpenAI from 'openai';

const openai = new OpenAI({
  apiKey: process.env.OPENAI_API_KEY,
});

const response = await openai.chat.completions.create({
  model: 'gpt-4',
  messages: [
    {
      role: 'system',
      content:
        "You are an AI tic-tac-toe player. You are always 'O' and I'm always 'X'.\n\nI'll provide you with my move as a number on this grid:\n\n0 | 1 | 2\n3 | 4 | 5\n6 | 7 | 8\n\nYou'll respond with only an array with an X in the position of my move, followed by your move, followed by an array with an O in the position of your move.\n\nIf one of us wins or it's a draw, tell me 'you win', 'I win', or 'draw'.\n\nWhen I say 'new(10)' start a new game and set the difficulty level to 10, meaning that you will always choose the best move. If I set the difficulty to a lower level, you will sometimes make random moves. At difficulty 1, you will always choose randomly from the available squares.",
    },
    {
      role: 'user',
      content: 'new(10)',
    }
```

FIGURE 5-8: Node.js code to get the next completion from the OpenAI API.

ChatGPT

The next step was to create my own API server that gets results from OpenAI and returns them to my client application. Since writing an API server is a fairly standard task, I decided to use Copilot Chat to generate it.

I started with the following prompt:

> I want to turn the code in server.js into an API server that I can send a new message to and have it appended to the messages array before submitting it to the OpenAI API. The server should return the response from the OpenAI API.

The code generated by Copilot was a good start. The complete code is shown in Listing 5-1.

LISTING 5-1: **The First Version of the Tic-Tac-Toe Server**

```javascript
import express from 'express';
import OpenAI from 'openai';
import 'dotenv/config';

const app = express();
const openai = new OpenAI({
  apiKey: process.env.OPENAI_API_KEY,
});

app.use(express.json());

app.post('/chat', async (req, res) => {
  const { message } = req.body;
  const response = await openai.chat.completions.create({
    model: 'gpt-4',
    messages: [
      {
        role: 'system',
        content:
          "You are an AI tic-tac-toe player. You are always 'O' and
          I'm always 'X'.\n\nI'll provide you with my move as a number
          on this grid:\n\n0 | 1 | 2\n3 | 4 | 5\n6 | 7 | 8\n\nYou'll
          respond with only an array with an X in the position of my
          move, followed by your move, followed by an array with an O
          in the position of your move.\n\nIf one of us wins or it's a
          draw, tell me 'you win', 'I win', or 'draw'.\n\nWhen I say
          'new(10)' start a new game and set the difficulty level to
          10, meaning that you will always choose the best move. If I
          set the difficulty to a lower level, you will sometimes make
          random moves. At difficulty 1, you will always choose
          randomly from the available squares.",
      },
      {
        role: 'user',
        content: message,
      },
    ],
  });
  res.json({ response });
});

app.listen(3000, () => {
  console.log('Server listening on port 3000');
});
```

Submitting follow-up prompts

At the bottom of Copilot's response, it explained the code it generated and suggested a follow-up prompt:

```
How can I test the API server?
```

This was going to be my next prompt anyway, so I clicked the suggested prompt and Copilot (correctly) suggested using curl or Postman to test it and gave instructions for using both, as shown in Figure 5-9, left.

The model also suggested another follow-up prompt, which seemed like an excellent idea to me, so I clicked that to ask for code for handling errors returned by the API server. The response to that prompt is shown in Figure 5-9, right.

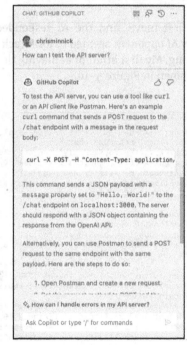
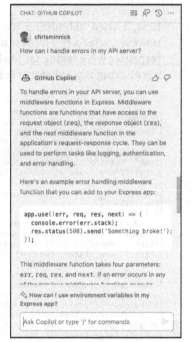

FIGURE 5-9: Suggestions for testing the API server (left) and for handling API server errors.

ChatGPT

Testing the server

Armed with Copilot's suggestions for testing and error handling, I had several tasks to work on before I could make the server work with the client app. First, I had to figure out whether the server works at all. From browsing the code, it looks like a standard Node.js API server that should be able to receive a message, pass it along to the OpenAI server, and return a response in JSON format.

Using the testing suggestions from Copilot, I started the server (using node server.js) and entered the following curl command into a new terminal window (all on one line):

```
curl -X POST -H "Content-Type: application/json" -d '
    {"message": "new(5)"}' http://localhost:3000/chat
```

This command should tell the AI tic-tac-toe game to start a new game with a difficulty level of 5. And the response I got from the server shows that was what it did:

```
"message":{"role":"assistant","content":"Understood.
We start a new game with a difficulty level of 5, which
means a mix of optimal and random moves. Your
move!"},"finish_reason":"stop"}],"usage":{"prompt_tokens":
199,"completion_tokens":29,"total_tokens":228}}}%
```

Next, I tried submitting my first move, and the AI responded appropriately. However, after a few moves, my AI opponent seemed to lose track of the game and responses were taking far too long. My first attempt at playing tic-tac-toe against the AI using my API server is shown in Figure 5-10.

chrisminnick — -zsh — 80×24
(base) chrisminnick@chris-mac ~ % curl -X POST -H "Content-Type: application/jso
n" -d '{"message": "new(5)"}' http://localhost:3000/chat
{"response":{"id":"chatcmpl-8DBMr5D7PkryjrYPpJY6yKxdMXgly","object":"chat.comple
tion","created":1698152653,"model":"gpt-4-0613","choices":[{"index":0,"message":
{"role":"assistant","content":"Understood. We start a new game with a difficulty
 level of 5, which means a mix of optimal and random moves. Your move!"},"finish
_reason":"stop"}],"usage":{"prompt_tokens":199,"completion_tokens":29,"total_tok
ens":228}}}
(base) chrisminnick@chris-mac ~ % curl -X POST -H "Content-Type: application/jso
n" -d '{"message": "0"}' http://localhost:3000/chat
{"response":{"id":"chatcmpl-8DBNTWqo7ke2U0PIvseupx4N7B4wG","object":"chat.comple
tion","created":1698152691,"model":"gpt-4-0613","choices":[{"index":0,"message":
{"role":"assistant","content":"['X', ' ', ' ', ' ', ' ', ' ', ' ', ' ', ' '],\n4
,\n['X', ' ', ' ', ' ', 'O', ' ', ' ', ' ', ' ']"},"finish_reason":"stop"}],"usa
ge":{"prompt_tokens":196,"completion_tokens":42,"total_tokens":238}}}
(base) chrisminnick@chris-mac ~ % curl -X POST -H "Content-Type: application/jso
n" -d '{"message": "2"}' http://localhost:3000/chat
{"response":{"id":"chatcmpl-8DBXm5v0RBfyPn4WcS5AuAo1kJsSM","object":"chat.comple
tion","created":1698153330,"model":"gpt-4-0613","choices":[{"index":0,"message":
{"role":"assistant","content":"[\"X\", 2, \"O\", 4]"},"finish_reason":"stop"}],"
usage":{"prompt_tokens":196,"completion_tokens":12,"total_tokens":208}}}
(base) chrisminnick@chris-mac ~ %

FIGURE 5-10:
My AI opponent
loses track of its
instructions.

Microsoft Corporation

The problem is that, although this code works, it doesn't have any way to keep track of the state of the game. Each request will only send the latest move from the client to OpenAI. Also, the AI would benefit from some examples of the response format that I'm looking for.

REMEMBER

Giving the AI examples of correct responses is called *few-shot prompting*. For details on this type of prompting, see Chapter 4.

Implementing few-shot prompting on the server

To give the AI more context, I wrote a series of messages (using the OpenAI playground) to simulate a correctly played game between the AI assistant and a human user. I then hard-coded those into the server, as shown in Figure 5-11.

```
10    messages: [
11      {
12        role: 'system',
13        content:
14          "You are an AI tic-tac-toe player. You are always 'O' and I'm always 'X'.\n\nI'll
              provide you with my move as a number on this grid:\n\n0 | 1 | 2\n3 | 4 | 5\n6 |
              7 | 8\n\nYou'll respond with only an array with an X in the position of my move,
              followed by your move, followed by an array with an O in the position of your
              move.\n\nIf one of us wins or it's a draw, tell me 'you win', 'I win', or 'draw'.
              \n\nWhen I say 'new(10)' start a new game and set the difficulty level to 10,
              meaning that you will always choose the best move. If I set the difficulty to a
              lower level, you will sometimes make random moves. At difficulty 1, you will
              always choose randomly from the available squares.",
15      },
16      {
17        role: 'user',
18        content: 'new(10)',
19      },
20      {
21        role: 'assistant',
22        content: 'new game',
23      },
24      {
25        role: 'user',
26        content: '0',
27      },
28      {
29        role: 'assistant',
30        content:
31          "['X', ' ', ' ', ' ', ' ', ' ', ' ', ' ', ' ']\nMy move: 4\n['X', ' ', ' ', ' ',
```

FIGURE 5-11: Giving more context to the AI.

I then restarted the server and attempted to play a new game using the `curl` command. The new game started correctly, but on my first move, the AI responded that I should start a new game to continue playing, as shown in Figure 5-12.

This happened because the previous prompts in the conversation are not being sent to the server. Since the server has no way of tracking sessions between an individual user and the AI, the best place to implement session state is on the client.

```
chrisminnick — -zsh — 80×24
(base) chrisminnick@chris-mac ~ % curl -X POST -H "Content-Type: application/jso
n" -d '{"message": "new(5)"}' http://localhost:3000/chat
{"response":{"id":"chatcmpl-8DBhY15NMUhdRYR0EeoN1Gh9vdtwF","object":"chat.comple
tion","created":1698153936,"model":"gpt-4-0613","choices":[{"index":0,"message":
{"role":"assistant","content":"new game, level 5"},"finish_reason":"stop"}],"usa
ge":{"prompt_tokens":502,"completion_tokens":6,"total_tokens":508}}}
(base) chrisminnick@chris-mac ~ % curl -X POST -H "Content-Type: application/jso
n" -d '{"message": "0"}' http://localhost:3000/chat
{"response":{"id":"chatcmpl-8DBhsBeis5AhuWni3Ewu1IxmVAKAi","object":"chat.comple
tion","created":1698153956,"model":"gpt-4-0613","choices":[{"index":0,"message":
{"role":"assistant","content":"Please start a new game to continue playing."},"f
inish_reason":"stop"}],"usage":{"prompt_tokens":499,"completion_tokens":9,"total
_tokens":508}}}
(base) chrisminnick@chris-mac ~ %
```

FIGURE 5-12:
The AI doesn't
remember the
last command.

Before working on the client, however, I have to set up the server to combine the prompts that are hard-coded on the server with the prompts that come from the client. I stored the system prompt and the example game in a variable, and then prepended that to the messages that the client app sends to the server.

I also simplified the example game so the AI is returning only the number of the square where it wants to place a O. This change makes the client app easier to code and has the additional benefit of greatly reducing the number of tokens necessary for playing a game.

The finished server app is shown in Listing 5-2.

LISTING 5-2: **My Finished API Server**

```
import express from 'express';
import OpenAI from 'openai';
import 'dotenv/config';
import cors from 'cors';

const app = express();
const openai = new OpenAI({
  apiKey: process.env.OPENAI_API_KEY,
});

app.use(express.json());
app.use(cors());
```

```javascript
app.post('/chat', async (req, res) => {
  const context = [
    {
      role: 'system',
      content:
        "You are an AI tic-tac-toe player. You are always 'O' and
        I'm always 'X'.\n\nI'll provide you with my move as a number
        on this grid:\n\n0 | 1 | 2\n3 | 4 | 5\n6 | 7 | 8\n\nYou'll
        respond with only your move, which must not be a number that
        has already been played in the current game.\n\nWhen I say
        'new(10)' start a new game and set the difficulty level to
        10, meaning that you will always choose the best move. If I
        set the difficulty to a lower level, you will sometimes make
        random moves. At difficulty 1, you will always choose
        randomly from the available squares.",
    },
    {
      role: 'user',
      content: 'new(10)',
    },
    {
      role: 'assistant',
      content: 'new game, level 10',
    },
    {
      role: 'user',
      content: '0',
    },
    {
      role: 'assistant',
      content: '4',
    },
    {
      role: 'user',
      content: '1',
    },
    {
      role: 'assistant',
      content: '2',
    },
    {
      role: 'user',
      content: '6',
    },
```

(continued)

LISTING 5-2: *(continued)*

```
    {
      role: 'assistant',
      content: '8',
    },
    {
      role: 'user',
      content: '5',
    },
    {
      role: 'assistant',
      content: '3',
    },
    {
      role: 'user',
      content: '7',
    },
  ];
  const newMessage = req.body.messages;
  const messages = [...context, ...newMessage];
  const response = await openai.chat.completions.create({
    model: 'gpt-4',
    messages: messages,
    temperature: 0.5,
    max_tokens: 255,
    top_p: 1,
    frequency_penalty: 0,
    presence_penalty: 0,
  });
  res.json({ response });
});

app.listen(3000, () => {
  console.log('Server listening on port 3000');
});
```

Improving the client

To make the client application send my moves to the server and get the AI's moves back from the server, I wrote a new function named getAIMove(). This function sends the API server all the moves in the current game and gets back the AI's new move.

I also created a function named startNewGame() that takes the level of difficulty and passes the command to the server to start a new game. The complete code for the client-side script is shown in Listing 5-3.

LISTING 5-3: **The Client-Side JavaScript**

```javascript
let board = ['', '', '', '', '', '', '', '', ''];
let currentPlayer = 'X';
let isGameOver = false;
let messageHistory = [];

function startNewGame(levelOfDifficulty) {
  board = ['', '', '', '', '', '', '', '', ''];
  currentPlayer = 'X';
  isGameOver = false;
  messageHistory = [];
  messageHistory.push({
    role: 'user',
    content: 'new(' + levelOfDifficulty + ')',
  });
  document.querySelectorAll('.cell').forEach((cell) => (cell.
        innerHTML = ''));
  const response = getAIMove(messageHistory);
  return response;
}

function makeMove(index) {
  if (board[index] === '' && !isGameOver) {
    board[index] = currentPlayer;
   document.getElementsByClassName('cell')[index].innerHTML =
        currentPlayer;
    messageHistory.push({
      role: 'user',
      content: index.toString(),
    });

    if (checkWin()) {
      alert(currentPlayer + ' Wins!');
      isGameOver = true;
      return;
    }
    if (checkDraw()) {
      alert('Draw!');
```

(continued)

LISTING 5-3: *(continued)*

```
      isGameOver = true;
      return;
    }
    aiMove(messageHistory); // Player is X, AI is O
  }
}

async function getAIMove(message) {
  // This function will send a message to the API server
  // The message will contain each previous move and the user's
        latest move
  // The API server will return the AI's next move
  const response = await fetch('http://localhost:3000/chat', {
    method: 'POST',
    headers: {
      'Content-Type': 'application/json',
    },
    body: JSON.stringify({
      messages: message,
    }),
  });
  const data = await response.json();
  document.getElementById('message').innerHTML =
    data.response.choices[0].message.content;
  return data.response.choices[0].message.content;
}

async function aiMove(messageHistory) {
  let move = await getAIMove(messageHistory);
  messageHistory.push({
    role: 'assistant',
    content: move.toString(),
  });
  board[move] = 'O';
  document.getElementsByClassName('cell')[move].innerHTML = 'O';
  if (checkWin()) {
    alert('O Wins!');
    isGameOver = true;
  }
}

function checkWin() {
  let winCombos = [
```

```
      [0, 1, 2],
      [3, 4, 5],
      [6, 7, 8],
      [0, 3, 6],
      [1, 4, 7],
      [2, 5, 8],
      [0, 4, 8],
      [2, 4, 6],
    ];
    for (let i = 0; i < winCombos.length; i++) {
      if (
        board[winCombos[i][0]] &&;
        board[winCombos[i][0]] === board[winCombos[i][1]] &&;
        board[winCombos[i][0]] === board[winCombos[i][2]]
      ) {
        return true;
      }
    }
    return false;
}

function checkDraw() {
  return board.every((cell) => cell !== '');
}
```

Once I finished writing the client-side script and updating the HTML page to add the Start Game button, I tested the game. After a little debugging, the game worked and I could play tic-tac-toe with GPT-4 through my web browser.

However, after several games, it became apparent that although GPT-4 knows the rules of tic-tac-toe, it is terrible at strategy. I won every game, even when I set the level of difficulty to 10 and I played wrong, as shown in Figure 5-13.

The GPT models are language models and are not well-equipped to handle reasoning.

Moving logic from AI to the client

When integrating responses from an AI into an app, consider whether parts of the response from the AI can be done in your client- or server-side code. If so, you can reduce the complexity of the instructions to the AI as well as the number of interactions between your application and the AI. This will have multiple benefits, including reduced costs for AI usage, improved performance, and allowing the AI to focus on fewer tasks, which may improve its accuracy.

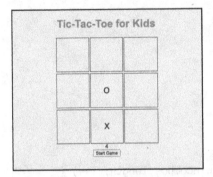
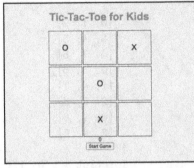
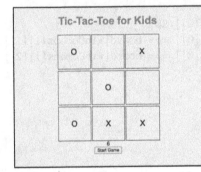
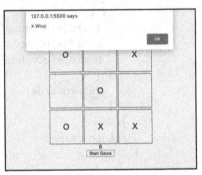

ChatGPT

FIGURE 5-13:
GPT-4 is no good
at tic-tac-toe.

Because the level of difficulty simply adjusts the number of random responses, making random moves seems like a natural thing to take off the AI's plate. My idea was to handle the level of difficulty on the client side, and not even prompt the AI for random moves.

To accomplish this, I went back to the completely random tic-tac-toe move code that ChatGPT generated and modified it so that the selected level of difficulty would determine how frequently moves are generated randomly.

First, I revised the system prompt to eliminate the description of the levels of difficulty. Here's my new prompt:

```
{
    role: 'system',
    content:
        "You are an AI tic-tac-toe player. You are always
        'O' and I'm always 'X'.\n\nI'll provide you with
        my move as a number on this grid:\n\n0 | 1 | 2\n3
        | 4 | 5\n6 | 7 | 8\n\nYou'll respond with only
        your move, which must not be a number that has
        already been played in the current game.\n\nWhen I say
        'new()' start a new game.",
}
```

Then, to start writing the random move functionality, I entered the following comment at the beginning of the getAIMove() function:

```
/*
  Use the value of difficulty to decide whether to
  query the API for a move or use a random move.
  If difficulty is 10, always query the API
  If difficulty is 0, always use a random move
  If difficulty is between 0 and 10, use a random move
  10 - difficulty percent of the time
  and use the best move difficulty percent of the time
*/
```

The modified function I wrote with the help of Copilot is shown in Listing 5-4.

LISTING 5-4: **The new getAIMove() Function**

```
async function getAIMove(message) {
  /*
  Use the value of difficulty to decide whether to
  query the API for a move or use a random move.
  If difficulty is 10, always query the API
  If difficulty is 0, always use a random move
  If difficulty is between 0 and 10, use a random move
  10 - difficulty percent of the time
  and use the best move difficulty percent of the time
  */
  let random = Math.random();
  if (random < difficulty / 10) {
    const response = await fetch('http://localhost:3000/chat', {
      method: 'POST',
      headers: {
        'Content-Type': 'application/json',
      },
      body: JSON.stringify({
        messages: message,
      }),
    });
    const data = await response.json();
    document.getElementById('message').innerHTML =
      data.response.choices[0].message.content;
    return data.response.choices[0].message.content;
  }
```

(continued)

LISTING 5-4:   *(continued)*

```
let move = Math.floor(Math.random() * 8);
while (board[move] !== '') {
  move = Math.floor(Math.random() * 8);
}
document.getElementById('message').innerHTML = move.toString();
return move.toString();
}
```

With this new prompt and function, I could set the difficulty (in the script at first, and then through the use of a slider input in the HTML) and adjust the percentage of moves made by GPT-4 versus moves randomly generated in the client application.

The AI still couldn't play tic-tac-toe worth a darn, however, even with the difficulty level set to 10.

TECHNICAL STUFF

It may be possible, though better prompting, to get GPT-4 to be good at tic-tac-toe. Email me at chris@minnick.com if you figure it out!

REMEMBER

You can find the complete code for the tic-tac-toe game on this book's website at www.dummies.com/go/codingwithaifd.

Tips and Tricks for Code Generation

The results you get from a generative AI model will vary widely, based on your prompts, the context and input you provide to the model, the specific LLM you use, the temperature and other settings provided to the model, and more.

As you become more comfortable working with an AI coding assistant, you'll start to become more familiar with what it can and can't do. If you follow certain practices, however, you can get the LLM to generate good code more reliably. In this section, I tell you some of the tips and tricks that I've found to be most helpful, as well as a few practices that will end up costing you more time than it's worth to use the AI.

I mention and use many of these best practices elsewhere in this book, so consider this section your handy reference as you're getting started with AI-assisted coding.

Don't stop coding

While AI can generate complete functions, or even working programs, it works best when you take the lead. Keep your skills up-to-date and use AI as a tool to help you write more code, rather than as a tool that will write your code for you. Not only will the AI learn from you and write better code, but you'll also be able to fully understand the code you're writing, which is essential to creating high-quality software.

Be specific

When prompting a coding assistant to generate code, or when asking a question about how to do something, be as specific as possible. When you're exploring an idea that you don't yet know how to code, it can be helpful to start with a vague prompt to generate ideas. But once you understand the problem and the domain, ask for details.

Think in steps

Complex requests are much more likely to result in unacceptable responses. Instead, break down every problem into its smallest units. Instead of saying, "How do I write an Instagram clone?" start with a plan (which you should consider writing as an SRS) and then with a small piece, such as the new user signup page.

Ask follow-up questions

If you're unsure about how a piece of generated code works or if a response is unexpected, ask the AI assistant to clarify, explain, or try again. For example, if a function generated by the AI doesn't look quite right to you, but you don't know exactly what's wrong with it, ask the AI to provide several other ways that the function might be written. Just as you might watch several YouTube videos before finding the best solution to a problem, having your AI assistant generate options can be a great way to figure out what will work best. If you don't like the responses one AI assistant gives you, try another AI assistant. Or try feeding the code generated by one AI assistant to another one, asking it to improve the code.

Check the official documentation

Remember that coding assistants are trained on publicly available code, and the LLM behind the assistant may have a training data cutoff date. As a result, code generated by an LLM may use deprecated syntax, an older version of a library, or libraries that are no longer recommended. If a code assistant uses syntax or a library that you're not familiar with, check the official documentation to make sure you're using it correctly.

Use examples and context

Although the latest LLMs have amazing capabilities, they aren't mind readers. If you want the output from a request to be in a specific format, give the AI an example of that format. If the code you ask the AI to generate will integrate with some other function or service, provide the relevant information to the AI as context.

Prioritize security

Chatbots and coding assistants may use your input to train the underlying model. To be certain that no sensitive or personally identifying information will show up in suggestions given to other users of the LLM, always anonymize sensitive data. For example, if you ask the AI to summarize a long email, remove or change the email addresses and names from the email before submitting it as input to an LLM.

Keep learning

Working with a chatbot or a coding assistant is a great way to get answers to coding questions, but it's no substitute for staying up-to-date the same way programmers always have — by talking with other programmers, engaging in online forums on StackOverflow, Reddit, and Hacker News, watching videos, taking classes, and reading high-quality books like the one you have in front of you!

Keep your tools updated

AI coding tools are evolving quickly. Make sure that you have the latest version of whatever tools you're using. If you learn about a new tool that seems promising (through any of the sources mentioned in the preceding tip), try it out. If a new tool or IDE works better for you than the one you've been using, consider switching to it.

Be mindful of AI's limitations

As you see repeatedly in this book, LLMs aren't perfect or omniscient. They were trained on a lot of data and can make predictions based on patterns they find. If you're writing code that's unlike anything the AI has seen before, it will be of little help to you.

Chapter 6

Formatting and Improving Your Code

N o software developer or team of software developers gets it right the first time. The software may function perfectly now, but often decisions made during the writing of the software or in the gradual process of upgrading the software that will cause problems later on.

In this chapter, you learn how to use AI coding assistants to help clean up your code.

Using AI Tools for Code Formatting

How your code is formatted and the decisions you make in the design of software directly affect how maintainable it is and how easy it will be to improve it in the future. Having good and consistent design and formatting also means that you don't need to think as hard to figure out what's going on in a program. An experienced programmer can look at blocks of well-written code, even if they've never seen it before, and quickly start to figure out what it does.

The first step in making your code more readable is to properly and consistently indent and format your lines of code and functions. To automate this step, we'll be using a simple form of rule-based AI, rather than a language model. Using a rule-based tool will always be more predictable than using a machine learning model, and that's exactly what's needed for this task.

Rule-based AI systems are the original form of AI. They operate using a list of conditions (or if-then statements) rather than by making predictions (as models do).

Setting up your formatting tools

Using a code formatter extension, you can have VS Code format your code as you work. Many good automated code formatters are available. One popular code formatter is Prettier.

Prettier calls itself an opinionated code formatter, which means you'll have little control over how Prettier formats your code but it will do it consistently. The benefit to using an opinionated code formatter like Prettier versus one that you must configure is that anyone who uses Prettier has their code formatted using the same style, which eliminates the need for standardizing the details of formatting among the members of a team.

Follow these steps to install and enable the Prettier extension in VS Code:

1. **Open the Extensions panel in VS Code and use it to search for and select Prettier.**

    Several extensions in the Extensions marketplace have names that start with *prettier*. Choose the official one (which should come up first in the results), which is published by Prettier, as shown in Figure 6-1.

2. **Press Ctrl+plus (+), (Command++ in macOS) to open the VS Code Settings screen.**

    You can open Settings also by choosing File ⇨ Preferences (Code ⇨ Settings in macOS).

3. **In the Settings search box, type** formatter.

    Settings related to code formatting will appear on the Settings page.

4. **Under the Default Formatter setting, select Prettier.**

5. **Scroll down the list of settings and select the boxes next to Editor: Format on Paste and Editor: Format on Save, as shown in Figure 6-2.**

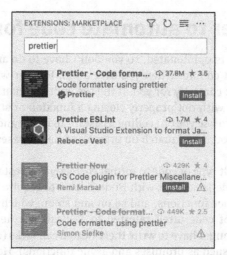

FIGURE 6-1:
Installing Prettier.

Prettier

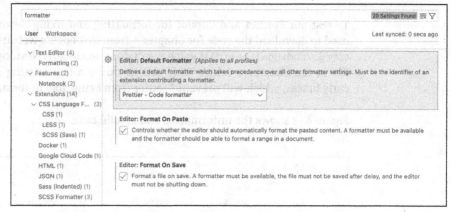

FIGURE 6-2:
Enabling Prettier
and automatic
formatting.

Prettier

6. **Choose File ➪ Auto Save to turn on automatic saving.**

Enabling autosave makes VS Code automatically save your files whenever you navigate to a different tab or when the focus moves away from the current file (such as when you type in Terminal or switch to a browser window to test your code).

7. **Close the Settings screen.**

Congratulations! You now have a code formatter installed. You'll never need to worry about whether you use tabs or spaces to indent your code again — a huge timesaver. Let's try it out.

Using Prettier to automate code formatting

As mentioned, Prettier is opinionated, so you don't have to do anything to make use of it except to start coding. When you save a file, Prettier will automatically and magically format it correctly for you. If the file isn't automatically formatted, you've made a mistake with not properly closing a function or statement. At that point, you might want to use your AI coding assistant to locate and fix the problem rather than manually count and match up braces and parentheses.

One particularly difficult type of code to format correctly is a nested callback function. Writing server-side JavaScript with Node.js used to require extensive use of functions passed to other functions, and so on and so on, which creates a nearly undecipherable mess of code often referred to as "callback hell." Fortunately, Node.js developers no longer have to write these nested callbacks (due to abstracted ways of writing them, such as promises and async functions). However, if you're a Node.js developer, there's no getting around having to work with legacy code that includes nested callbacks.

To test out Prettier and Copilot for formatting and fixing nested callbacks, you need to download the code for Chapter 6 from this book's website (www.dummies. com/go/codingwithaifd) if you haven't done so already. Next, open the nested.js file in the Chapter 6 folder. This code includes a few missing parentheses and curly braces, which will prevent Prettier from being able to format it correctly.

Figure 6-3 shows the unformatted and invalid code.

```
 nested.js 3, U  ✕

chapter06 >  nested.js > ...
   1    fs.readdir(source, function (err, files) {if (err) {console.
        log('Error finding files: ' + err);} else {files.forEach
        (function (filename, fileIndex) {console.log(filename);gm
        (source + filename).size(function (err, values) {if (err)
        {console.log('Error identifying file size: ' + err); else
        {console.log(filename + ' : ' + values);aspect = values.
        width / values.height;widths.forEach(function (width,
        widthIndex) {height = Math.round(width / aspect);console.log
        ('resizing ' + filename + 'to ' + height + 'x' + height;this.
        resize(width, height).write(dest + 'w' + width + '_' +
        filename,function (err) {if (err) console.log('Error writing
        file: ' + err);});}.bind(this));}}});});});}
   2    });
   3
```

FIGURE 6-3: A mess of unformatted code containing syntax errors.

Prettier

Surely no one would ever purposefully write something like this, right? However, you might need to debug code that's been *minified*, which is the process of removing unnecessary characters (such as comments and whitespace) so that the code takes up less space. If minified code contains an error, your code formatter won't be able to properly parse it.

Prettier does attempt to give you a clue as to the problem. Click Prettier in the bottom-right corner of VS Code. A window opens and displays a list of problems encountered while trying to format the code, as shown in Figure 6-4. If you don't see the Prettier link in the bottom toolbar, right-click the toolbar and select Prettier from the list of status bar links.

FIGURE 6-4:
Viewing problems Prettier discovered.

```
OUTPUT  ...                          Prettier              ∨  ≣  🔒  🗂  ∧  ✕
}
["ERROR" – 7:20:33 AM] Error formatting document.
["ERROR" – 7:20:33 AM] Unexpected token (1:285)
> 1 | fs.readdir(source, function (err, files) {if (err) {console.log
('Error finding files: ' + err);} else {files.forEach(function
(filename, fileIndex) {console.log(filename);gm(source + filename).
size(function (err, values) {if (err) {console.log('Error
identifying file size: ' + err); else {console.log(filename + ' : '
+ values);aspect = values.width / values.height;widths.forEach
(function (width, widthIndex) {height = Math.round(width / aspect);
console.log('resizing ' + filename + 'to ' + height + 'x' + height;
this.resize(width, height).write(dest + 'w' + width + '_' + filename,
function (err) {if (err) console.log('Error writing file: ' +
```

Prettier

The errors reported by Prettier are usually not immediately helpful, however. For example, Prettier indicates that there's an unexpected token. This could mean that the code has an extra character or a missing character, but you still need to search through the code and figure out exactly what "token" is the problem.

A better way to find the problem that's preventing this code from working and being formatted is to ask an AI assistant to do it for you. Follow these steps:

1. **Open the incorrectly formatted and invalid code in VS Code.**

2. **Make a backup of your code by copying it to another file.**

   It's impossible to know what an AI tool will do before trying it, so it's essential to have a way to get back to how the code was before you applied the brush.

TIP

   You could also commit the code to your source code repository immediately before using any tools in the Brushes panel. Alternatively, you can simply undo the changes made by Copilot by pressing Ctrl+Z.

3. **Select the entire code block, and then right-click inside it and choose Copilot ⇨ Fix This, as shown in Figure 6-5.**

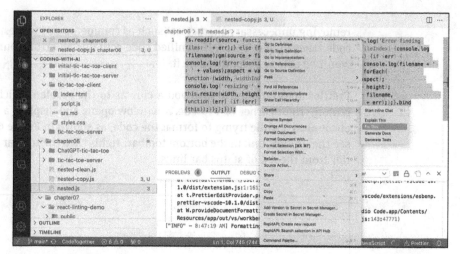

Microsoft Corporation

FIGURE 6-5:
Asking Copilot to fix your code.

Copilot lists the errors it found and shows you the changes it proposes making, as shown in Figure 6-6. In my case, Copilot indicates that parentheses are missing and two variables are unused. It also shows the prompt that it wrote to fix the code.

4. **Since we're concerned only with syntax errors (the missing parentheses) at this point, delete the parts of the prompt that deal with the unused variables and click the regenerate icon (circular arrow).**

This time, Copilot fixes just the syntax errors, as shown in Figure 6-7.

5. **To apply the changes to your code, click Accept.**

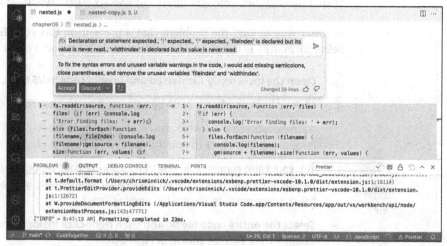

FIGURE 6-6:
Copilot suggests fixes.

Microsoft Corporation

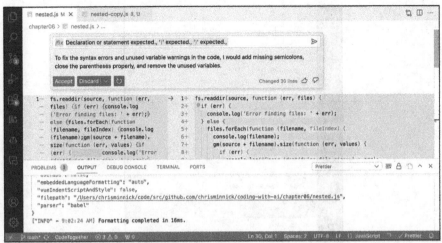

FIGURE 6-7:
Copilot fixed the
syntax errors.

The next thing we need to find out is whether Copilot changed anything else in the code while it was fixing the issue. In the files you downloaded from the book's website, the nested-clean.js file is a known good version of the code. I fixed the issues in this file by hand and verified that the code works. To find out if Copilot changed anything in the code while fixing the bugs, you can compare the code Copilot fixed with this known good file.

To automate comparing the files, you can use the file comparison tool built into VS Code. File comparison tools are commonly known as *diff tools*, because they check for differences. Follow these steps to use VS Code's diff tool:

1. **In File Explorer in VS Code, click nested-clean.js and then hold down the Ctrl key (Windows) or the Command key (on macOS) and click nested.js.**

   Both files are selected.

2. **Right-click the selected files and choose Compare Selected from the menu, as shown in Figure 6-8.**

   The diff panel appears, as shown in Figure 6-9.

If the diff panel doesn't show any differences between the two files, you know that Copilot solved the problems with the code and didn't change the code in any other way. If the two files are different, look at the differences and determine whether you need to fix them. It's possible that the two files differ in unimportant ways, such as line breaks. If the differences are significant, fix them manually or revert to your copy of the code and try using Copilot to fix the errors again.

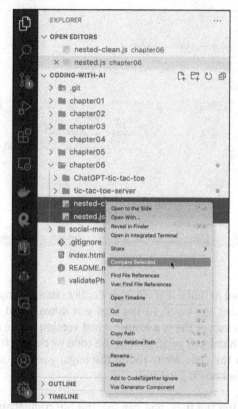

FIGURE 6-8:
Selecting files
to compare.

Microsoft Corporation

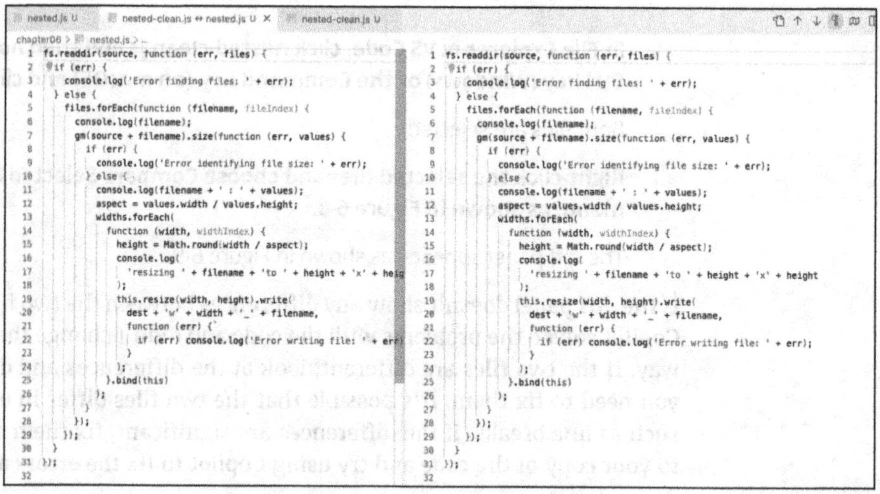

FIGURE 6-9:
The diff panel
in VS Code.

Microsoft Corporation

REMEMBER

Knowing when to use AI tools versus a traditional rule-based tool is just as important as knowing how to use AI tools. Because you can't ever fully trust the output from a machine learning model, if you want certainty (as in the case of checking for differences between files), use a rule-based tool.

Refactoring with AI

Programmers call the process of going back into a program to make changes that improve the structure of the program without changing the functionality *refactoring*. Refactoring is an essential process in the lifecycle of software. In this section, you learn how AI tools can help to identify potential issues in your programs that can benefit from refactoring and then how to use AI to help fix those issues.

Recognizing code smells

A *code smell,* as defined by software development gurus Kent Beck and Martin Fowler, is "a surface indication that usually corresponds to a deeper problem in the system." No one wants smelly code.

Most code smells are the result of novice programmers or rushed coding. As mentioned, you should think of your AI coding assistants as interns. Your coding intern will make many mistakes due to their inexperience and their lack of knowledge about your expectations. AI is no different. In fact, it's likely that AI coding assistants will write more bad code more consistently than a junior programmer because all it knows or can know is the open-source software it was trained on, which may not always be of the highest quality.

TIP

Many of the code smells listed in this section are described in more detail in Martin Fowler's classic book *Refactoring*, 2nd Edition (Addison-Wesley).

A bad smell in your code, like a bad smell in the bottom drawer of the refrigerator from vegetables left too long, can quickly lead to rot. *Code rot* is the process whereby your code degrades over time, and small problems in the design or implementation of previously written code start to affect how productive you and your team can be moving forward.

Code smells don't necessarily have to be fixed immediately, but they can be indicators that something larger is wrong that does need fixing. Code smells are grouped into the following categories:

» Dispensables

» Bloaters

» Abusers

» Couplers

» Change preventers

I explain each of these categories in the following sections.

Dispensables

Dispensable code smells are unnecessary code that should be removed from your source code. Examples of dispensables include the following:

» **Comment:** Comments are necessary in any source code, but they should be necessary and useful. Specifically, comments should explain why your code is the way it is, rather than how the code works. The code itself should be easy enough to read to explain the how.

» **Duplicate code:** Duplicate code often makes its way into code because you (or another programmer working on the code) were in a hurry or as a result of a lack of communication.

» **Lazy class:** Functions or classes that don't do much in a program may be better off being combined into other code. For example, if you have a function that formats a date string in a particular format and is used by only one other function, it's better to combine the date string function with the function where it's used.

» **Dead code:** Dead code may have had a purpose at one point but not now.

» **Oddball solution:** When you have two solutions to the same problem in your code, one of those solutions is an oddball solution and should be eliminated.

Bloaters

Bloaters are places in your code where the size of a function or other unit of code is much bigger than it should be. Bloaters generally happen over time as requirements are added and a program ages. Examples of bloaters include the following:

» **Large class or method:** A single class or function in a program should do only one thing. When a class starts having more than one purpose, it's a good indicator that it should be broken apart into multiple classes.

» **Long parameter list:** A function that takes a large number of parameters is difficult to read and may be unnecessarily complex. A large number of parameters may indicate that the function is trying to do too many things.

» **Primitive obsession:** *Primitive variables* hold single values rather than references to multiple values (as in the case of objects or arrays). A large number of primitive variables in a function may indicate that they can be combined into an object. For example, if you have primitives for firstName, lastName, streetAddress, state, and so forth, consider whether they should be combined into a single object (perhaps named user or customer).

Abusers

Abusers (often referred to as object–orientation abusers) are situations where solutions don't take full advantage of the possibilities of good software design practices. For example:

» **Switch statement:** A switch statement is often preferred over a complex if/else statement. However, overdependence on the use of switch statements may indicate that a developer is relying on less-than-optimal coding practices.

» **Temporary field:** A temporary field is a variable in a class or function used only under certain circumstances. It may be better to extract the variable into a separate class.

» **Conditional complexity:** This code smell is similar to the switch statement one. A large block of conditional code, such as a large chain of if/else statements, indicates that the code may be unnecessarily complex.

Couplers

Couplers are code smells that happen when code is too tightly interdependent. Coupling software too tightly makes it more difficult to change it in the future. Examples of couplers include the following:

» **Inappropriate intimacy:** In this coupler, a method depends too much on the implementation details of another method or class.

» **Indecent exposure:** Indecent exposure occurs when a class exposes its internal details, violating the principle of encapsulation.

>> **Feature envy:** A method that accesses the data of another object more than its own is said to have feature envy.

>> **Message chain:** A message chain occurs when one object requests another object which requests another, and so on. Message chains may create unnecessary dependencies between objects.

>> **Middleman:** A middleman is a class that exists only to delegate work to another class. When this is the case, consider eliminating the middleman.

Change preventers

Change preventers are smells that hinder change. Examples of change preventers are

>> **Divergent change:** This smell occurs when a class requires many changes in response to changes outside itself.

>> **Shotgun surgery:** This one occurs when multiple classes require small changes in response to a change.

Additional categories of code smells

In addition to the code smells just described, there are many other categories of code smells that you should be aware of, including the following:

>> **Global data:** While it's a myth that all global data is a code smell, the presence of a large amount of data in the global scope may indicate a larger problem. Global variables are a cause of other code smells.

>> **Magic number:** A magic number is hard-coded into a program and difficult for anyone except the creator of the software to decipher.

>> **Inconsistent name:** You should have conventions regarding how to name things such as functions, classes, and variables. The conventions you use don't matter as much as being consistent.

>> **Uncommunicative name:** Meaningless variable names are an easy code smell to prevent if you take your time when defining the variables. A good practice is to always name variables using multiple words. For example, name is a smelly variable name, but firstName is much more communicative.

>> **Type embedded in name:** Examples of variable names that exhibit this type of smell include quantityInt and priceInt. This bad practice can lead to code that's difficult to change. For example, if you use these variable names in an app for a sandwich store, what happens when the owner of the store decides

to start selling half sandwiches or increases the price by 25 cents? You can simply update the variable's type to allow for decimals, but updating every instance of the variable name in your program may require changes in many different places.

Detecting code smells with Copilot

Code smells are typically identified during a process called a *code review*. In this section, you use AI to do a quick code review.

It's common for AI-generated code to contain bad coding practices and code smells. Because AI code assistants don't really know how to code, every mistake made in their training data may show up in response to your prompts about coding. On the positive side, however, large language models also have information about how to code correctly, even if they don't always do it themselves.

One way to use AI to check for code smells is to use the GitHub Copilot Chat feature. Follow these steps:

1. **Open the code you want to check in VS Code, along with any related files (and the SRS if you have one).**

   I'm going to use the tic-tac-toe game from Chapter 5.

2. **Clicking the Chat icon in the left panel of VS Code.**

   The Copilot chat window appears.

3. **Enter the following prompt into Copilot Chat:**

   ```
   Does this program contain any code smells?
   List and explain them.
   ```

In response to my prompt, Copilot returns a list of three code smells it said may be present in the tic-tac-toe game:

>> **Magic number:** The program sets an initial value for the level of difficulty using the following statement:

   ```
   let difficulty = 10;
   ```

   Copilot is correct in saying that this is a magic number.

>> **Long function:** Copilot suggests that the startNewGame( ) function may be a long function because it's doing several things. Again, Copilot is correct.

» **Global data:** At the beginning of the program, several global variables are declared. The program might be made more robust by declaring these inside a function or a class instead.

Copilot's full initial response is shown in Figure 6-10.

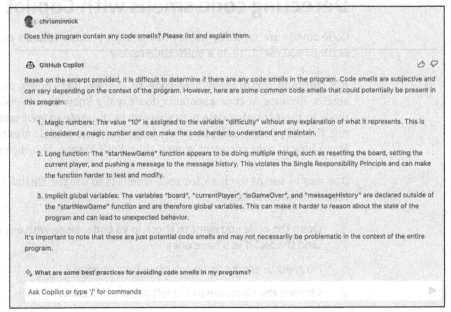

FIGURE 6-10:
Using Copilot
Chat to
review code.

Any language model's responses contain a certain amount of randomness, so it's often helpful to ask the same question more than once. Before asking Copilot to review my code again, I cleared the preceding prompt and response by clicking the Clear button at the top of the Copilot chat window, as shown in Figure 6-11.

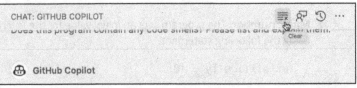

FIGURE 6-11:
Clearing the
previous chat.

The second time I prompted Copilot, it came back with the same three code smells it had detected previously, plus a new one. The fourth problem it detected, correctly, is a lack of comments. Copilot's explanation of the comments code smell is shown in Figure 6-12.

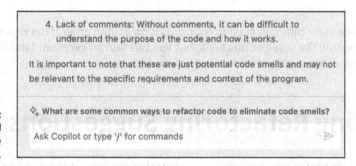

4. Lack of comments: Without comments, it can be difficult to understand the purpose of the code and how it works.

It is important to note that these are just potential code smells and may not be relevant to the specific requirements and context of the program.

✧ What are some common ways to refactor code to eliminate code smells?

Ask Copilot or type '/' for commands

GitHub, Inc.

FIGURE 6-12: Copilot detected that my code lacks comments.

Just to see what would happen, I asked Copilot one more time. This time, it came back with five code smells, four of which it said the code didn't have. It did produce one new issue worth looking into: inconsistent naming. Figure 6-13 shows Copilot's response about the inconsistent naming issue.

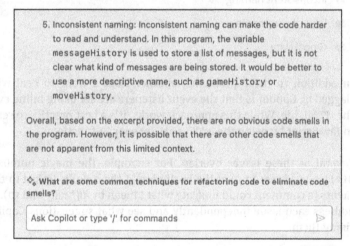

5. Inconsistent naming: Inconsistent naming can make the code harder to read and understand. In this program, the variable `messageHistory` is used to store a list of messages, but it is not clear what kind of messages are being stored. It would be better to use a more descriptive name, such as `gameHistory` or `moveHistory`.

Overall, based on the excerpt provided, there are no obvious code smells in the program. However, it is possible that there are other code smells that are not apparent from this limited context.

✧ What are some common techniques for refactoring code to eliminate code smells?

Ask Copilot or type '/' for commands

GitHub, Inc.

FIGURE 6-13: Copilot pointed out the inconsistent naming in the program.

Refactoring safely

Refactoring your code has the potential to cause new problems. For this reason, it's important to proceed slowly and carefully and to keep proper backups at every point in the process so that you can undo your work.

The best way to keep a history of changes you make is to use a version control system, to make changes to the code in a new branch of the repository, and to fully test your code after making changes and before merging it back into the main branch of your repository.

TIP

The most common version control system among programmers is Git. Using Git is beyond the scope of this book, but you can find an excellent (and free) book about Git at https://git-scm.com/book/en/v2.

Generating Refactoring Suggestions

Once you've found issues in your code that are in need of refactoring, the next step is to figure out what to do about them. Here is the current list of potential issues that Copilot detected in the tic-tac-toe game:

>> Long function

>> Magic numbers

>> Inconsistent naming

>> Lack of comments

>> Global data

In addition to these problems, another issue I want to deal with that wasn't flagged by Copilot is that the event listeners are set using inline event listeners in the HTML file. While this approach works, it's a best practice to set event listeners in JavaScript by using the addEventListener() function.

Several of these issues overlap. For example, the magic number issue (where difficulty is set to 10 at the beginning of the code) is linked to the lack of comments (a comment could indicate what I mean by *difficulty* and 10). However, I will address each issue independently and see what suggestions Copilot Chat has for fixing them.

Setting event listeners correctly

Asking AI for help with correctly setting event listeners presents a problem, which I suspect is the same reason why the AI didn't flag this as an issue in the first place. The problem is that this refactor will involve changes to more than one file. Copilot takes other files into consideration when generating suggestions for the file you're currently working on, but it might not suggest changes to other files to fix a problem in the current file.

I know how I would approach fixing this issue, but I want to see how Copilot would approach the problem. With index.html open in VS Code and the JavaScript file open in another tab, I prompt Copilot Chat with the following:

> How can I set the event listeners inside script.js
> rather than inside the HTML?

The code portion of the response, shown in Figure 6-14, was exactly what
I needed.

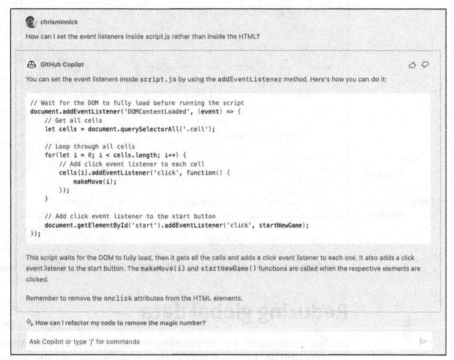

chrisminnick

How can I set the event listeners inside script.js rather than inside the HTML?

GitHub Copilot

You can set the event listeners inside `script.js` by using the `addEventListener` method. Here's how you can do it:

```
// Wait for the DOM to fully load before running the script
document.addEventListener('DOMContentLoaded', (event) => {
    // Get all cells
    let cells = document.querySelectorAll('.cell');

    // Loop through all cells
    for(let i = 0; i < cells.length; i++) {
        // Add click event listener to each cell
        cells[i].addEventListener('click', function() {
            makeMove(i);
        });
    }

    // Add click event listener to the start button
    document.getElementById('start').addEventListener('click', startNewGame);
});
```

This script waits for the DOM to fully load, then it gets all the cells and adds a click event listener to each one. It also adds a click event listener to the start button. The `makeMove(i)` and `startNewGame()` functions are called when the respective elements are clicked.

Remember to remove the `onclick` attributes from the HTML elements.

How can I refactor my code to remove the magic number?

Ask Copilot or type '/' for commands

GitHub, Inc.

FIGURE 6-14:
Copilot's
suggestion for
refactoring the
event listeners.

I implemented the suggestion. My program still works as expected, so I check my
code into the repository and am ready to move on to the next problem.

TIP

Just as it can be beneficial to ask another coder how they would approach a problem that you already have an answer to, prompting AI can sometimes give you a
different perspective or bring something new to your attention.

Removing the magic number

After its response regarding the event listeners, Copilot generated the following
follow-up question:

> How can I refactor my code to remove the magic number?

I agree with Copilot that fixing this issue next would be a good idea. To see what solution Copilot would generate, I clicked the suggested prompt. Copilot's response seems reasonable, as shown in Figure 6-15.

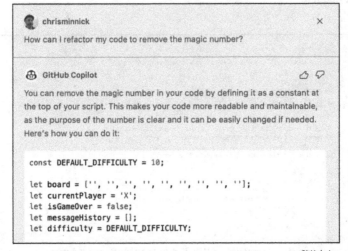

FIGURE 6-15: Copilot's suggestion for fixing the magic number.

I implemented the solution and can now move on to the next issue.

Reducing global data

Copilot's suggestion for eliminating the global data is to encapsulate the data and functionality of the game into a class. It even provides the necessary code for me to start to implement this solution myself, as shown in Figure 6-16.

Copilot's suggestion wasn't quite right, however, because it didn't include the fact that the startNewGame() function needs to be an async function. But during the implementation of the solution, it did start out by suggesting the correct code for the startNewGame() function, as shown in Figure 6-17.

After seeing Copilot's initial code, I got too confident in it and ended up trusting and accepting each of Copilot's suggestions to see if it would rewrite the program as a class correctly. It didn't.

I restored my last known working code and tried it again, but this time I disabled Copilot and did the conversion to a class myself.

To remove global data, you can encapsulate your data inside a class or an object. Here's an example of how you can do it using a class:

```
class Game {
  constructor() {
    this.DEFAULT_DIFFICULTY = 10;
    this.board = ['', '', '', '', '', '', '', '', ''];
    this.currentPlayer = 'X';
    this.isGameOver = false;
    this.messageHistory = [];
    this.difficulty = this.DEFAULT_DIFFICULTY;
  }

  makeMove(i) {
    // implementation of makeMove
  }

  startNewGame() {
    // implementation of startNewGame
  }
}
```

FIGURE 6-16:
The start of the solution to the global data.

```
1   class Game {
2     constructor() {
3       this.DEFAULT_DIFFICULTY = 10;
4       this.board = ['', '', '', '', '', '', '', '', ''];
5       this.currentPlayer = 'X';
6       this.isGameOver = false;
7       this.messageHistory = [];
8       this.difficulty = this.DEFAULT_DIFFICULTY;
9     }
10
11    async startNewGame() {
12      this.board = ['', '', '', '', '', '', '', '', ''];
        this.currentPlayer = 'X';
        this.isGameOver = false;
        this.messageHistory = [];
        this.messageHistory.push({
          role: 'user',
          content: 'new',
        });
        document.querySelectorAll('.cell').forEach((cell) => (cell.innerHTML = ''));

        const response = await fetch('http://localhost:3000/chat', {
```

FIGURE 6-17:
Copilot seemed to write most of the code correctly.

TIP

I'm purposefully making mistakes here so you don't have to! Check every suggestion from GenAI carefully, and don't accept a suggestion blindly without understanding and approving it.

Fixing long functions

The startNewGame() function has more than one purpose. It currently resets the global variables, resets the tic-tac-toe grid, sends a message to the OpenAI API to tell it to start a new game, and writes the server's response to the screen before returning the response.

I asked Copilot chat to fix the `startNewGame()` function so that it didn't have too many tasks. The solution it came back with was to break up `startNewGame()` into three functions, but its solution discarded the most important part of the functionality of `startNewGame()`, which is the starting of a new game.

I then posed the same question to GPT-4, which gave me a much better suggestion for how to break apart the function. The code GPT-4 generated for `startNewGame()` simply invokes three other functions, like this:

```
async startNewGame() {
    this.resetGameState();
    this.clearBoardDisplay();
    await this.postNewGameMessage();
}
```

TIP

If one language model isn't giving you the results you want, try another. If neither one is of any help, you may need to change your prompt or break the task into smaller pieces.

Fixing inconsistent naming

I had high hopes for how a language model might improve my naming of variables and functions. I prompted Copilot with the following:

```
How can I refactor this program to make the
naming consistent?
```

The AI responded with several general tips and best practices and three concrete suggestions, as shown in Figure 6-18. I agreed with two of the three suggestions and implemented them, and then I asked the question again.

The second time I asked, it returned two different suggestions. I agreed with one of them and implemented it, and then asked the question again. The third time, it returned the same advice regarding best practices but then suggested that I rename two variables that it had already given suggestions for (but with different and, in my opinion, worse suggestions). It seemed I had hit the point of diminishing returns with my repeated questioning.

My next action was to look through the code and see if there were any additional names that I thought could be improved. I decided that the remaining names were all adequate.

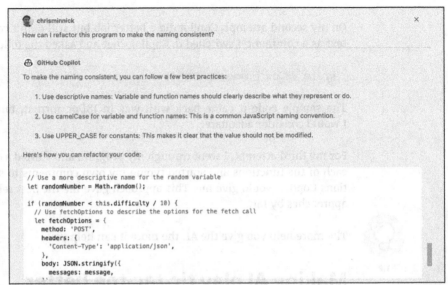

FIGURE 6-18:
Generating tips
for making
names consistent
in the program.

GitHub, Inc.

TIP

If you ask a leading question, such as "What's wrong with my code?" or "How can I fix my code?" a language model will often respond with an answer that assumes something is wrong with your code rather than telling you that there isn't anything wrong with it. It doesn't hurt to ask, but trust your own judgment in the end.

Lack of comments

The final thing I wanted Copilot's help with was the documentation and comments in my program. Since I already knew that the program needed more documentation, I decided to try Copilot's generate docs tool.

I selected the first method in my class, right-clicked it, and chose Copilot ⇨ Generate Docs. Copilot wrote a description of the method, but it used an incorrect symbol to mark it as a comment and was wordy and repetitive, as shown in Figure 6-19.

```
# This code initializes the game and sets up all of the event
# listeners. It also sets up the slider and the event listener
# that changes the difficulty level when the slider is moved.

init() {
    document.addEventListener('DOMContentLoaded', (event) => {
        let cells = document.querySelectorAll('.cell');
        cells.forEach((cell, i) => {
            cell.addEventListener('click', () => this.makeMove(i));
        });
        document.
```

FIGURE 6-19:
Copilot Labs
failed at its first
documentation
attempt.

On my second attempt, Copilot did a better job but still didn't correctly mark the text as a comment. I switched to Copilot Chat and asked the following:

```
Write JSDoc comments for this program.
```

The sample code it came back with was in JSDoc format, but it wasn't what I would consider adequate.

For my third attempt, I went through my program and started a code block before each of the functions and started typing my own comments to see what suggestions Copilot would give me. This approach gave me the best results of the three approaches by far.

TIP

The more help you give the AI, the more it can help you.

Making AI play tic-tac-toe better

The last issue I wanted to deal with in the program was to see if Copilot could give me suggestions for how to make GPT-4 better at playing tic-tac-toe. I opened the file containing the Node.js program that interacts with GPT-4 and prompted Copilot with the following:

```
How can I modify my prompt to GPT-4 to make it be
better at playing tic-tac-toe?
```

Copilot suggested using the following prompt:

```
You are a highly skilled AI trained to play tic-tac-toe.
You are playing against a human opponent. Your goal is
to win or draw the game. You are expected to make
optimal moves based on the current state of the game
board. The board positions are numbered from 0 to 8,
starting from the top left corner and going to the
right and then down. The board is represented as a list
of nine elements, each of which can be "X", "O", or ""
(for an empty space).
```

Excited to finally play to a draw against the AI, I implemented the suggestion and started the server and the client.

My AI opponent still wasn't any good at playing tic-tac-toe, and I won every game no matter how hard I tried to lose. Darn.

At this point, I felt good about the refactoring that I'd been able to do, if not about AI's capability to play tic-tac-toe. The complete program is shown in Listing 6-1.

LISTING 6-1: **The Refactored Tic-Tac-Toe Game**

```
class TicTacToeGame {
  constructor(difficulty = 10) {
    this.DEFAULT_DIFFICULTY = difficulty;
    this.board = ['', '', '', '', '', '', '', '', ''];
    this.currentPlayer = 'X';
    this.isGameOver = false;
    this.messageHistory = [];
    this.difficulty = this.DEFAULT_DIFFICULTY;
    this.init();
  }
  /**
   * Initialize the game by adding event listeners
     to the DOM
   */
  init() {
    document.addEventListener('DOMContentLoaded', (event) => {
      let cells = document.querySelectorAll('.cell');
      cells.forEach((cell, i) => {
        cell.addEventListener('click', () => this.makeMove(i));
      });
      document
        .getElementById('start')
        .addEventListener('click', () => this.startNewGame());
    });

    let slider = document.getElementById('slider');
    document.getElementById('difficulty').innerHTML =
      'Level of difficulty: ' + slider.value;
    slider.addEventListener('change', (e) => {
      document.getElementById('difficulty').innerHTML =
        'Level of difficulty: ' + e.target.value;
      this.difficulty = e.target.value;
    });
  }
  /**
   * Start a new game by resetting the game state
     and clearing the board
   * Then post a new game message to the server
   */
```

(continued)

LISTING 6-1:   *(continued)*

```javascript
  async startNewGame() {
    this.resetGameState();
    this.clearBoardDisplay();
    await this.postNewGameMessage();
  }

  /**
   * Reset the game state
   */
  resetGameState() {
    this.board = ['', '', '', '', '', '', '', '', ''];
    this.currentPlayer = 'X';
    this.isGameOver = false;
    this.messageHistory = [{ role: 'user', content: 'new' }];
  }
  /**
   * Clear the board display
   */
  clearBoardDisplay() {
    document.querySelectorAll('.cell').forEach((cell) => (cell.innerHTML = ''));
  }

  /**
   * Post a new game message to the server
   */
  async postNewGameMessage() {
    try {
      const response = await fetch('http://localhost:3000/chat', {
        method: 'POST',
        headers: { 'Content-Type': 'application/json' },
        body: JSON.stringify({ messages: this.messageHistory }),
      });

      const data = await response.json();
      this.updateMessageDisplay(data.response.choices[0].message.content);
    } catch (error) {
      console.error('Failed to post new game message:', error);
      this.updateMessageDisplay('Error starting a new game. Please try again.');
    }
  }

  /**
   * Update the message display
   * @param {string} message
   */
  updateMessageDisplay(message) {
    document.getElementById('message').innerHTML = message;
  }
```

```
/**
 * Make a move on the board
 * @param {number} index
 */
makeMove(index) {
  if (this.board[index] === '' && !this.isGameOver) {
    this.board[index] = this.currentPlayer;
    document.getElementsByClassName('cell')[index].innerHTML =
      this.currentPlayer;
    this.messageHistory.push({ role: 'user', content: index.toString() });

    if (this.checkWin()) {
      alert(this.currentPlayer + ' Wins!');
      this.isGameOver = true;
      return;
    }
    if (this.checkDraw()) {
      alert('Draw!');
      this.isGameOver = true;
      return;
    }
    this.aiMove(); // Player is X, AI is O
  }
}


/**
 * Check whether someone has won the game
 * @returns {boolean}
 */
checkWin() {
  const winCombos = [
    [0, 1, 2],
    [3, 4, 5],
    [6, 7, 8],
    [0, 3, 6],
    [1, 4, 7],
    [2, 5, 8],
    [0, 4, 8],
    [2, 4, 6],
  ];
  return winCombos.some((combo) => {
    return (
      this.board[combo[0]] &&
      this.board[combo[0]] === this.board[combo[1]] &&
      this.board[combo[0]] === this.board[combo[2]]
    );
```

(continued)

LISTING 6-1:   (continued)

```
    });
  }

  /**
   * Check whether the game is a draw
   * @returns {boolean}
   */
  checkDraw() {
    return this.board.every((cell) => cell !== '');
  }

  /**
   * Make a move for the AI
   */
  async aiMove() {
    let move = await this.getAIMove(this.messageHistory);
    this.messageHistory.push({ role: 'assistant', content: move.toString() });
    console.log(move);
    this.board[move] = 'O';
    document.getElementsByClassName('cell')[move].innerHTML = 'O';
    if (this.checkWin()) {
      alert('O Wins!');
      this.isGameOver = true;
    }
  }

  /**
   * Get a move from the AI
   * @param {array} message
   * @returns {string}
   */
  async getAIMove(message) {
    /*
      Use the value of difficulty to decide whether to
      query the API for a move or use a random move.
      If difficulty is 10, always query the API
      If difficulty is 0, always use a random move
      If difficulty is between 0 and 10, use a random move
      10 - difficulty percent of the time
      and use the best move difficulty percent of the time
    */
    let randomNumber = Math.random();
    if (randomNumber < this.difficulty / 10) {
      const response = await fetch('http://localhost:3000/chat', {
        method: 'POST',
        headers: {
          'Content-Type': 'application/json',
        },
```

```
        body: JSON.stringify({
          messages: message,
        }),
      });
      const data = await response.json();
      let messageElement = document.getElementById('message');
      messageElement.innerHTML = data.response.choices[0].message.content;
      return data.response.choices[0].message.content;
    }
    let randomMove = Math.floor(Math.random() * 8);
    while (this.board[move] !== '') {
      randomMove = Math.floor(Math.random() * 8);
    }
    document.getElementById('message').innerHTML = move.toString();
    return randomMove.toString();
  }
}

// Create a new game
new TicTacToeGame();
```

Chapter **7**

Finding and Eliminating Bugs

The term *debugging* as it relates to computers dates back to Admiral Grace Hopper, who worked at Harvard University in the 1940s. A colleague of hers found a moth stuck in a computer that was keeping it from working correctly, and she remarked that they were "debugging" the system.

TECHNICAL STUFF

Although glitches in mechanical systems were called *bugs* as early as 1887, when Thomas Edison used the term, Grace Hopper is attributed with introducing the term as it relates to computers and computer programming.

Today, you're much less likely to encounter physical bugs that will keep your programs from working correctly, but these defects in your code are still just as pesky and sometimes as difficult to spot.

In this chapter, you learn how to use AI tools to assist you with the process of debugging your code.

Knowing Your Bugs

Before you can remove bugs from code, you need to locate them, identify them, and document them. In this section, you discover how to perform all three tasks.

Strategies for detecting bugs

Many different methods are used to detect bugs in software. The most effective strategies for detecting bugs are

>> **Code reviews:** Reviewing code with peers on a regular basis often catches problems that a single developer working alone can't. Performing code reviews with an AI assistant is covered in Chapter 6.

>> **Automated testing:** Automated testing makes sure that new functionality doesn't break existing code. This type of testing helps detect software errors early in the development cycle. Automated testing with AI assistance is covered in Chapter 9.

>> **Static code analysis:** Static code analysis analyzes your code as you write it. I cover static code analysis in the "Preventing Bugs with Linting" section in this chapter.

>> **Debugging tools:** Debugging tools allow developers to step through and inspect code and variables while a program is running. They're essential to figuring out the root causes of a bug. AI-assisted debugging is covered in the "Detecting Bugs with AI" section of this chapter.

>> **Logging and monitoring:** Logging of errors and performance monitoring provide software developers with detailed information about how well the software runs after it's deployed to a production environment.

Identifying common types of bugs

Earth contains an estimated 6 to 10 million different types of bugs, which make up 90 percent of animal forms. Fortunately, software bugs don't come in nearly as many different varieties and, in most cases, aren't as omnipresent.

The most commonly occurring types of software bugs follow:

>> **Syntax errors** are incorrect or missing characters in the code that prevent the program from compiling or running.

>> **Runtime errors** don't prevent the program from compiling but will cause it to crash.

>> **Functional bugs** happen when something in the software doesn't operate as intended, such as a search box that doesn't search.

>> **Logical bugs** are issues related to the business logic and are generally the result of poorly written code, such as a value assigned to the wrong variable.

>> **Workflow bugs** have to do with the user's navigation of the software application. One example of a workflow bug is a link that doesn't bring a user to the correct page on a website.

>> **Unit-level bugs** are simple, easy-to-fix bugs contained in a single unit of code. An example of a unit-level bug is a problem with the input validation for an email address field.

>> **System-level integration bugs** are more complex bugs in which individual units of code each function correctly but behave unexpectedly when working together. This type of bug can be difficult and time-consuming to track down and fix. For example, if two software components expect different data formats, they might not be able to exchange data correctly.

>> **Out-of-bound bugs** are issues that happen as a result of a user interacting with the software's user interface in an unintended way, such as a user entering in an input field a larger value than the system expects.

>> **Security bugs** are problems that make the software vulnerable to malicious attacks or to another type of risk, such as exposing user data to unauthorized users.

WARNING

Although security bugs might not prevent normal usage of the software, they're the highest priority bugs and should be fixed immediately.

CAN YOU WRITE BUG-FREE SOFTWARE?

Most coding bugs result from what we used to refer to as human error. With the advent of AI-assisted coding, AI assistants might be just as likely to be the cause of bugs. All software of any complexity has bugs. The aim to create bug-free software is unrealistic and will lead to missed deadlines and cost overruns.

Some of the most famous projects failed because of impossible quality requirements. For example, the Federal Aviation Administration's project to write new air traffic control software in the 1980s and 1990s was originally proposed as a project that would start in 1982 and be completed in 1996 at a cost of $2.5 billion. By the time the project was canceled in 1994, the cost estimate had risen to $7 billion and segments of the project were behind schedule by as much as 8 years. One of the many causes for the project's failure was that the FAA demanded 99.99999% reliability, which was considered by many to be unrealistic.

AI-assisted bug reporting with Jam

Bug reporting is how software developers and software development teams document and track bugs and potential bugs with software. Bug reports typically describe the current functioning of some aspect of the software and how it should perform.

Following are some characteristics of a good bug report:

» Contains visual evidence of the defect

» Has sufficient detail for a developer to be able to reproduce the conditions that led to the bug report

» Describes only one bug, rather than lumping several issues together

» Is filed in a standard and defined way (such as through a bug tracker)

The quality of a bug report often depends on the reporter's level of experience with the software, how much time they take to accurately describe the issue, and their writing ability. AI-assisted debugging tools can help users and testers accurately describe an issue and can help developers to reproduce and even fix reported bugs.

Jam (`https://jam.dev`) is a Chrome browser extension that simplifies the process of reporting a bug on websites and web applications. It integrates with an AI chatbot to provide developers with additional information about how to resolve the bug.

To start using Jam, go to `https://jam.dev/jamgpt` and install the browser plug-in. Next, click the Jam icon that appears in your browser to display the screen shown in Figure 7-1.

To start reporting a bug on any website you visit, you can capture a screenshot, record a video of the active browser tab or your desktop, and use the instant replay feature, which attaches a screen capture of your most recent interactions with the active browser tab.

Bug reports created using Jam can be shared in several ways, including using a link, via email, or as an issue in a GitHub repository. In Figure 7-2, I am creating a bug report in the repository for one of my websites.

Once you have used the Jam extension to create a bug report, you can open the report on the Jam website or send the bug report to one of the platforms Jam integrates with, such as GitHub, Asana, Jira, or Slack.

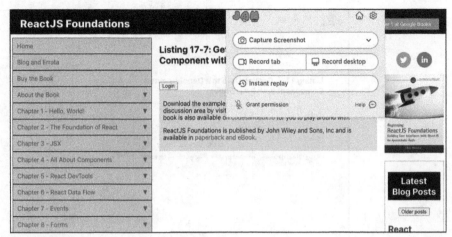

FIGURE 7-1:
Reporting a bug
with Jam.

JamGPT

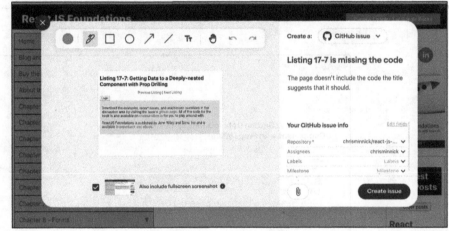

FIGURE 7-2:
Creating a bug
report and
opening a
GitHub issue.

JamGPT

Jam provides several types of data about the conditions in the browser when the bug was reported, including what actions the user took, what network requests led to the screen where the bug was reported, and information about the user's web browser and operating system, as shown in Figure 7-3.

The JamGPT tab, on the right side of the screen, gives you access to a chatbot that can access all the information about the bug report. When you open the JamGPT tab, the chatbot asks if you'd like it to analyze the bug report and make recommendations, as shown in Figure 7-4.

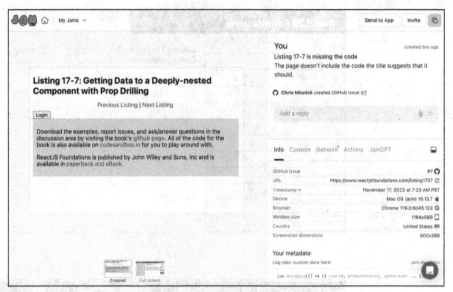

FIGURE 7-3:
Debugging
with Jam.

JamGPT

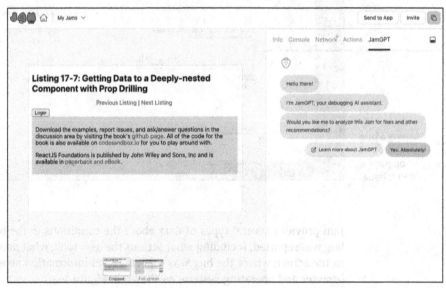

FIGURE 7-4:
JamGPT offers
to help you.

JamGPT

After you ask JamGPT to help, it analyzes the bug report and suggests a possible fix. JamGPT can't make the fix for you, but its suggestions may be helpful in locating the problem, as shown in Figure 7-5.

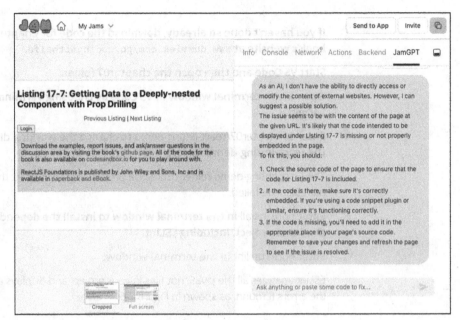

FIGURE 7-5:
JamGPT suggests
possible
solutions.

Preventing Bugs with Linting

Since debugging can be a frustrating and time-consuming process, it's a good idea to do everything you can do to eliminate the need for debugging in the first place.

In Chapter 6, you use Prettier to automatically format your code. Formatting your code in a consistent way is an important step in writing quality code, but it's far from the only thing you can do to reduce the need for debugging.

In Chapter 1, you learn about static code analysis tools, which are also known as linters. Most linters work in a similar way to code formatter tools. They use a list of rules to check your code before you compile or run it. Whereas *code formatters* are concerned with the tabs, spaces, and line breaks in your code, *linters* are concerned with the syntax of your code and your adherence to good coding conventions.

REMEMBER

Debugging fixes problems that occur while your code is running. Linting fixes problems in your code that exist when the code isn't running (which is why linters are a *static* code analysis tool). Ideally, linting can eliminate the need for debugging.

Installing a linter

The most popular linter for JavaScript code is ESLint. Follow these steps to install and try out ESLint.

1. If you haven't done so already, download the code for Chapter 7 from this book's website at www.dummies.com/go/codingwithaifd.

2. Start VS Code and then open the chapter07 folder.

3. Open a new terminal window in VS Code by choosing Terminal ⇨ New Terminal.

4. Enter cd chapter07/react-linting-demo to change the working directory to the react-linting-demo folder.

   The react-linting-demo folder contains a project written in React that already has ESLint installed.

5. Enter npm install in the terminal window to install the dependencies of the React project, including ESLint.

6. Enter npm run lint in the terminal window.

   ESLint analyzes all the JavaScript files in your project and displays a report of the errors it found, as shown in Figure 7-6.

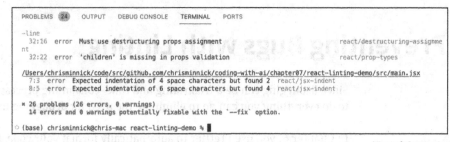

FIGURE 7-6:
ESLint reports on errors it found in your code.

TIP

If you don't know JavaScript or React, some of the errors reported by ESLint won't make much sense. But fear not! Understanding React and JavaScript isn't important to understanding how to use a linter and how to extend the capabilities of a linter with AI.

Installing the ESLint extension

To make VS Code highlight errors in your code reported by ESLint, you need to install the ESLint extension. Follow these steps:

1. In VS Code, click the Extensions icon on the left to open the Extensions panel.

2. In the search field at the top of the Extensions panel, search for ESLint.

The first result when you enter **ESLint** should be the official ESLint extension from Microsoft, as shown in Figure 7-7.

3. **Click the Install button for the ESLint extension.**

4. **Return to the tab for the App.js file.**

Now that the ESLint extension is installed, the errors reported by ESLint will be underlined with red squiggly lines, as shown in Figure 7-8.

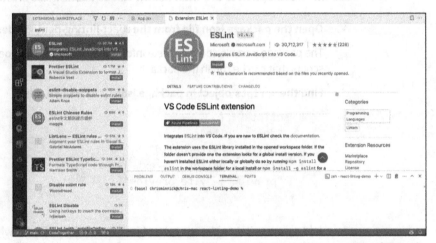

Microsoft Corporation

FIGURE 7-7: The ESLint VS Code extension.

Microsoft Corporation

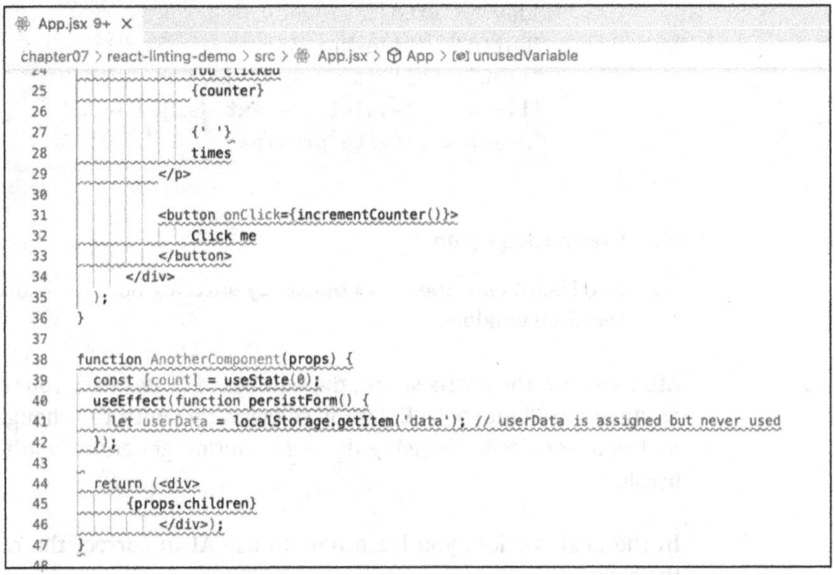

FIGURE 7-8: The ESLint extension highlights linting errors.

TECHNICAL STUFF

As far as I know, the technical term for red squiggly lines is *red squiggly lines*. I've never heard anyone refer to them by any other name.

Fixing your code with a linter

After ESLint reports the errors it finds, it includes a message saying that some of the errors are potentially fixable by using the `--fix` option. Follow these steps to use the `--fix` option to see what ESLint can do about these errors.

1. **Open the package.json file from the react-linting-demo folder.**

   The package.json file contains meta information, a list of dependencies, and scripts that can be run in the package.

2. **Find the `scripts` object in package.json. It looks like this:**

   ```
   "scripts": {
     "dev": "vite",
     "build": "vite build",
     "lint": "eslint . --ext js,jsx",
     "preview": "vite preview"
   },
   ```

3. **Add a new script to the `scripts` object that will run ESLint with the `--fix` option, as shown in bold:**

   ```
   "scripts": {
     "dev": "vite",
     "build": "vite build",
     "lint": "eslint . --ext js,jsx",
     "lintfix": "eslint . --ext js,jsx --fix",
     "preview": "vite preview"
   },
   ```

4. **Save package.json.**

5. **Run ESLint with the `--fix` option by entering** npm run lintfix **in the terminal window.**

After you run the lintfix script, the number of issues with your code may go down, as shown in Figure 7-9. ESLint is conservative with the changes it automatically makes to your code, so using the `--fix` option generally won't cause anything to break.

In the next section, you learn how to use AI to correct the remaining issues in the code.

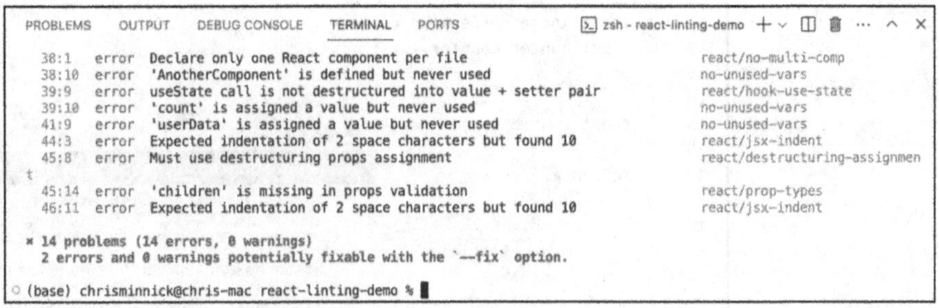

FIGURE 7-9:
Some problems
were fixable
using `--fix`.

Microsoft Corporation

Combining linting with AI

If you hover your mouse pointer over any code with a red squiggly line, you'll see a Quick Fix link in the pop-up window, as shown in Figure 7-10.

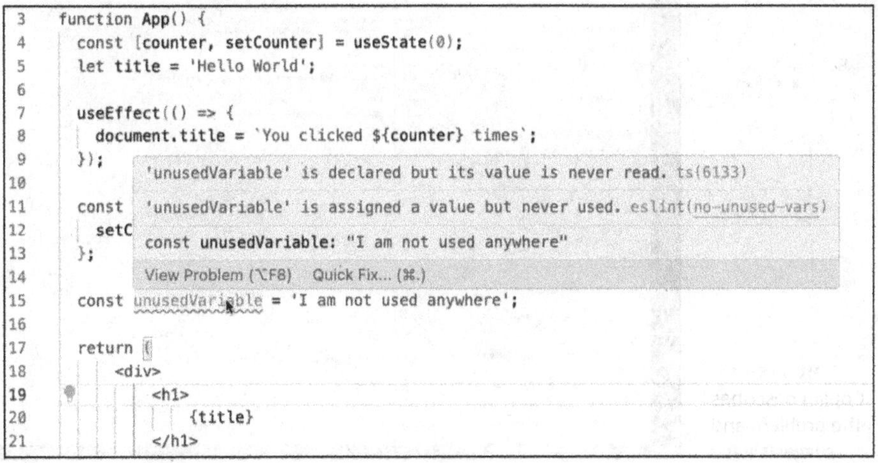

```
3    function App() {
4      const [counter, setCounter] = useState(0);
5      let title = 'Hello World';
6
7      useEffect(() => {
8        document.title = `You clicked ${counter} times`;
9      });
10
11     const   'unusedVariable' is declared but its value is never read. ts(6133)
12       setC
13     };      'unusedVariable' is assigned a value but never used. eslint(no-unused-vars)
14
15     const unusedVariable = 'I am not used anywhere';   const unusedVariable: "I am not used anywhere"
16
17     return (    View Problem (⌥F8)   Quick Fix... (⌘.)
18       <div>
19         <h1>
20           {title}
21         </h1>
```

FIGURE 7-10:
Viewing the
Quick Fix link.

Microsoft Corporation

Click the Quick Fix link to reveal your options for automatically fixing the problem, as shown in Figure 7-11.

If you have GitHub Copilot installed, you'll see options to fix or explain the error using Copilot. To find out more information about the error and to see how Copilot would go about fixing it, click the Explain Using Copilot option. The Copilot Chat pane appears, with an explanation (sometimes in far more detail than is necessary) of the problem and a proposed solution, as shown in Figure 7-12.

If you agree with Copilot's suggestion, you can either implement the fix yourself or use the Fix Using Copilot feature in the Quick Fix pop-up menu to have Copilot implement the fix itself.

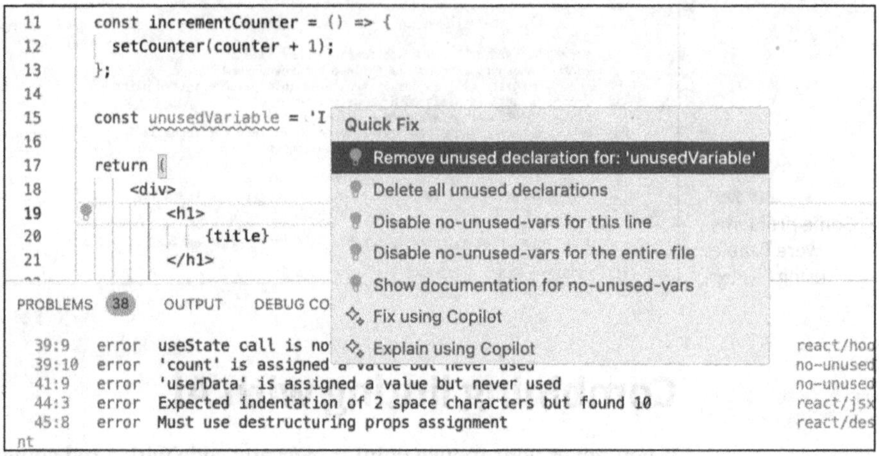

```
11      const incrementCounter = () => {
12        setCounter(counter + 1);
13      };
14
15      const unusedVariable = 'I  ┌─────────────────────────────────────────────────
16                                 │  Quick Fix
17      return (                   │  💡 Remove unused declaration for: 'unusedVariable'
18          <div>                  │  💡 Delete all unused declarations
19      💡      <h1>               │  💡 Disable no-unused-vars for this line
20              {title}            │  💡 Disable no-unused-vars for the entire file
21          </h1>                  │  💡 Show documentation for no-unused-vars
                                   │  ✧ Fix using Copilot
PROBLEMS  38    OUTPUT   DEBUG CO  │  ✧ Explain using Copilot
                                   └─────────────────────────────────────────────────
  39:9   error   useState call is no                                      react/hoo
  39:10  error   'count' is assigned a value but never used               no-unused
  41:9   error   'userData' is assigned a value but never used            no-unused
  44:3   error   Expected indentation of 2 space characters but found 10  react/jsx
  45:8   error   Must use destructuring props assignment                  react/des
nt
```

FIGURE 7-11:
The Quick Fix
options.

Microsoft Corporation

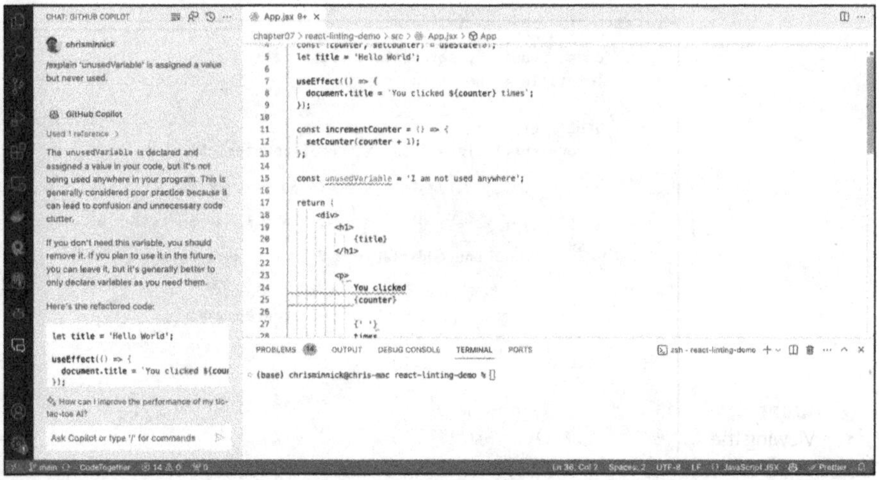

FIGURE 7-12:
Copilot describes
the problem and
suggests a fix.

Microsoft Corporation

If you click the Fix Using Copilot option, a window opens above the code in question with the change that Copilot wants to make to your code. You can either Accept or Discard the change. Figure 7-13 shows what appeared when I asked Copilot to fix the unused variable problem in my code.

Your original code is shown on the left and the proposed new code is shown on the right. Red highlighted code on the left will be removed if you apply the changes. Green highlighted code on the right will be added to your file if you apply the change. The areas on the right marked with diagonal lines represent blank space that won't be in the code when you accept it. (Copilot adds these lines to make the changed code align with the original code.)

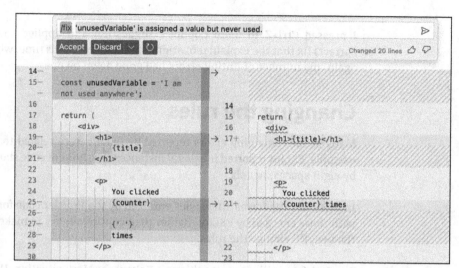

FIGURE 7-13:
Copilot prompts
you to accept or
decline a change.

Microsoft Corporation

As you can see from Figure 7-13, Copilot may try to make much bigger changes to your code than just fixing the single error you requested. In the case of the unused variable, the correct fix would have been to simply remove the single line of code containing the unused variable.

When I reviewed the proposed changes, I saw that Copilot was fixing several issues with the code at once. I was curious as to whether my number of linting errors would decrease by more than just one if I applied the fixes, so I accepted the proposed changes.

After Copilot made its "fixes," I ran ESLint again to see how many errors Copilot fixed. However, ESLint reported that my code now had seven more errors than it did before Copilot tried to fix things, as shown in Figure 7-14.

```
PROBLEMS  21     OUTPUT    DEBUG CONSOLE    TERMINAL    PORTS

   21:18  error  ` times      ` must be placed on a new line
   21:18  error  Missing JSX expression container around literal string: "times"
   24:7   error  Missing an explicit type attribute for button
   24:7   error  Expected indentation of 8 space characters but found 6
   24:44  error  `Click me` must be placed on a new line
   24:44  error  Missing JSX expression container around literal string: "Click me"
   29:1   error  Declare only one React component per file
   29:10  error  'AnotherComponent' is defined but never used
   30:9   error  useState call is not destructured into value + setter pair
   30:10  error  'count' is assigned a value but never used
   32:9   error  'userData' is assigned a value but never used
   35:15  error  `{props.children}` must be placed on a new line
   35:16  error  Must use destructuring props assignment
   35:22  error  'children' is missing in props validation

✖ 21 problems (21 errors, 0 warnings)
  10 errors and 0 warnings potentially fixable with the `--fix` option.

○ (base) chrisminnick@chris-mac react-linting-demo %
```

FIGURE 7-14:
That's the last
time I ask Copilot
to fix something.

Microsoft Corporation

I pressed Ctrl+Z to undo Copilot's suggestion and applied the obvious (and correct) fix that the Explain tool originally suggested. This time, when I ran ESLint again, my number of linting errors had gone down by one.

Changing the rules

Many of the remaining errors reported by ESLint were related to style rules. For example, ESLint reported in several instances that lines of code should be indented by eight spaces, not six.

In this case, the formatting styles enforced by the Prettier code formatter conflict with those checked by ESLint. Rather than continually try to make peace between the two, I'll change the rules.

Star Trek fans will recognize this as a Kobayashi Maru situation. When faced with a no-win scenario, be like Captain Kirk and change the rules.

REMEMBER

In matters of code formatting, if your linter and your code formatter disagree, adjust the rules of the linter.

To make ESLint ignore code indentation, you can modify its configuration file. The project-wide settings for ESLint are in a file named .eslintrc, which is at the root of your project directory. Depending on how you set up your project, .eslintrc may have an extension, such as .cjs or .mjs.

The .eslintrc file contains a configuration object with various properties. You can read about all the properties in .eslintrc by going to `https://eslint.org/docs/latest/use/configure/`. The property that you can use to adjust what ESLint reports as an error is the `rules` property. In this React project, the `rules` property currently contains only one rule, as shown in Figure 7-15.

```
  App.jsx 9+, M      .eslintrc.cjs  ×
chapter07 > react-linting-demo >  .eslintrc.cjs > [@] <unknown>
  6        'plugin:react/jsx-runtime',
  7        'plugin:react-hooks/recommended',
  8        'plugin:react/all',
  9     ],
 10     ignorePatterns: ['dist', '.eslintrc.cjs'],
 11     parserOptions: { ecmaVersion: 'latest', sourceType: 'module' },
 12     settings: { react: { version: '18.2' } },
 13     plugins: ['react-refresh'],
 14     rules: {
 15        'react-refresh/only-export-components': [
 16          'warn',
 17          { allowConstantExport: true },
 18        ],
 19     },
 20   };
 21
```

FIGURE 7-15: The rules property in .eslintrc.

Microsoft Corporation

ESLint rules modify the default behavior of ESLint and ESLint plugins. A rule starts with the name of a rule, followed by the severity level of that rule. ESLint has three levels of severity for rules:

>> Off or 0 disables a rule.

>> Warn or 1 turns the rule on, but only as a warning, meaning that it won't stop your code from compiling but it should be addressed.

>> Error or 2 turns the rule on as an error that will prevent your code from compiling.

When you run ESLint, the name of each rule that your code violates is displayed on the right side of the linting report and the severity of the rule violation is on the left, as shown in Figure 7-16.

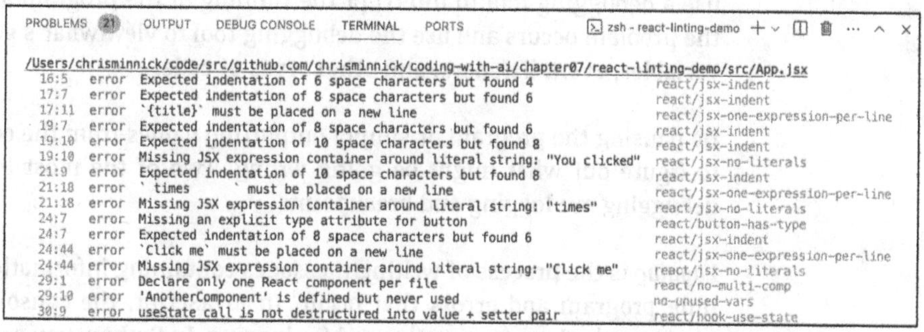

FIGURE 7-16: Viewing the name and default severity of rules.

Microsoft Corporation

When your linting report shows something as an error but you consider it a non-critical problem or not an error, copy the name of the rule from your lint report and add it to the `rules` object. For example, Figure 7-17 shows how to disable the `jsx-indent` rule that's currently conflicting with Prettier.

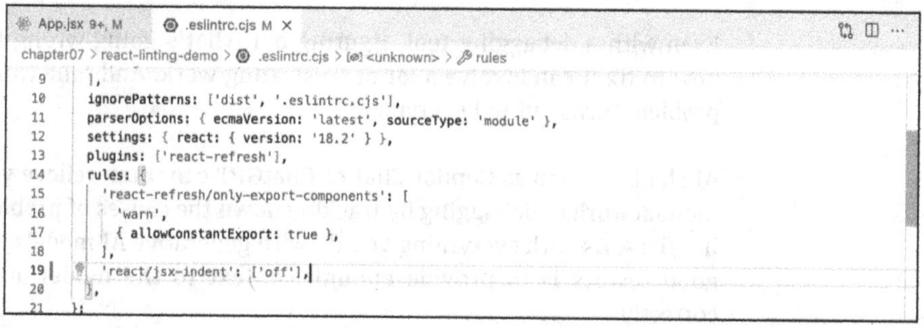

FIGURE 7-17: Adjusting a rule's severity.

Microsoft Corporation

To fix the remaining issues, I disabled several other rules that conflicted with Prettier or that I don't consider to be a problem, deleted an unused function, and corrected my use of React's useState() function.

Detecting Bugs with AI

Although using a code linter and a code formatter can help you write better code and avoid many common bugs, problems that aren't caught during development will be found in the process of testing or by the end users of the software.

Non-AI debugging tools take many different forms, but they generally all work the same way. When something isn't working as you expect in your code, you can use a debugging tool to interrupt the running of the program at the point where the problem occurs and use the debugging tool to view what's going on with your variables, event listeners, and other types of code.

By pausing the program or simply outputting values from the code, you can start to figure out what might be going wrong. Two of the most important tools in debugging are logging and breakpoints.

Logging is the process of writing messages containing information about the running program and errors that occur. In JavaScript, the console module and its log() method are frequently used for logging. In Python, you can use the print() statement or the logging module.

Breakpoints are spots in your code where you indicate (with the debugger) that you want the execution of the program to pause while you inspect the program's variables. Web browsers have a debugging tool you can use when debugging JavaScript code running in a browser. Figure 7-18 shows the debugging tool built into Google Chrome.

Even with a debugging tool, figuring out what's going wrong in a program and how to fix it can involve a lot of frustrating work. And nine times out of ten, the problem turns out to be a typo.

AI chatbots such as Copilot Chat or ChatGPT can often relieve you of some of the manual work of debugging by tracking down the causes of problems and suggesting fixes. As with everything you do with generative AI models, the key to getting good results is to provide enough context to the model and prompt the AI correctly.

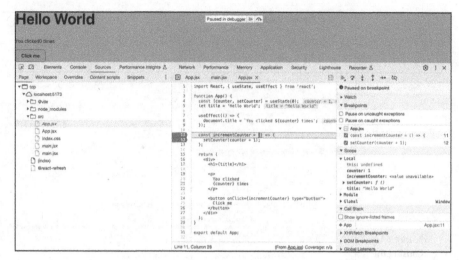

FIGURE 7-18: Chrome's JavaScript debugger.

The following listing shows a Python function containing at least two simple unit-level bugs:

```python
def calculate_average(numbers):
    total = 0
    for number in numbers:
        if not isinstance(number, (int, float)):
            raise TypeError("Invalid data type. All values must
                be numbers.")
        total += number
    average = total / len(numbers)
    return average
```

In terms of syntax, `calculate_average()` is fine. However, the problem here is that the function expects to receive a list of numbers, but it doesn't check whether the argument passed to it is a list. As written, if you pass a value to this function that isn't a list, it will raise a `TypeError`, indicating that the values must be numbers, which isn't actually the problem. Also, if you pass an empty list to the function, it will raise a `ZeroDivisionError`.

Figure 7-19 shows how to run the function and cause the `TypeError`.

For my first attempt to get an AI chatbot to fix the bug, I opened a file containing the function in VS Code and typed **/fix** in Copilot Chat. Copilot Chat identified the `ZeroDivisionError` problem, as shown in Figure 7-20, but it didn't address the issue of what happens when you pass the function a value that isn't a list.

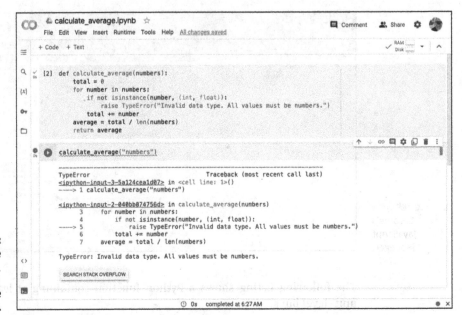

FIGURE 7-19:
Causing the
`calculate_`
`average()`
function to raise
an error.

FIGURE 7-20:
Copilot fixed
one issue.

I updated my code with Copilot's suggestion, as well as with an example of calling the function with a string, and asked Copilot to fix it again. This time, Copilot correctly pointed out that I was calling the function incorrectly and showed me how to call it with a list of numbers, but it didn't address the issue with the function.

I followed up with the following prompt:

```
How can I fix the function so it doesn't raise an
error when it doesn't get a list?
```

With this direct question, Copilot responded with code that fixes the problem I wanted to fix. The corrected code follows:

```
def calculate_average(numbers):
    if not isinstance(numbers, list):
        return "Error: Input should be a list of numbers."
    if len(numbers) == 0:
        return None
    total = 0
    for number in numbers:
        if not isinstance(number, (int, float)):
            raise TypeError("Invalid data type. All values must
    be numbers.")
        total += number
    average = total / len(numbers)
    return average

print(calculate_ave rage('a'))
```

Automating Bug Fixes with AI

In a perfect world, it would be possible for an AI assistant to automatically scan your code and suggest fixes, instead of relying on manual bug detection or pasting code into a chatbot. By integrating AI-powered bug detection and fixes into your software development lifecycle, you can find and correct many types of bugs and security problems that can't be detected by linters and that you never would have thought to ask your AI coding assistant about.

Introducing Snyk

Snyk (https://snyk.io/) is a platform that integrates with many popular software development tools and version control systems to scan, prioritize, and fix security vulnerabilities and certain other kinds of bugs. The tools and platforms Snyk integrates with include the following:

- » Popular IDEs, such as VS Code, WebStorm, Android Studio, and Eclipse

- » Source control systems, including GitHub, Bitbucket, and GitLab

- » Container registries, including Amazon ECR, Docker Hub, and Azure ACR

- » Kubernetes

- » Continuous integration platforms, including AWS CodePipeline, Azure Pipelines, Bitbucket Pipelines, and GitHub Actions

- » Notification and ticketing systems, such as AWS CloudTrail Lake, Jira, and Slack

Because Snyk integrates with so many tools, it's possible to customize how you use it so it becomes an integral part of your workflow.

Follow these steps to sign up for Snyk and use it to detect bugs and vulnerabilities in a code repository:

1. **Go to** https://app.snyk.io/login.

   You see a button for signing up with GitHub and several alternative ways to sign up below it, as shown in Figure 7-21.

2. **Click the GitHub link (or the signup method of your choice).**

   Whichever method you choose, make sure you have code on the platform that you want to check for bugs and vulnerabilities.

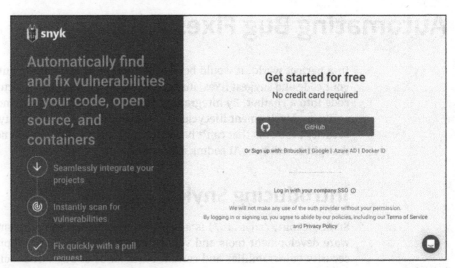

FIGURE 7-21:
The Snyk
signup page.

Snyk Limited

3. **Step through the process of signing up for Snyk and giving it access to the service you chose for signing up.**

Once you've giving Snyk permission to read from your repositories, you'll see the page where you can import and scan your first project, as shown in Figure 7-22.

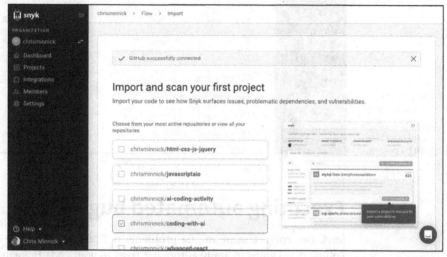

FIGURE 7-22: Snyk's import and scan a project page.

4. **Select a repository you want to import, and then click the Import and Scan button.**

You'll be taken to your project list.

5. **Click the name of your imported project to expand it.**

After a short time, any issues that Snyk detects will appear, along with a severity ranking, as shown in Figure 7-23.

6. **Click the filename of the first file with detected issues to see more information about the bugs.**

In the case of my repository, the problem was the package.json file, which had some out-of-date dependencies containing security vulnerabilities.

FIGURE 7-23:
Snyk shows bugs and prioritizes them by severity.

Executing automated bug fixes

Snyk can correct some of the problems it finds in your code or dependencies. Follow these steps to apply automatic fixes to your code repository:

1. **On the left, click the Dashboard link.**

   The dashboard displays a list of your projects and a Fix Vulnerabilities link for each issue that Snyk can fix automatically.

2. **Click the Fix Vulnerabilities link next your project or one of your files.**

   Snyk displays the issues it can automatically fix and offers to open a pull request, as shown in Figure 7-24. A *pull request (PR)* suggests and explains a specific change to a code repository; it doesn't change anything in your repository until the owner of the repository approves the PR.

3. **Select or deselect issues you want Snyk to fix, and then click the Open a Fix PR button.**

   GitHub displays the pull request Snyk generated, as shown in Figure 7-25.

4. **Read through the information provided by Snyk about the bugs and vulnerabilities, and look at its proposed changes carefully before scrolling to the bottom of the PR and clicking the Merge Pull Request button.**

After the bug fixes are merged into your repository, you can pull the changed code into your local code and run tests to verify that it still works as expected.

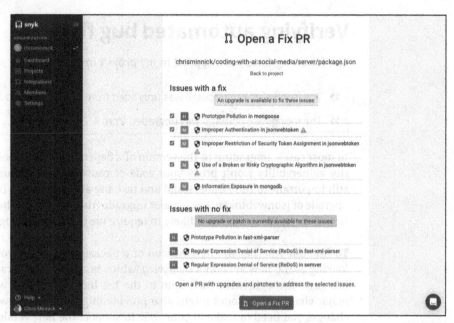

FIGURE 7-24:
Snyk offers to
open a PR.

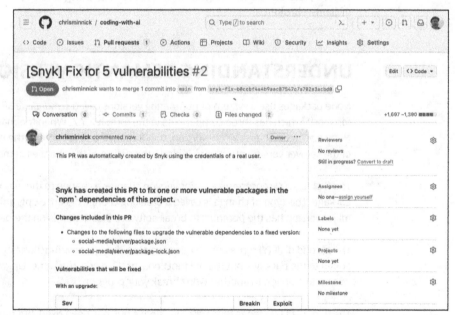

FIGURE 7-25:
Snyk opens a pull
request for its
recommended
fixes.

Verifying automated bug fixes

The following fixes were applied to my project in the preceding section:

>> The jsonwebtoken package was upgraded from version 8.5.1 to 9.0.0.

>> The mongoose package was upgraded from 6.7.1 to 6.12.0.

In most cases, upgrading to the version of a dependency that doesn't have a security vulnerability won't break your code or cause additional bugs. However, it's still important to fully understand and test any automated bug fixes. Because the upgrade of jsonwebtoken was a major upgrade (the number on the far left changed from 8 to 9), it's much more likely to require me to fix something else in my code.

To find out whether the new version of a package will break your code, start by looking at the new version's *changelog*, which is a list of the versions the package has gone through, with each item in the list indicating what was changed. For major changes, packages might also provide migration notes, which explain the changes you need to make to your code to support the new version.

Figure 7-26 shows the migration notes for migrating from version 8 to version 9 of jsonwebtoken.

UNDERSTANDING SEMANTIC VERSIONING

Node packages use a system of numbering versions called *semantic versioning* (*semver* for short), which has three components in the format X.Y.Z. When the maintainer of a Node package releases a new version, they'll change one or more of the components of the semver version number to indicate the nature of the changes in the new version.

The first digit (X) represents a major version change: a change to the way you use the package. This type of change is called a breaking change because upgrading to a new major version has the potential to break software that depends on the package.

The second digit (Y) represents a minor version change: new functionality has been added to the package, but the old functionality still works the same. Upgrading from one minor version to another won't break your program.

The third digit (Z) stands for a patch version: a bug has been fixed, but no new functionality has been added to the package. You should always upgrade to the latest patch version.

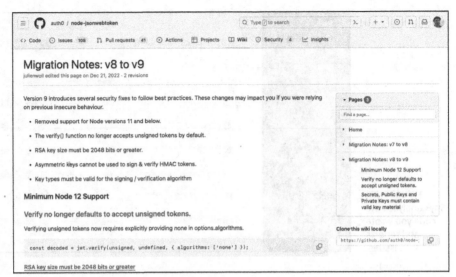

FIGURE 7-26:
The migration notes for version 9 of jsonwebtoken.

Once you've made any necessary upgrades to your code specified in the migration notes or the changelog, you should rerun your tests to make sure they still pass. (Testing and getting AI's help with writing tests is covered in Chapter 9.)

Knowing when to automate

Upgrading an out-of-date dependency with a security problem is a natural fit for automation. (Other types of bugs can't be automated quite as easily.)

In addition to checking your project's dependencies, Snyk also checks your code to find common problems that may represent security bugs. In the list of issues in the Projects view in Snyk, you may see an item labeled Code Analysis, as shown in Figure 7-27. If there are issues related to the code analysis, practices were found in your code that may be security vulnerabilities.

You can click Code Analysis and then click through the list it displays to see more information. For example, Figure 7-28 shows a detected code issue in the AI tic-tac-toe game described in Chapter 5.

To find out more information about the bug and get a potential solution, click the Fix Analysis button in the top-right corner of the screen. The Fix Analysis screen explains how to fix the bug and shows you a similar solution to the issue implemented in a different repository from Snyk's training data, as shown in Figure 7-29.

FIGURE 7-27:
Snyk analyzes the
code you wrote
and reports
issues.

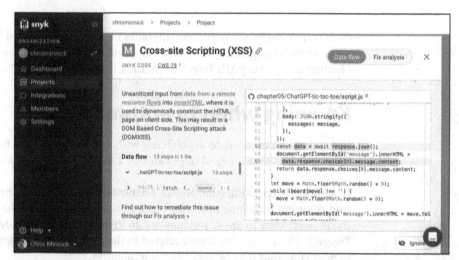

FIGURE 7-28:
A bug was
detected in the
tic-tac-toe game.

Unlike AI chatbots, Snyk doesn't provide the solution to your problem. However, by looking at how the problem was fixed in another project, you can figure out how to fix it in your code. In this case, the problem was that the use of the DOM innerHTML property to set data in the browser that comes directly from a remote source could potentially expose the client application to a cross-site scripting (XSS) attack.

To fix the problem, I changed the property to set the text in the browser to innerText, which causes the browser to display any code that's part of the server's response as plain text, without trying to interpret it.

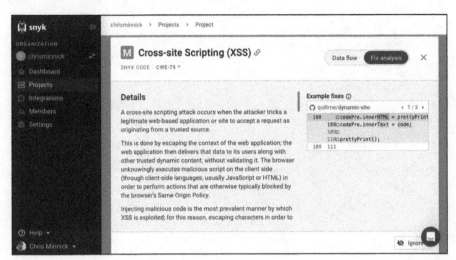

FIGURE 7-29:
Snyk provides a
potential fix.

Snyk Limited

Chapter **8**

Translating and Optimizing Code

After you have a working program, you might want to translate it to another programming language or improve the code's quality or efficiency. Both tasks should be done carefully, if at all.

Code translation and code optimization are related topics because both seek to change the code in some way without changing its functionality and purpose. In this chapter, you discover how AI tools can help.

Translating Code to Other Languages

The most common form of code translation is *compilation*, in which native code written by programmers is translated into machine code that can be run by the CPU. Compilation is a necessary and reliable process.

Translating code from one high-level programming language to another, however, is a process fraught with danger. If you do it for the wrong reason (such as thinking the new language is cooler than the old language), you could end up with a time-consuming project that doesn't provide any benefit to the users of the software or, worse, provides fewer functions than the original code. (Does it sound as though I have experience with these scenarios?)

Good reasons exist for translating code between high-level languages. The most common reason is that the hardware or operating system the software requires doesn't have a compiler for the current programming language. For example, if you want a web app (written in HTML, CSS, and JavaScript) to run natively on a mobile device, you need to translate it. Or, if you have a legacy application built using an obsolete programming language that you want to use on modern hardware, you'll likely need to translate the app.

Preparing your code for translation

If you're translating code between two libraries or frameworks but using the same underlying language (such as translating a web app written using Angular to one that uses React), your chances of getting good results are much higher than if you're translating between programming languages. In either case, however, you can do several things prior to the translation to help the process go more smoothly.

Most of the steps for preparing your code for translation are simply good coding practices:

>> **Back up your original code.** The most essential step is to make sure you can always revert to the original language — either to modify your AI-assisted translation approach or to handle at least part of it manually.

>> **Comment and document your code thoroughly.** The AI assistant may be able to use your comments and documentation to interpret the purpose of the code.

>> **Clean and refactor the code.** Remove any unnecessary or redundant code and simplify complex parts of the code as much as possible.

>> **Ensure a consistent coding style.** Use a linter and a code formatter to ensure that your code has consistent naming conventions, indentation, and bracket placement.

>> **Use descriptive variable and function names.** Descriptive names can help the AI to better understand the structure and purpose of your code.

>> **Address language-specific features.** When translating between programming languages, a common big problem occurs when features and conventions used in one language aren't present in the other language. Reducing the use of these features or simply being aware of the program's use of them will help you identify and fix issues with the translated code.

>> **Modularize your code.** By breaking your code into small and modular components, you help the AI to translate your code more efficiently. If your code is written as a collection of independent modules, it also allows you to translate the source code in smaller chunks, which may improve accuracy and simplify troubleshooting.

Exploring translation strategies

To see how well large language models handle translation between programming languages, let's start with a simple JavaScript function:

```javascript
// converts an array to an HTML unordered list
function makeUnorderedList(array) {
  let listItems = array.map(element => {
    return `<li>${element}</li>`;
  });
  return `<ul>${listItems.join("")}</ul>`;
}
```

There's nothing tricky about this function. When you give it an array, it converts the array into an HTML bulleted list. Figure 8-1 shows the makeUnorderedList() function in action.

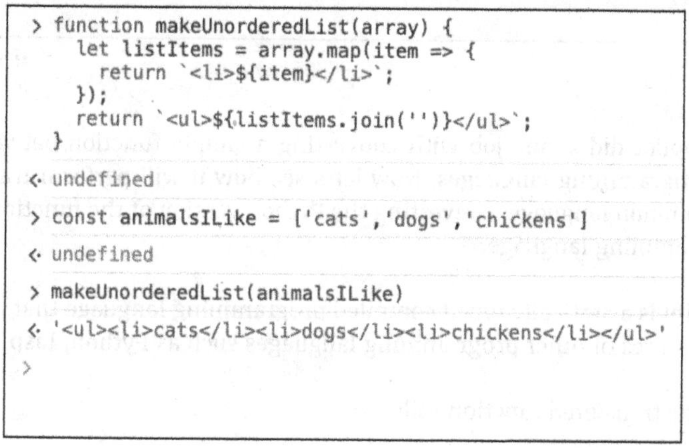

```javascript
> function makeUnorderedList(array) {
    let listItems = array.map(item => {
      return `<li>${item}</li>`;
    });
    return `<ul>${listItems.join('')}</ul>`;
  }
<- undefined
> const animalsILike = ['cats','dogs','chickens']
<- undefined
> makeUnorderedList(animalsILike)
<- '<ul><li>cats</li><li>dogs</li><li>chickens</li></ul>'
>
```

FIGURE 8-1:
The JavaScript version of makeUnorderedList() running in the browser console.

Microsoft Corporation

You can use Copilot Chat to translate code from one language to another. With a file containing just the makeUnorderedList() function open in VS Code, give Copilot Chat the following prompt:

```
translate this function to python.
```

Copilot's translation follows:

```python
def make_unordered_list(array):
    list_items = [f"<li>{element}</li>" for element in array]
    return f"<ul>{".join(list_items)}</ul>"
```

This solution seems fine. To test it out, enter it into Google Colab and run the function. The result, which is shown in Figure 8-2, is what I expected.

```
[1]  def make_unordered_list(array):
         list_items = [f"<li>{element}</li>" for element in array]
         return f"<ul>{''.join(list_items)}</ul>"

[2]  rooms = ['kitchen','living room','dining room']

     make_unordered_list(rooms)

         '<ul><li>kitchen</li><li>living room</li><li>dining room</li></ul>'
```

FIGURE 8-2: Testing the translated function.

Copilot did a fine job with converting a simple function between two common programming languages. Now let's see how it will perform translating to a less common language, converting the Python version of the function to the Nim programming language.

TECHNICAL STUFF

Nim is a statically typed compiled programming language that combines the best features of other programming languages such as Python, Lisp, and Ada.

The translated function follows:

```nim
import strutils

proc makeUnorderedList(array: seq[string]): string =
  var listItems = ""
  for element in array:
```

```
        listItems = listItems & "<li>" & element & "</li>"
      return "<ul>" & listItems & "</ul>"
```

I don't know Nim (yet), but at first glance, this result looks reasonable. I asked Copilot for an example of how to use the function, and it produced an example and said what the output would be, as shown in Figure 8-3.

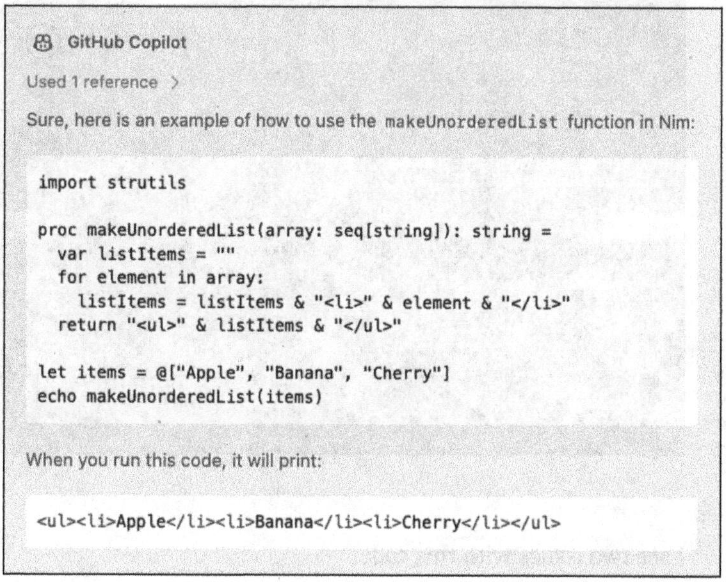

⑧ GitHub Copilot

Used 1 reference ›

Sure, here is an example of how to use the `makeUnorderedList` function in Nim:

```
import strutils

proc makeUnorderedList(array: seq[string]): string =
  var listItems = ""
  for element in array:
    listItems = listItems & "<li>" & element & "</li>"
  return "<ul>" & listItems & "</ul>"

let items = @["Apple", "Banana", "Cherry"]
echo makeUnorderedList(items)
```

When you run this code, it will print:

```
<ul><li>Apple</li><li>Banana</li><li>Cherry</li></ul>
```

FIGURE 8-3:
Copilot's example code and the predicted result of running it.

To verify whether Copilot's Nim code works and produces the expected output, copy the example code into the Nim Playground at `https://play.nim-lang.org/`. The output was exactly what Copilot said it would be, as shown in Figure 8-4.

WARNING

Although this simple example produces correct results, I don't know whether this is the best way to write this function in Nim. Unless you're just experimenting, don't ask an AI assistant to convert code to a language you don't know.

The leap from JavaScript to Nim seemed to be a success. Now I want to find out whether Copilot can help with something I have a daily use for: converting JavaScript to TypeScript. Unfortunately, on the first attempt, Copilot only had partial success:

```
converts an array to an HTML unordered list
function makeUnorderedList(array: any[]) {
  let listItems = array.map((element) => {
```

```
    return `<li>${element}</li>`;
  });
  return `<ul>${listItems.join("")}</ul>`;
}
```

GitHub, Inc.

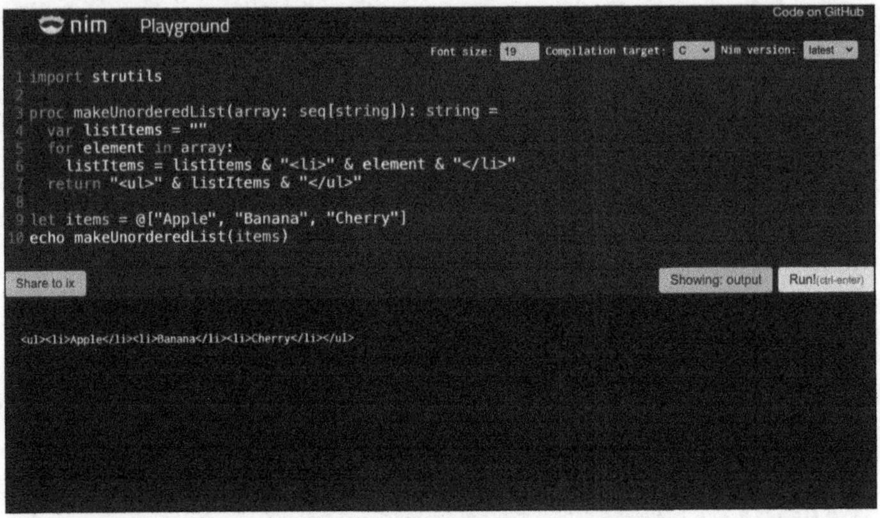

FIGURE 8-4:
Our first
Nim program
works great!

I see two issues with this code:

» The comment isn't marked as a comment.

» The parameter accepted by makeUnorderedList() is annotated as being of
type any[].

Because the original function doesn't specify what data type the elements of the
array should be, this translation is technically correct. However, a human programmer would have used a more specific type.

I asked Copilot to do the translation again, and the result this time was better but
still not right:

```
converts an array to an HTML unordered list
function makeUnorderedList(array: string[]): string {
  let listItems: string[] = array.map((element) => {
    return `<li>${element}</li>`;
  });
  return `<ul>${listItems.join("")}</ul>`;
}
```

In this translation, the comment still isn't marked as a comment, and the type annotations for the return value from the function and for listItems are unnecessary. I tried the translation again and got a nearly perfect result, except that the comment was stripped out:

```
function makeUnorderedList(array: string[]) {
  let listItems = array.map((element) => {
    return `<li>${element}</li>`;
  });
  return `<ul>${listItems.join("")}</ul>`;
}
```

WARNING

It's likely that Copilot will handle simple translations much better by the time you read this, especially if the model it uses is upgraded. However, this experiment demonstrates that it's not possible or wise to trust an AI translation unless you know the target language.

Translating a complete program using GPT-4

GPT-4 is much larger and more capable of difficult tasks than the model behind Copilot. To see how GPT-4 would perform with a complex translation, I used the OpenAI Playground to create a code translation assistant. I gave the model the following system prompt:

```
You are an expert JavaScript programmer. Translate my
code from a web app to a mobile app written in React
Native.
```

The web app I wrote to test my new translation assistant uses a single React component that gives the user an input field where they can type a GitHub username, as shown in Figure 8-5. When the user clicks the Get Repositories link, the app uses the GitHub API to fetch and display a list of the user's GitHub repositories.

In the OpenAI Playground, I pasted the code for the app's single component, plus the code for rendering it into a user prompt. I selected the GPT-4 model and set the temperature to 0.5 so the model would favor more accurate predictions over creativity. To make sure the response didn't get cut off, I set the maximum length to a far higher value than I expected would be necessary. My prompt and settings are shown in Figure 8-6.

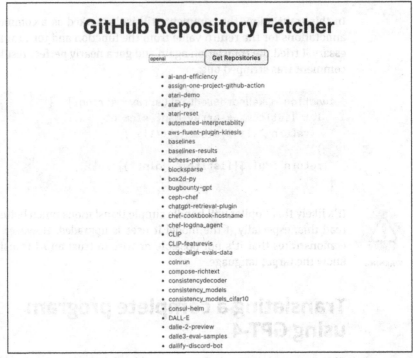

GitHub Repository Fetcher

openai | Get Repositories

- ai-and-efficiency
- assign-one-project-github-action
- atari-demo
- atari-py
- atari-reset
- automated-interpretability
- aws-fluent-plugin-kinesis
- baselines
- baselines-results
- bchess-personal
- blocksparse
- box2d-py
- bugbounty-gpt
- ceph-chef
- chatgpt-retrieval-plugin
- chef-cookbook-hostname
- chef-logdna_agent
- CLIP
- CLIP-featurevis
- code-align-evals-data
- coinrun
- compose-richtext
- consistencydecoder
- consistency_models
- consistency_models_cifar10
- consul-helm
- DALL-E
- dalle-2-preview
- dalle3-eval-samples
- dallify-discord-bot

FIGURE 8-5:
A web app for
fetching GitHub
repository
names.

GitHub, Inc.

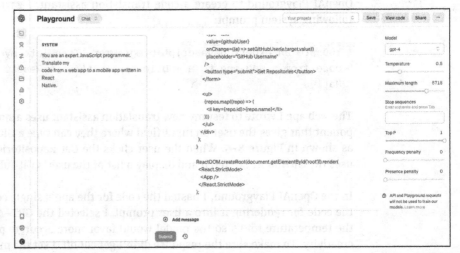

FIGURE 8-6:
Setting up a
translation
request in
OpenAI
Playground.

ChatGPT

I submitted the prompt and got back the converted component, which I copied and pasted into a React Native template and ran. Except for a minor styling issue on iOS, it worked perfectly on both iOS and Android devices, as shown in Figure 8-7.

FIGURE 8-7:
The GitHub
Repository
Fetcher mobile
app on iOS (left)
and Android
(right) devices.

GitHub, Inc.

Verifying translated code

Translating code from one language to another and verifying that the translated code runs is just the beginning of the process of ensuring that the translation is accurate. Especially if you translated the code with the help of an AI assistant, the new code has to go through many more steps before you can deploy it.

You should treat translated code the same as freshly written code. The process for verifying your translated app involves the following steps:

>> **Understand the source code:** Take the time to fully understand the source code of the translated app as well as the original code before moving on to the next steps. AI chatbot tools may be able to help you better understand the code. (Chatbots are covered in Chapters 3 and 4.)

>> **Test:** The translation might have introduced new bugs to your program. Take the tests you wrote for the original code and adapt them to the new code. AI may be helpful with translating the tests for the new code. (Testing is covered in Chapter 9.)

- » **Conduct code reviews:** Conduct code reviews, ideally with the help of another human programmer as well as with an AI assistant. (Conducting a code review with AI is covered in Chapter 11.)

- » **Do a static code analysis:** Use a linter with your new code to check for potential syntax, formatting, and style issues. (Static code analysis is covered in Chapter 7.)

- » **Cross-reference output:** Provide both versions of the app with the same input and check that they produce identical output for data processing or calculation tasks. (Testing tools and techniques that can help with this task are covered in Chapter 9.)

- » **Document:** Check the documentation and comments in the new code to verify that they're still accurate, and update them as needed. (Creating documentation with AI assistance is covered in Chapter 10.)

- » **Conduct a security review:** Different languages and runtime environments have different security vulnerabilities. For example, the security concerns associated with a web app are very different from those of an Android or iOS app. For this reason, you need to conduct a security review of the translated code. A tool such as Snyk (which is covered in Chapter 7) can be helpful with conducting this review.

REMEMBER

The tools and processes used for verifying translated code are the same as those used to write and optimize original code.

Optimizing Your Code with AI

Poorly optimized code works correctly but isn't efficient or functioning well or as expected. Almost all code can be improved. You might want to optimize code to make it run faster, to improve its quality, or to make it work within the limitations of the hardware or other environmental factors.

Python is one of the most commonly used programming languages and is particularly popular and useful when working with machine learning. However, Python is notoriously slow when compared to other programming languages. When you combine Python's slowness with the processing and memory requirements of machine learning tasks, the result can be a program that takes a very long time to run and monopolizes the resources of your computer while running.

However, slowness in the running of a program isn't just the fault of the language, compiler, and underlying hardware. The decisions you make during coding can affect a program's performance to a greater extent.

Identifying opportunities for improving performance takes time and experience. Code optimization starts with *profiling*, which is a technique that detects how long each function in your program takes to run and how often it's executed. Profiling will tell you what areas of your program are in need of optimization. A tool that does profiling is called a *profiler*.

By combining the job of a traditional profiler with suggestions from an AI chatbot, you can find out what code runs slowly and get suggestions for possible improvements.

Getting code optimization suggestions

Scalene is a CPU, GPU, and memory profiler for Python that profiles code and offers AI-powered proposed optimizations.

TECHNICAL
STUFF

I installed and ran Scalene on macOS. The Windows version of Scalene doesn't support all the same features as the Linux or macOS version at the time of this writing.

Before you can install Scalene, you need to have Python installed and configured. Because Scalene makes use of OpenAI's models, you also need to have an OpenAI account with a positive balance to use the AI features. To find out how to get an OpenAI account and an API key, see Chapter 4.

Then follow these steps to install Scalene and test it out:

1. **Visit the GitHub repository for Scalene at** https://github.com/plasma-umass/scalene **to read more about it.**

2. **On macOS, Linux, or Windows Subsystem for Linux (WSL2), use the following pip command to install the Scalene package:**

    ```
    pip install -U scalene
    ```

3. **Clone the Scalene GitHub repository to a convenient place on your computer by entering the following command in a terminal window:**

    ```
    git clone https://github.com/plasma-umass/scalene
    ```

    The GitHub repository contains a directory of Python files which we'll use to test Scalene.

4. **Open the Scalene GitHub repository in VS Code.**

5. **In the Extensions panel in VS Code, find and install the Scalene VS Code extension, as shown in Figure 8-8.**

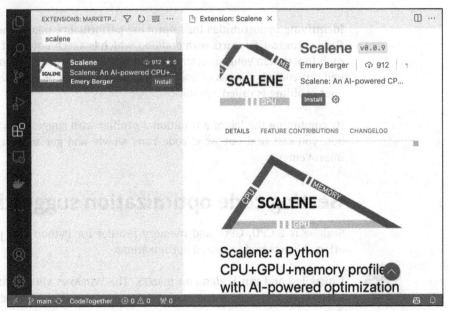

FIGURE 8-8:
Installing the
Scalene VS Code
extension.

6. Open test/testme.py in VS Code.

This program doesn't do anything useful, but we can use it to demonstrate what Scalene can do.

7. Press Command+Shift+P (macOS) or Ctrl+Shift+P (Windows) to open the VS Code command palette.

8. Type Scalene **in the command palette until you see the Scalene: AI-Powered Profiling. . . command. Click that command to run it.**

A message appears in VS Code telling you that Scalene is profiling your code. When it finishes, a report opens in VS Code, as shown in Figure 8-9.

9. Look through the report.

On my computer, the program took 10.646 seconds to run and used a maximum of 20.536 MB of memory.

Note the lines of code with a lightning or fireworks icon to the left. The fireworks icon indicates that Scalene has proposed optimizations for that line or region of code; click the icon to view the optimizations. The lightning icon causes Scalene to propose optimizations for the lines of code that it didn't find optimizations for originally, or to attempt to generate different code for lines for which it did propose an optimization.

10. To enter your OpenAI API key into Scalene, click the Advanced Options link (under the Scalene logo at the top of the Scalene report), as shown in Figure 8-10.

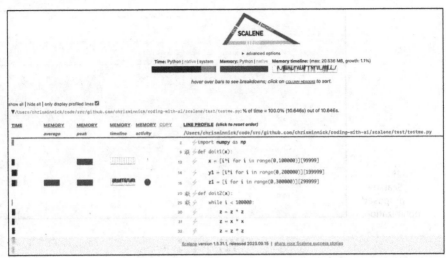

FIGURE 8-9:
Scalene's report
for testme.py.

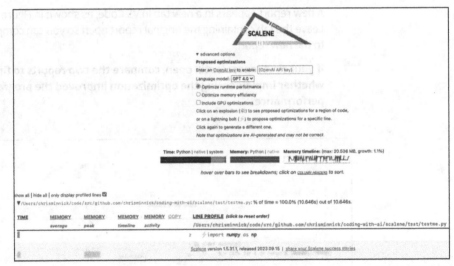

FIGURE 8-10:
Opening the
advanced options
to input an
API key.

11. In the input field in the advanced options area, paste your OpenAI API key, and then close the advanced options by clicking the Advanced Options link again.

12. Click a fireworks icon in Scalene's report.

After a short time, a proposed optimization appears below the line marked with the fireworks icon, as shown in Figure 8-11.

13. Review the proposed optimization.

If you want to see a different proposal, click the fireworks icon again.

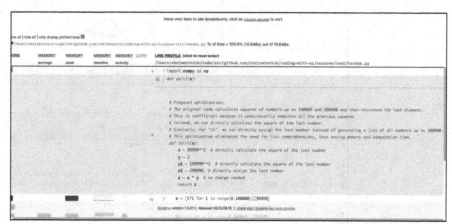

FIGURE 8-11:
Scalene's
proposed
optimization.

Microsoft Corporation

14. Once you find an optimization that makes sense to you, implement it in your code and run Scalene again.

A new report appears in a new tab in VS Code, as shown in Figure 8-12. Leave the tab containing the original report open so you can compare it to the new report.

15. If your first report is still open, compare the two reports to find out whether implementing the optimization improved the program's performance.

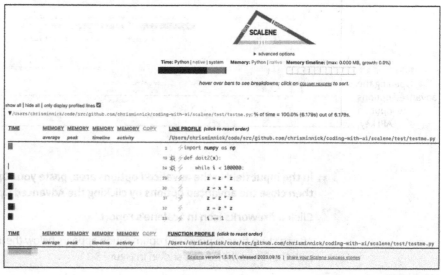

FIGURE 8-12:
Profiling your
optimized code.

Microsoft Corporation

The testme.py file was designed to be as inefficient as possible to demonstrate Scalene. But, by optimizing just the first function, I was able to reduce the memory to 0 MB and the execution time by about 4.5 seconds.

Avoiding premature optimization

The best time to optimize your code is when you're first writing it. However, this isn't always possible. As software is written and requirements change, inefficiencies and bad code have a way of creeping in. See Chapter 6 to learn about the types of problems (also known as code smells) that can exist in source code, many of which can negatively affect performance.

Before you optimize your code for performance, decide whether optimization is worthwhile. If a program is working correctly and you identify a refactoring that could make it run faster, proceed with caution to avoid what programmers call "premature optimization." The preeminent computer scientist Donald Knuth, author of *The Art of Computer Programming*, famously declared that "Premature optimization is the root of all evil." (Someone else said, "Absolute statements are the root of all evil.")

What Knuth meant is that programmers should be careful that they're not worrying about efficiency more than necessary. Shaving a few microseconds from a process at the cost of multiple hours of work and potentially introducing new bugs isn't worth the effort — especially because faster CPUs will likely result in a more significant performance improvement in a short time and without additional programming work.

However, if the users of your application report slow performance or other deficiencies in the software, making optimizations to address this feedback should be your top priority.

Avoiding premature optimization

The best time to optimize your code is when you're first writing it. However, this isn't always possible. As software is written and requirements change, inefficiencies and bad code have a way of creeping in. See Chapter 6 to learn about the types of problems (also known as code smells) that can exist in source code, many of which can negatively affect performance.

Before you optimize your code for performance, decide whether the optimization is worthwhile. If a program is working correctly and you identify a refactoring that could make it run faster, proceed with caution to avoid what programmers call "premature optimization." The preeminent computer scientist Donald Knuth, author of "The Art of Computer Programming," famously declared that "premature optimization is the root of all evil." (Someone else said, "Absolute statements are the root of all evil.")

What Knuth means is that programmers should be careful that they're not worrying about efficiency more than necessary. Shaving a few microseconds from a process at the cost of multiple hours of work and potentially throwing new bugs isn't worth the effort — especially because faster CPUs will likely result in a more significant performance improvement in a short time and without additional programming work.

However, if the users of your application report slow performance or other deficiencies, the software making optimizations to address this feedback should be your top priority.

3
Testing, Documenting, and Maintaining Your Code

Generate tests and verify your code's functionality.

Learn to write high-quality documentation with the help of AI assistants.

Uncover ways to use AI to make your code more maintainable.

Chapter **9**

Testing Your Code

O f all the programming tasks that AI can help with, testing is perhaps the safest. That's because running a test doesn't affect your code or the software design— it merely checks whether the software operates how it was designed.

Writing tests with AI assistance, however, is not always reliable. As you learn in this chapter, the quality of the tests and testing advice that you get from AI depends on your prompts to the AI model and how well you know which tasks are better handled by people.

Test automation is the process of using software separate from the software being tested to control the running of tests. Prior to the 1980s, most software testing was done by testers, people who would use the software to confirm that it worked. In the late 1980s, testers used tools to record their interactions with the software and replay a test at any time. This process was known as *record and playback testing*.

The third major change to testing happened in the 1990s, when much of testing became script-driven. Rather than testing software by using it, testers began automating testing tasks by writing scripts using programming languages. As a result, testing became more flexible but also more technical, requiring the skills of software developers rather than software testers. Starting in the 2010s, AI tools to assist with testing software began to emerge. Testing with AI-assistance can make testing and the writing of tests easier, which will once again allow non-programmers to participate in the process (as well as programmers, of course).

Writing a Test Plan

A *test plan* describes what you're planning to test, how it will be tested, and a schedule for testing. You can use a test plan also to list the risks anticipated in the project so testing can be prioritized accordingly.

Deciding between formal and agile

Traditional methods of testing, in which testing is a discrete phase of the software development lifecycle that involves predefined steps, are best used when the requirements are precise, such as writing software for airplanes, spaceships, or the IRS. For such mission-critical software applications, a formal test plan that specifies the who, what, where, when, and how of the testing phase should be created and followed.

Most software development today follows an agile methodology, in which software development and testing are done iteratively, rather than as a linear step-by-step process.

In agile software development, a test plan focuses on continuous testing. Recognizing that requirements change and that no plan is perfect, agile testing emphasizes flexibility and adaptability in the testing process. The goal of an agile test plan is to test the software to ensure that it meets the needs of the end users, as specified in the user stories and acceptance criteria. (User stories are covered in Chapter 5.)

Whether a test plan is a formal document or an agile plan will depend on the type of software you're building and the software development methodology used by your employer.

Stepping through the test planning process

Although testing is increasingly an integral part of the software development process, additional testing also needs to be done when the software is fully functional. For the purposes of creating a plan, it's helpful to think of testing as a project that's separate from software development, whether or not it actually is.

On small projects and personal projects, you'll do all the development and testing yourself. On large projects, developers are still involved in testing, but the job of creating a test plan and formally declaring the product "tested" falls to the quality assurance (QA) team.

Creating a test plan usually involves the following steps:

>> **Analyze the software.** Review the software's documentation, speak with the developers, and gain a thorough understanding of the software to be tested.

>> **Define your testing strategy.** Specify the goals and objectives of the testing project.

>> **Determine the testing scope.** Define what is to be tested and what methodologies you will use to test it. Examples of methodologies include unit testing, system testing, performance testing, and security testing.

>> **Define the test criteria.** Define the *exit criteria,* which are the conditions under which the testing will be deemed successful or failed, and the *suspension criteria,* which are the conditions under which testing should be suspended.

>> **Prepare the test environment.** Figure out the resources you need (such as software, hardware, and operating systems) to conduct the testing.

>> **Create a test schedule.** Divide the testing process into tasks and activities and create a series of deadlines.

>> **Identify the test deliverables.** Determine the deliverables of the testing process: the test plan, the test creation, and finally the test report.

You can jump-start the test plan process with the help of an AI assistant. Although you'll need to revise and expand on the AI-generated plan, the AI model might provide ideas you hadn't considered.

Figuring out how to fully test a program requires a developer to understand not only the functions being tested but also the testing framework used to write the tests. Although creating tests should be an integral part of the software development process, it's often so difficult and time-consuming to write good tests that testing becomes an afterthought.

Most developers I know would happily outsource testing to AI so they could focus more on the fun part of software development — namely, writing code.

Understanding the role of AI in test planning

You can use AI in several ways during the test planning process. Some of the tasks that AI can perform include the following:

>> Simulate user behavior to identify failure or success patterns.

>> Analyze the software's requirements to generate test steps to validate them.

>> Explain the code and identify functionality that needs to be tested.

>> Write test cases.

Following are the benefits of using AI to create a test plan:

>> **Automated analysis:** An AI system can quickly analyze vast amounts of data, including complex codebases and test results.

>> **Subtle pattern detection:** AI is capable of detecting patterns and anomalies that might be overlooked by humans.

>> **Future issues prediction:** By using historical data, AI can predict future failures and allow for proactive test planning.

>> **Risk assessment:** AI can identify high-risk areas of code and help to prioritize testing efforts.

>> **Scenario simulations:** AI can simulate various testing scenarios to identify the most effective approaches.

Identifying core functionalities

Before you can test software, you need to understand what the software does. For complex software or software you didn't write, it's helpful to document the core functionalities that will be tested before you start to make a plan for how to test them.

A software requirements specification (SRS), if available, can give you a good start for identifying what the software was originally designed to do. However, it's likely that the requirements changed during the software development process. Having an AI assistant explain the functionality of the software can also serve as a guide for documenting functionality.

In Chapter 5, I create a tic-tac-toe game with the help of AI. As it stands now, the game only partially meets the requirements specified in the SRS. To start figuring out how to test the game, the first step is to identify the areas of functionality in the game.

I opened the JavaScript file for the client app and prompted Copilot Chat with the following:

```
@workspace What are the core functionalities in this
tic-tac-toe game?
```

Copilot responded with an accurate list and descriptions of each of the functionalities in the tic-tac-toe game, as shown in Figure 9-1.

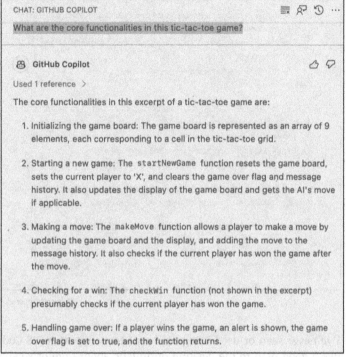

FIGURE 9-1:
Copilot identified the functionalities of the tic-tac-toe game.

Generating test scenarios

Next I gave Copilot the following prompt:

```
@workspace Tell me how I should test this program.
```

Copilot responded with a list of proposed tests for each of the functions in the program, as shown in Figure 9-2.

The last piece of advice Copilot gave in response to my prompt was

```
You can use the integrated unit test support
in Visual Studio Code to write and run these tests.
```

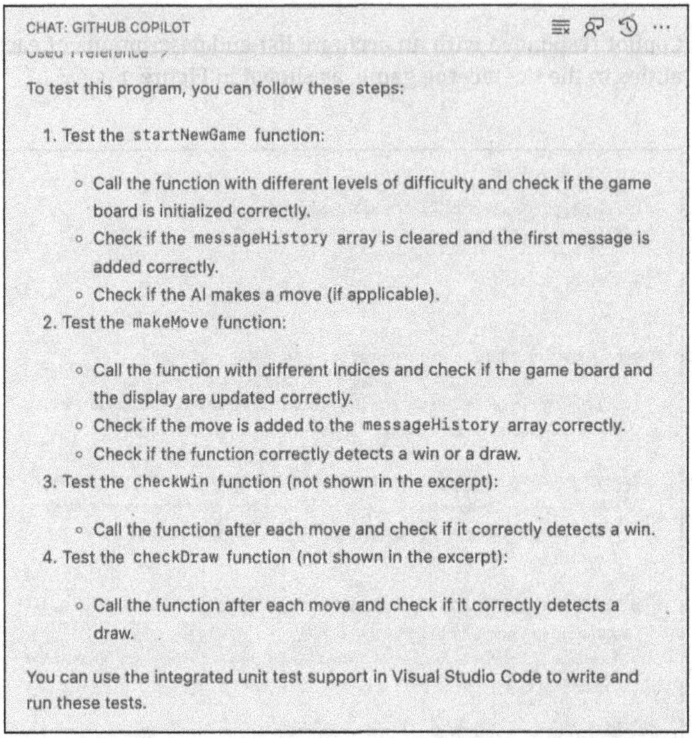

To test this program, you can follow these steps:

1. Test the `startNewGame` function:

   - Call the function with different levels of difficulty and check if the game board is initialized correctly.
   - Check if the `messageHistory` array is cleared and the first message is added correctly.
   - Check if the AI makes a move (if applicable).

2. Test the `makeMove` function:

   - Call the function with different indices and check if the game board and the display are updated correctly.
   - Check if the move is added to the `messageHistory` array correctly.
   - Check if the function correctly detects a win or a draw.

3. Test the `checkWin` function (not shown in the excerpt):

   - Call the function after each move and check if it correctly detects a win.

4. Test the `checkDraw` function (not shown in the excerpt):

   - Call the function after each move and check if it correctly detects a draw.

You can use the integrated unit test support in Visual Studio Code to write and run these tests.

FIGURE 9-2:
Copilot creates a list of test cases.

Microsoft Corporation

I've never seen or used integrated unit test support in VS Code, but this sounds like a good plan to me. Feeling optimistic about Copilot's capability, I ask it the following question:

```
How can I use the integrated unit test support for
Visual Studio Code to write and run these tests?
```

In its response, Copilot gave me some incomplete instructions for installing a testing framework but didn't make any further mention of integrated test support in VS Code. After searching the VS Code documentation, I discovered that VS Code doesn't have integrated unit test support. This advice was just Copilot improvising!

In the following sections, I show you how to set up unit test support in your project, write your first tests, and make the best use of AI for testing.

Working with a Testing Framework

A *testing automation framework* is a piece of software that provides tools for writing tests and an environment for running tests. Many testing frameworks are available, and a software project may need to use several different frameworks to perform various kinds of testing.

Developers are most likely to be involved with *unit testing*, a software testing method in which individual modules of a software application are tested to determine whether they're fit for use. In unit testing, developers create tests (also known as specs) that describe and test the output of functions by comparing the expected output of the function with the actual output of the function. This comparison between expected output and actual output is known as an *assertion*.

Fully testing an individual function in a program usually requires multiple assertions, with each assertion testing an aspect or possible output of the function. The collection of tests for a single function or module is called a *test suite*.

The most popular testing framework for writing and running unit tests for JavaScript code is Jest (https://jestjs.io). Jest runs in the Node.js runtime environment. If you don't have Node.js installed, go to https://nodejs.org/ to download and install it before moving on to the next section.

Installing Jest

In this section, you install the Jest testing framework. But first, if you haven't done so already, download the code for this book from www.dummies.com/go/codingwithaifd and open the chapter09 folder in VS Code.

TIP

If you want to skip the process of setting up Jest and get straight to learning how to write tests, open the tic-tac-toe-client-final folder in a terminal window and run npm install. I've already done the hard parts of setting up Jest for you in that folder, so you can skip the remaining steps in this section and go straight to the section titled "Running Jest."

To install Jest, follow these steps:

1. **Open a new terminal window, and enter the following to switch to the proper folder:**

```
cd tic-tac-toe-client
```

Make sure to use the version of the game in the Chapter 9 folder. This version contains additional bug fixes and optimizations that aren't in the version in the Chapter 6 folder.

2. **Enter the following command in the terminal to initialize a Node project in your client directory:**

```
npm init
```

3. **Answer the questions posed by the** `npm init` **script. (You can accept the default answer to each question.)**

Your answers are used to configure the Node.js package. Note that you can come back later and change your responses by editing the package.json file.

4. **Install Jest by entering the following command in the terminal window:**

```
npm install jest --save-dev
```

5. **Install the JSDom environment:**

```
npm install jest-environment-jsdom --save-dev
```

JSDom is a browser-like environment in which Jest will run your tests to simulate running them in an actual web browser.

6. **Create a base config for Jest:**

```
npx jest --init
```

The Jest init script will ask you a few questions. The questions, along with the settings I chose, are:

```
Would you like to use Jest when running "test" script in
    "package.json"? yes
Would you like to use Typescript for the configuration
    file? no
Choose the test environment that will be used for testing
    jsdom (browser-like)
Do you want Jest to add coverage reports? yes
Which provider should be used to instrument code for
    coverage? v8
Automatically clear mock calls, instances, contexts and
    results before every test? yes
```

Once you've answered the questions, Jest will create a file named jest.config.js in your project.

Because Jest runs in Node, it's possible that your project will contain syntax that's not supported by Node. To account for that, you have to install a few more packages.

7. Enter the following in your terminal window:

```
npm install babel-jest @babel/preset-env @babel/core
   --save-dev
```

Babel is a JavaScript *transpiler,* which converts code from one version of a language to another. In this case, you'll be using Babel to convert the code designed to run in the browser to code that will run in Node.

8. Configure the babel-jest plug-in:

a. *Open jest.config.js.* You'll see a lot of commented-out instructions.

b. *Find the commented-out instruction that starts with transform: and uncomment it.* The transform instruction is where you can specify filename patterns to match and then change those files before testing. In our case, we'll be transpiling JavaScript files using the babel-jest plug-in.

c. *Change the transform instruction to the following:*

```
transform: {
   '\\.[jt]sx?$': 'babel-jest',
}
```

9. Configure Babel by creating a file in your project named babel.config.json and adding the following content to it:

```
{
    "env": {
        "test": {
            "presets": [
                "@babel/preset-env"
            ]
        }
    }
}
```

Whew! That wasn't so bad, was it? Move on to the next section to learn how to run Jest and how to write your first tests.

Running Jest

Now that the Jest test framework is installed and configured, the next step is to run it. To run Jest, enter `npm test` in the terminal window.

Jest looks through your project (everything in the current Node.js package) for test suites to run. Right now, this project doesn't have any tests, so Jest responds with a "No tests found" message, as shown in Figure 9-3.

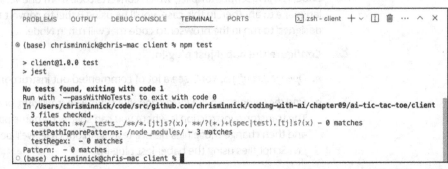

Microsoft Corporation

FIGURE 9-3: Jest responds that it couldn't find any tests.

In addition to pointing out that there aren't any tests in the project, the report also indicates the folder it checked, the number of files in the project, and the filenames in which it's looking for tests. By default, Jest looks for tests in the following files:

» JavaScript or TypeScript files in a folder named __tests__ (that's two underscores, followed by the word *tests* followed by two more underscores).

» JavaScript or TypeScript files with .spec. in their name before the file extension, such as MyComponent.spec.js.

» JavaScript of TypeScript files with .test. in their name before the file extension, such as MyComponent.test.js.

Generating test cases

In Copilot Chat, the `/tests` command generates tests for the code you've selected in the code editor. Follow these steps to use `/tests`:

1. **Make sure that both script.test.js and script.js are open in VS Code.**

2. **In script.js, select the `checkWin()` function.**

   The `checkWin()` function checks whether either player has won the game.

3. Enter /tests in Copilot Chat.

Copilot automatically prefaces the /tests command with @workspace, and then attempts to generate tests for the checkWin() function, as shown in Figure 9-4.

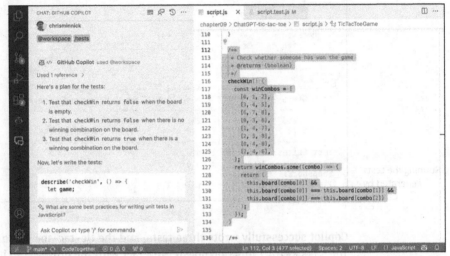

FIGURE 9-4: Copilot generated tests for the checkWin() function.

Microsoft Corporation

REMEMBER

The @workspace command is a Copilot agent that instructs Copilot to consider all the files in the current VS Code workspace while generating a response. You learn about agents in Chapter 4.

Copilot suggested three tests for the checkWin() function:

>> Test that checkWin() returns false when the board is empty.

>> Test that checkWin() returns false when the board does not have a winning combination.

>> Test that checkWin() returns true when the board has a winning combination.

These tests seem to cover every condition possible with the function, so let's create a test suite and add them to it. To start setting up a test suite for the script.js file in the tic-tac-toe game, I created a file named script.test.js and added the following import statement to it:

```
import { TicTacToeGame } from './script';
```

I copied the tests generated by Copilot and pasted them into script.test.js after the import statement and ran npm test. The result is shown in Figure 9-5.

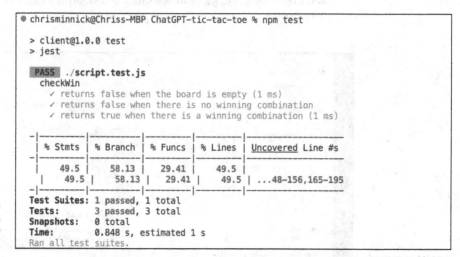

```
● chrisminnick@Chriss-MBP ChatGPT-tic-tac-toe % npm test

  > client@1.0.0 test
  > jest

  PASS  ./script.test.js
    checkWin
      ✓ returns false when the board is empty (1 ms)
      ✓ returns false when there is no winning combination
      ✓ returns true when there is a winning combination (1 ms)

  -|-----------|-----------|-----------|-----------|-------------------
   | % Stmts   | % Branch  | % Funcs   | % Lines   | Uncovered Line #s
  -|-----------|-----------|-----------|-----------|-------------------
   |    49.5   |   58.13   |   29.41   |   49.5    |
   |    49.5   |   58.13   |   29.41   |   49.5    | ...48-156,165-195
  -|-----------|-----------|-----------|-----------|-------------------
  Test Suites: 1 passed, 1 total
  Tests:       3 passed, 3 total
  Snapshots:   0 total
  Time:        0.848 s, estimated 1 s
  Ran all test suites.
```

FIGURE 9-5:
Running the tests generated by Copilot.

Copilot successfully wrote three tests, and the tic-tac-toe game passed all three! The checkWin() function doesn't interact with the browser, so it's a perfect candidate for creating simple tests. The checkDraw() function checks whether all the squares are filled without either player winning. It's also very simple, and you can use the same approach to generate tests for that function. Follow these steps:

1. **Making sure that script.test.js is still open in the neighboring tab, select the checkDraw() function in script.js.**

2. **In Copilot Chat, enter /tests and press Enter.**

   The first time I ran /tests, I had selected checkDraw() and its comment. Copilot returned tests for other functions in the program in addition to checkDraw(). Next, I selected just the checkDraw() function (without its documentation) and entered /tests again. This time it gave me the response I wanted.

Copilot suggested the following tests for the checkDraw() function:

» Test that checkDraw() returns false when the board is empty.

» Test that checkDraw() returns false when the board is partially filled.

» Test that checkDraw() returns true when the board is fully filled and there is no winner.

Again, this seems like a good plan. After providing a plan for testing checkDraw(), Copilot wrote tests for each suggested test case, as shown in Figure 9-6.

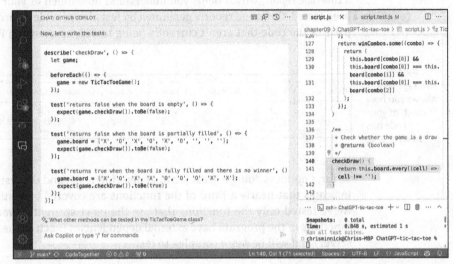

FIGURE 9-6: The tests Copilot suggests for checkDraw().

Microsoft Corporation

I copied the tests, pasted them in script.test.js, and ran the tests again. The result is shown in Figure 9-7.

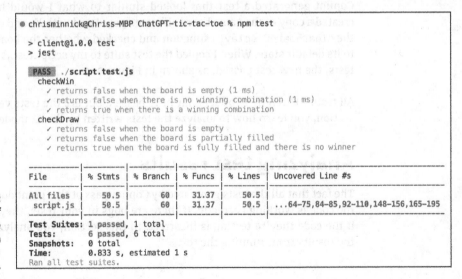

FIGURE 9-7: The result of running the tests for both checkDraw() and checkWin().

Reading a coverage report

Testing frameworks, such as Jest, can look at the tests you've written to generate a *coverage report*, which helps you understand how much of your source code has been tested. Coverage reports generated by Jest also provide information about the parts of the code that aren't currently being tested, as shown in Figure 9-8.

File	% Stmts	% Branch	% Funcs	% Lines	Uncovered Line #s
All files	50.5	60	31.37	50.5	
script.js	50.5	60	31.37	50.5	...64–75,84–85,92–110,148–156,165–195

So far, Copilot is doing a great job of generating tests, and the test coverage report indicates that nearly a third of the functions are covered by tests now. However, we've tested only the functions that are the most straightforward to test. Other functions in the program have external dependencies (such as the browser and the server) and will be more complex to test.

For example, the clearBoardDiplay() function, which resets the game board to its default state, interacts with the browser and requires a test that correctly queries the state of the board in the browser. To see whether Copilot was up to the task, I selected the function and ran the /tests command.

Copilot generated a test that looked similar to what I would have written. It created a copy of the game board elements populated with Xs and Os, and then ran the clearBoardDisplay() function and checked whether the board was restored to its default state. When I copied the test suite to my script.test.js file and ran the tests, the new test passed, as shown in Figure 9-9.

All tests written by Copilot so far have passed, but are the tests valid? In the next section, you learn how to analyze the tests written by the AI model.

Analyzing test results

The fact that all the tests generated by Copilot pass at this point doesn't mean that the code is working correctly. If there are bugs in your tests, they may pass even if the code they're testing is incorrect. In this section, you analyze the tests and the results from running the tests.

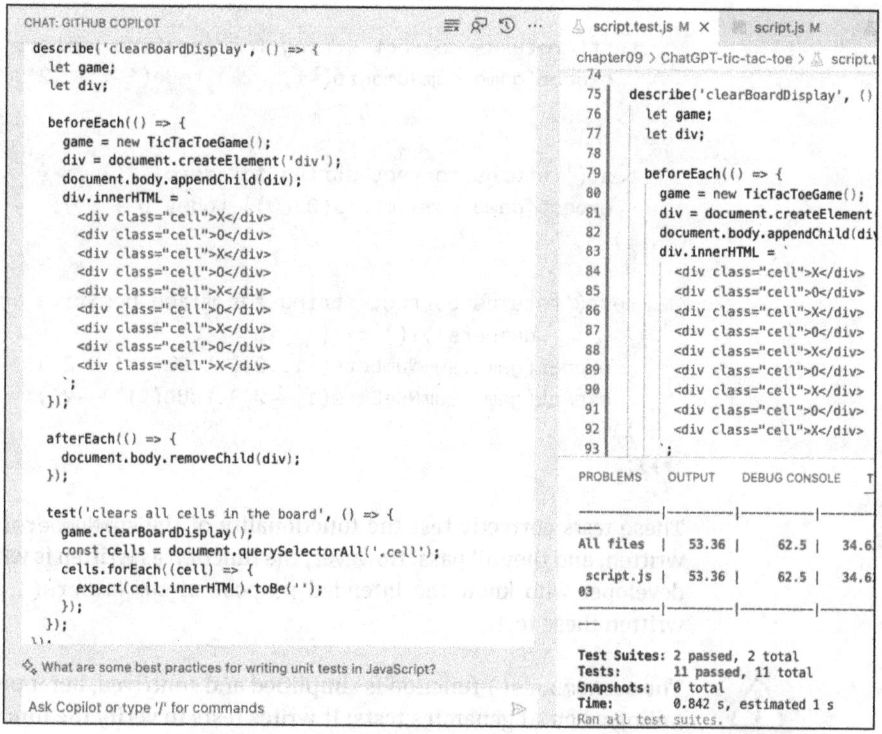

```
CHAT: GITHUB COPILOT                          ≡ ℛ ⊙ ···      △ script.test.js M ×      script.js M
describe('clearBoardDisplay', () => {              chapter09 > ChatGPT-tic-tac-toe > △ script.t
  let game;                                         74
  let div;                                          75    describe('clearBoardDisplay', ()
                                                    76      let game;
  beforeEach(() => {                                77      let div;
    game = new TicTacToeGame();                     78
    div = document.createElement('div');            79      beforeEach(() => {
    document.body.appendChild(div);                 80        game = new TicTacToeGame();
    div.innerHTML = `                               81        div = document.createElement
      <div class="cell">X</div>                     82        document.body.appendChild(di
      <div class="cell">O</div>                     83        div.innerHTML = `
      <div class="cell">X</div>                     84          <div class="cell">X</div>
      <div class="cell">O</div>                     85          <div class="cell">O</div>
      <div class="cell">X</div>                     86          <div class="cell">X</div>
      <div class="cell">O</div>                     87          <div class="cell">O</div>
      <div class="cell">X</div>                     88          <div class="cell">X</div>
      <div class="cell">O</div>                     89          <div class="cell">O</div>
      <div class="cell">X</div>                     90          <div class="cell">X</div>
    `;                                              91          <div class="cell">O</div>
  });                                               92          <div class="cell">X</div>
                                                    93        `;
  afterEach(() => {
    document.body.removeChild(div);               PROBLEMS    OUTPUT    DEBUG CONSOLE    T
  });
                                                  ----------|---------|---------|---------
  test('clears all cells in the board', () => {
    game.clearBoardDisplay();                     All files | 53.36 |    62.5 |    34.6
    const cells = document.querySelectorAll('.cell');  ---
    cells.forEach((cell) => {                     script.js | 53.36 |    62.5 |    34.6
      expect(cell.innerHTML).toBe('');            03
    });                                           ----------|---------|---------|---------
  });                                             ---
});
```

What are some best practices for writing unit tests in JavaScript?

```
Ask Copilot or type '/' for commands          ▷
```

```
Test Suites: 2 passed, 2 total
Tests:       11 passed, 11 total
Snapshots:   0 total
Time:        0.842 s, estimated 1 s
Ran all test suites.
```

Microsoft Corporation

FIGURE 9-9:
The test for
clearBoard-
Diplay()
passed.

If you write buggy code and ask a generative AI model to write a unit test for the buggy code, the model may give you a test that verifies the behavior of the code as it is — bugs and all. For example, consider the following function:

```
sumNumbers(num1, num2) {
  return `${num1} + ${num2}`;
}
```

As indicated by the name of the function, the intended purpose of this function is to add two numbers. However, it was written in such a way that will result in it returning a string.

I selected the sumNumbers() function and asked Copilot to write tests for it. Copilot provided the following tests:

```
describe('sumNumbers', () => {
  test('returns correct string for positive numbers', () => {
    expect(game.sumNumbers(1, 2)).toBe('1 + 2');
  });
```

```
test('returns correct string for negative numbers', () => {
  expect(game.sumNumbers(-1, -2)).toBe('-1 + -2');
});

test('returns correct string for zero', () => {
  expect(game.sumNumbers(0, 0)).toBe('0 + 0');
});

test('returns correct string for mixed positive and negative
      numbers', () => {
  expect(game.sumNumbers(-1, 2)).toBe('-1 + 2');
  expect(game.sumNumbers(1, -2)).toBe('1 + -2');
});
});
```

These tests correctly test the functionality of the sumNumbers() function as it's written, and they all pass. However, the function as written is wrong, and a human developer who knew the intended purpose of sumNumbers() would never have written these tests.

WARNING

The sumNumbers() function is simplified and contrived, but it points to a potential failing when AI generates tests: It writes tests to verify the function you have, not to verify that the function produces the results you want.

One strategy for solving this problem may be to properly document your functions before you generate tests. I added a comment describing the function, like this:

```
/**
 * Adds two numbers together.
 * @returns {number}
 */
sumNumbers(num1, num2) {
  return `${num1} + ${num2}`;
}
```

However, even with this comment, when I ran the /tests command Copilot still generated tests for the function as it was written rather than for what I intended the function to do.

For my next attempt, I specifically asked Copilot to generate a test that would check whether the function does what the description of the function specifies:

```
Write a test to verify that the sumNumbers function
does what it's supposed to do, as specified in its
JSDoc comment.
```

Even with this specific comment, Copilot still generated tests to verify that the function returns a string rather than a number, as shown in Figure 9-10.

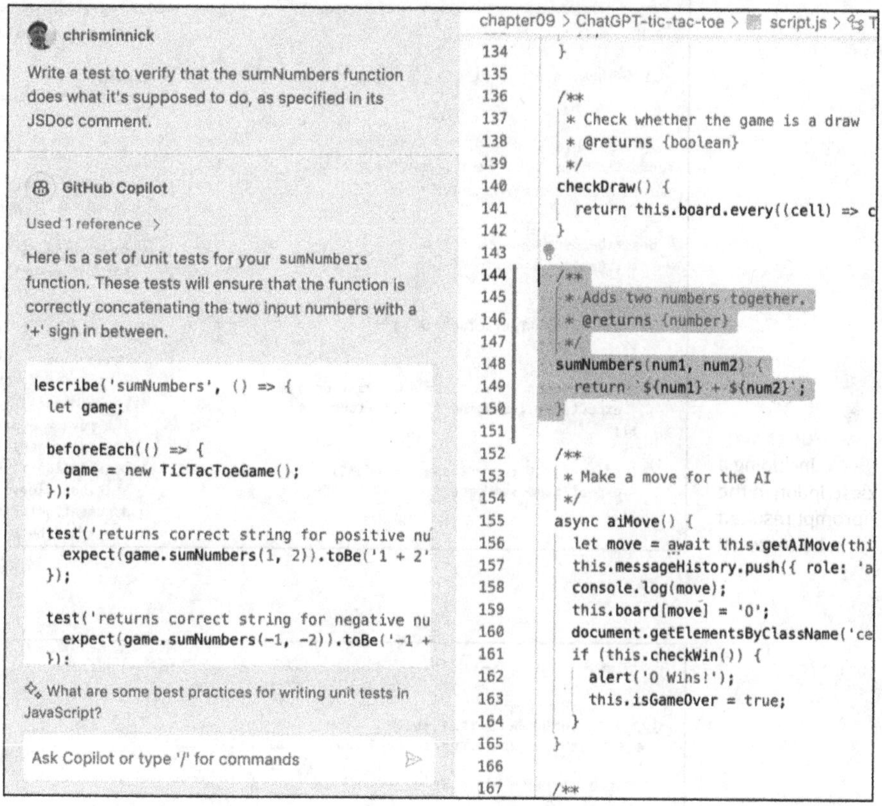

FIGURE 9-10: Copilot can't seem to get it right.

Microsoft Corporation

I decided to give it one more try. This time, I asked for exactly what I wanted, like this:

```
The sumNumbers function should take two numbers as
its arguments and return the sum of the two numbers.
Write tests to check whether this is what it does.
```

This time, Copilot wrote the tests I wanted, as shown in Figure 9-11.

I copied the tests to a file named sumNumbers.test.js and ran them. As expected, all three tests that Copilot generated failed, as shown in Figure 9-12.

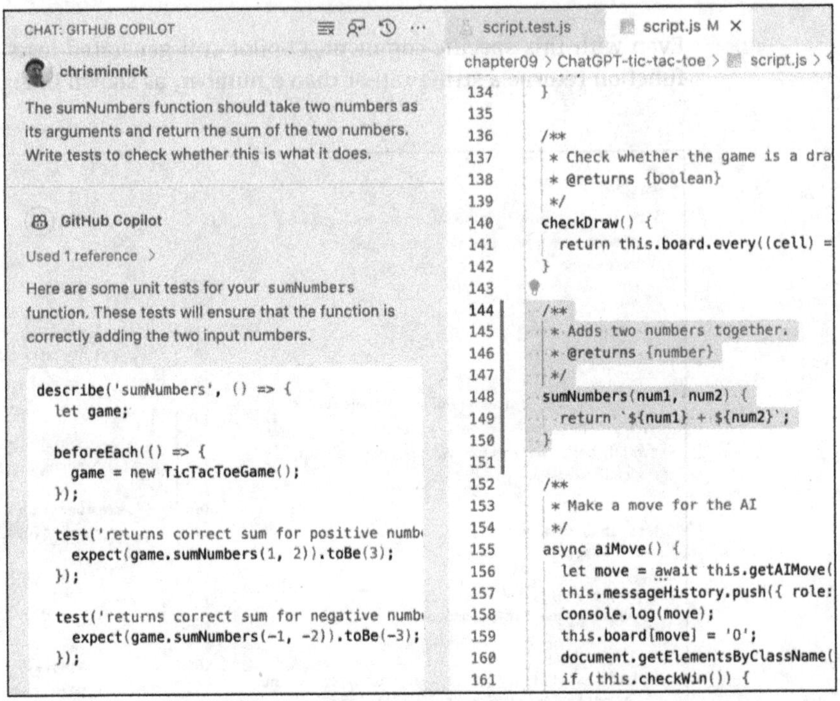

FIGURE 9-11:
Including a
description in the
prompt resulted
in better tests!

Microsoft Corporation

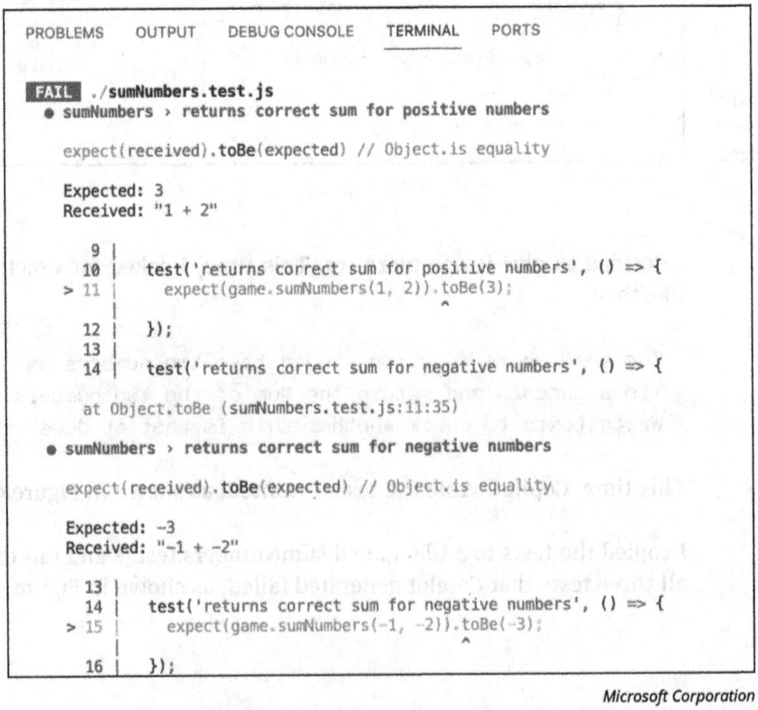

FIGURE 9-12:
The new tests
failed, as
expected.

Microsoft Corporation

I modified the sumNumbers() function to produce the correct output, then re-ran the tests. With the function fixed, the tests all passed, as shown in Figure 9-13.

```
PASS  ./sumNumbers.test.js
PASS  ./script.test.js
-----------|----------|----------|----------|----------|-------------------------------
File       | % Stmts  | % Branch | % Funcs  | % Lines  | Uncovered Line #s
-----------|----------|----------|----------|----------|-------------------------------
All files  |   52.4   |   60.86  |   32.69  |   52.4   |
 script.js |   52.4   |   60.86  |   32.69  |   52.4   | 16-31,39-41,48-52,57-58,64-75,84-85,92-110,156-164,173-203
-----------|----------|----------|----------|----------|-------------------------------

Test Suites: 2 passed, 2 total
Tests:       10 passed, 10 total
Snapshots:   0 total
Time:        0.971 s, estimated 1 s
Ran all test suites.
```

FIGURE 9-13:
With the function fixed, the tests pass.

Generative AI won't always write the tests you want. To understand why, it's important to always keep in mind that generative models can only make predictions that have a high likelihood of being correct.

REMEMBER

It's tempting to accuse a GenAI model of being bad at its job when it repeatedly gives the same wrong answer to a seemingly simple prompt. However, the problem is often that it's providing perfectly fine responses to the question you asked, and that asking the question correctly will result in the output you expect.

Test-Driven Development with AI

Because generative AI relies on context, getting AI to generate tests for functions that have bugs can be challenging. However, what if we turned the process on its head and asked AI to generate working code based on failing tests? This is the idea behind test-driven development, and it may be the best way to get an AI assistant to write exactly the code you need.

Test-driven development (TDD) is a software development practice that focuses on creating tests for functionality that doesn't yet exist. In test-driven development, the developer writes a test for a single unit of code, and then writes the code to make the test pass. No piece of code is written without a test being written first, so TDD (done correctly) results in 100 percent code coverage and higher-quality code.

The TDD process involves three steps, called the *TDD cycle*, which are repeated as often as necessary to build the desired software:

>> **Write a test.** Write a test that accurately describes a single piece of functionality, and then run the test to confirm that it fails (because the feature doesn't yet exist.) Also known as the red stage.

>> **Write code to pass the test.** Write the minimum code necessary to make the test pass. Also known as the green stage.

>> **Refactor.** Restructure both the code and the test to improve them.

After refactoring step, the cycle starts over with another test.

The developer's goal while practicing TDD is to build tests and software in small and tested pieces of code. Rather than focusing on writing the code correctly and then testing that it works, TDD emphasizes writing good tests and then writing the minimum amount of code to pass the tests, even if the code you write isn't ideal. After the code passes the test, you improve the code in the refactor stage.

Because AI is good at writing small amounts of code when given good instructions, TDD seems like a perfect match for working with an AI assistant. But there's a catch — you need to write the tests yourself. If you have AI write both the tests and the code, it's highly likely that both will be wrong. Writing tests in TDD is how you design the software, so it's important to get the tests right.

Technically, you don't need to write the tests entirely without AI assistance. Using Copilot's completion feature as you code is generally safe, as long as you verify and approve each autocompletion.

To find a feature that would be a good candidate to develop with TDD, I looked at the unfinished features in the tic-tac-toe game's SRS, which I generated using ChatGPT in Chapter 5. The biggest feature that I haven't yet created is specified under the heading Game History and Stats:

```
- The game will keep track of player stats such as:
  - Total games played.
  - Number of games won.
  - Number of games lost.
```

To start, I wrote a test to check whether the totalGamesPlayed variable increments after a game is played. Here's what I came up with:

```
describe('Game stats', () => {
  let game;
```

```
beforeEach(() => {
  game = new TicTacToeGame();
});
test('increments total games played after a game ends',
     () => {
  expect(game.totalGamesPlayed).toBe(0);
  game.isGameOver = true;
  game.updateGameStats();
  expect(game.totalGamesPlayed).toBe(1);
});
});
```

After writing the test, I ran Jest to confirm that this test failed. And it did, of course, as shown in Figure 9-14.

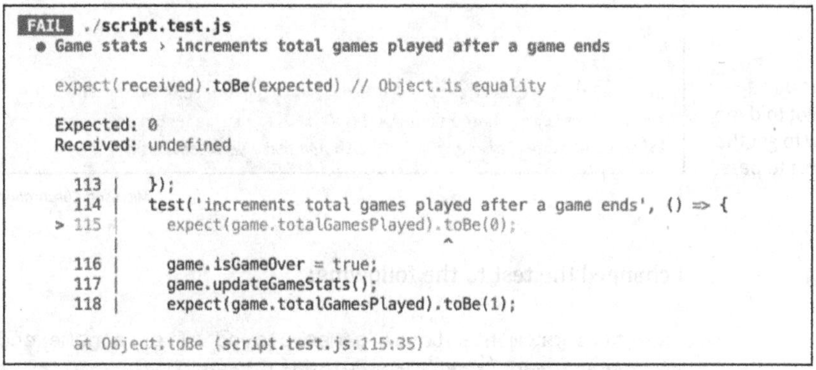

```
FAIL  ./script.test.js
  ● Game stats › increments total games played after a game ends

    expect(received).toBe(expected) // Object.is equality

    Expected: 0
    Received: undefined

      113 |    });
      114 |    test('increments total games played after a game ends', () => {
    > 115 |        expect(game.totalGamesPlayed).toBe(0);
          |                                      ^
      116 |        game.isGameOver = true;
      117 |        game.updateGameStats();
      118 |        expect(game.totalGamesPlayed).toBe(1);

      at Object.toBe (script.test.js:115:35)
```

FIGURE 9-14:
As expected, my
first tests failed.

Next, I opened my script.js, script.test.js, and srs.md files and prompted Copilot Chat with the following:

```
@workspace Write the code to pass this test:
```

After the prompt, I pasted my test in the chat window. Note that I used the @workspace command to tell Copilot to consider all the files in my project as references for its response, which is shown in Figure 9-15.

I implemented the suggested solution and ran my tests again. Everything passed, so I was ready to move on to refactoring.

One way to improve the test would be to simulate the ending of a game, rather than setting isGameOver to true manually. This improvement would make the test more representative of the actual usage of the class.

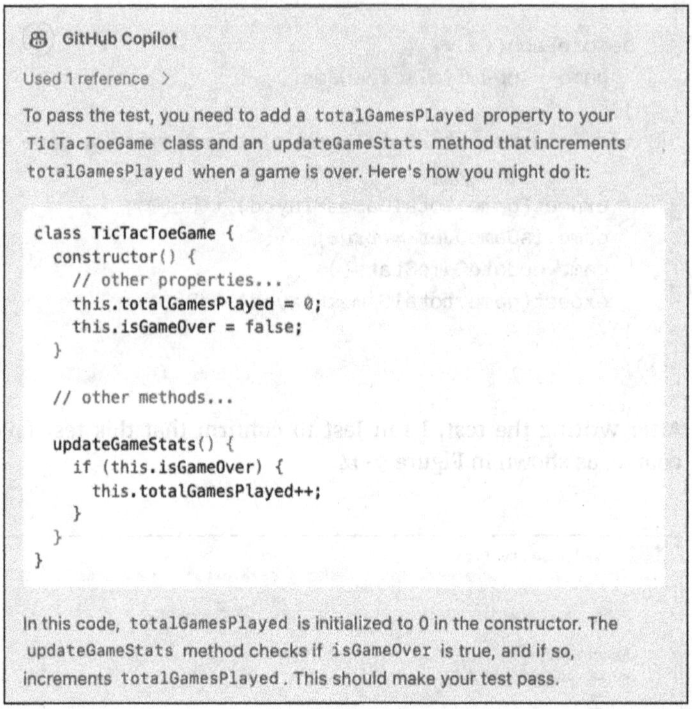

To pass the test, you need to add a `totalGamesPlayed` property to your `TicTacToeGame` class and an `updateGameStats` method that increments `totalGamesPlayed` when a game is over. Here's how you might do it:

```
class TicTacToeGame {
  constructor() {
    // other properties...
    this.totalGamesPlayed = 0;
    this.isGameOver = false;
  }

  // other methods...

  updateGameStats() {
    if (this.isGameOver) {
      this.totalGamesPlayed++;
    }
  }
}
```

In this code, `totalGamesPlayed` is initialized to 0 in the constructor. The `updateGameStats` method checks if `isGameOver` is true, and if so, increments `totalGamesPlayed`. This should make your test pass.

FIGURE 9-15:
Copilot told me
how to get the
test to pass.

Microsoft Corporation

I changed the test to the following:

```
test('increments total games played after a game ends', () => {
  expect(game.totalGamesPlayed).toBe(0);
  game.endGame()
  expect(game.totalGamesPlayed).toBe(1);
});
```

I ran the test again and it failed. I asked Copilot how to change the program to pass the test and it responded as shown in Figure 9-16.

This suggestion worked and my test passed. I felt pretty good about the test and the solution, so I moved on to refactoring. I checked everything carefully, and then wrote my next test.

WARNING

After you modify a test and implement the code to pass it, check for extraneous code. As you learn in Chapter 6, code that may have had a purpose at one time but is no longer used by the program is known as *dead code*. You should remove dead code during the refactoring stage of TDD.

FIGURE 9-16: Updating the game to pass the refactored test.

Microsoft Corporation

At this point, the endGame() method is never called in the normal playing of the game, so I decided to make ending the game the next bit of functionality to write. To see how Copilot would write the test, I prompted it with the following:

```
@workspace How can I write a unit test to check whether
the endGame method runs when a player wins?
```

For some unknown reason, Copilot responded that it can help with only programming-related questions, as shown in Figure 9-17.

I'm sure that I could refine my prompt to make Copilot understand what I was talking about, but I felt like my point about not asking AI to generate tests while doing TDD was proven, so I wrote the following test suite:

```
describe('Game end', () => {
  let game;
  beforeEach(() => {
    game = new TicTacToeGame();
```

```
  });
  test('sets isGameOver to true after a player wins', () => {
    expect(game.isGameOver).toBe(false);
    game.board = ['X', 'X', 'X', 'O', 'O', '', '', '', ''];
    game.checkWin();
    expect(game.isGameOver).toBe(true);
  });
});
```

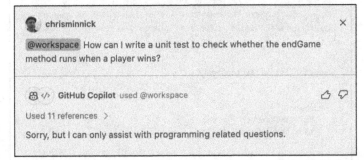

chrisminnick   ×

@workspace How can I write a unit test to check whether the endGame
method runs when a player wins?

GitHub Copilot used @workspace

Used 11 references >

Sorry, but I can only assist with programming related questions.

Microsoft Corporation

FIGURE 9-17:
Copilot seems to
be confused.

I tried several times to get Copilot Chat to generate the code I wanted. I prefaced
my prompt with @workspace to have it analyze all the files in my project. I gave it
just script.js for reference, and then I gave it just script.test.js. Each time, it stub-
bornly refused to provide what I considered an acceptable response. Rather than
continuing to argue with Copilot Chat, I decided it would be faster to just write this
code myself.

The correct answer is to call the endGame() function when one player wins.
Here's the revised checkWin() function, with the code I wrote to pass this test
shown in bold:

```
/**
 * Check whether someone has won the game
 * @returns {boolean}
 */
checkWin() {
  const winCombos = [
    [0, 1, 2],
    [3, 4, 5],
    [6, 7, 8],
    [0, 3, 6],
    [1, 4, 7],
    [2, 5, 8],
```

```
      [0, 4, 8],
      [2, 4, 6],
  ];
  const win = winCombos.some((combo) => {
    return (
      this.board[combo[0]] &&
      this.board[combo[0]] === this.board[combo[1]] &&
      this.board[combo[0]] === this.board[combo[2]]
    );
  });
  win ? this.endGame() : null;
  return win;
}
```

I implemented my solution, and the test passed. This leads to the most important lesson of this chapter: In AI-assisted TDD, if you know the right way (or even just an easy way) to get your test to pass, don't ask for AI assistance. Trust yourself.

Much more needs to be done to finish the functionality described in the Game History and Stats section of the SRS. If you want to experiment with AI-assisted TDD, you can find the complete code for the tic-tac-toe game as it stands now in the tic-tac-toe-final folder in the chapter09 folder of the code you downloaded for this book.

» **Commenting your code**

» **Creating diagrams**

» **Documenting APIs with AI**

Chapter **10**

Documenting Your Code

In every other chapter, you learn about using AI to translate natural language to code. In this chapter, you learn about using AI to translate code to natural language. Whether you're writing comments to describe a function or creating a manual for the users of your software, documenting your code (or the results of running your code) is the process of explaining what code does, or should do, in a language that can more easily be understood by your target audience (people).

Software documentation can be divided into two broad categories: internal documentation and external documentation. Every software project needs both types.

Internal documentation is generally created by software developers and project managers to help guide the development process. It may include administrative documentation, such as status reports and meeting notes, as well as developer documentation, such as requirements, comments, and software architecture diagrams.

External documentation includes everything end users of the software will need to deploy and use it. Examples of end-user documentation include README files, release notes, tutorials, FAQs, troubleshooting guides, system documentation, API documentation, and blog posts.

In this chapter, you learn how to use AI to create both internal and external documentation for software.

Working with Documentation Bots

Although you could use any of the GenAI tools you learned about in other chapters to create documentation, there are better options. Many software packages have been created specifically for creating and maintaining documentation, and most now feature an AI option.

Popular software documentation tools include the following:

>> Bit.ai (https://bit.ai) is a platform for teams and individuals to create, collaborate, and organize both internal and external documentation. Its AI chatbot, AI Genius, can be added to any paid plan.

>> Document360 (https://document360.com) offers a drag-and-drop interface for creating both internal and external documentation. It includes a generative AI chatbot, called Eddy, that provides answers from your documentation.

>> GitBook (https://gitbook.com) emphasizes collaboration and generates documentation in Markdown format. *Markdown* is a lightweight markdown format often used for writing documentation for projects that are primarily distributed as Git repositories (hosted on sites like GitHub, BitBucket, and GitLab). Markdown files have the .md extension. GitBook has an AI assistant that uses a chatbot to generate new content.

>> Notion (https://notion.so) is an all-in-one workspace tool that combines note-taking, project management, and documentation. It has an AI add-on that can generate content based on your documentation.

>> Nuclino (https://nuclino.com) focuses on simplicity and ease of use. It features an AI chatbot, called Sidekick, that can draft emails, translate content, craft marketing copy, and more.

>> Swimm (https://swimm.io) is designed for creating internal documentation. Its AI assistant, Swimm AI, can generate explanations of your code and help create code documentation.

Most of the software documentation tools that have added AI do so by fine-tuning a pretrained model using your code and making this fine-tuned model available through a chat interface. Rather than getting into the details of the non-AI features of a software documentation tool, let's explore how you can fine-tune a model yourself to create your own AI assistant.

Building your own documentation bot

In this section, you learn how to use the OpenAI platform site to build your own documentation-writing assistant. This assistant will be trained on the code you upload and will interpret your code to generate both internal and external documentation.

To get started, log into the OpenAI platform at `https://platform.openai.com`. Then go to the assistants interface by clicking the Assistants icon (robot) in the left navigation. (You can also go directly to `https://platform.openai.com/assistants`.) Follow these steps to set up and train a new assistant:

1. **Click the Create button on the Assistants page.**

The window shown in Figure 10-1 appears, where you can specify some options and upload files.

2. **Give your assistant a name, such as My Helpful Documentation Assistant.**

3. **In the Instructions text area, enter some instructions.**

Here's what I started with:

> You are an experienced technical writer who is also proficient in many different programming languages. You can interpret code and use your knowledge of programming and technical writing to create both internal and external software documentation.

FIGURE 10-1:
Starting the new assistant creation process.

ChatGPT

I will probably need to refine these instructions once I test the assistant, but this is a good start.

4. **Select a model.**

   At this point, the most recent GPT model is gpt-4-1106-preview, which is what I selected.

5. **In the Tools options, enable the Code Interpreter and Retrieval tools.**

   The Code Interpreter tool enables the assistant to write and run code. The Retrieval tool enables the assistant to retrieve content from the files you upload.

6. **Upload your project's files.**

   For my first test of the assistant, I deleted the node_modules folders from both the tic-tac-toe game's server and client, and I deleted the .env file from the server folder before making a .zip file and clicking the Add button in the Files area of the New Assistant window to upload it.

7. **Save your assistant, then click the Test button in the upper-right corner of the New Assistant window.**

   A new session will open in the Playground, as shown in Figure 10-2.

FIGURE 10-2:
Starting a documentation assistant session.

ChatGPT

Testing your documentation assistant

Congratulations, you have a new assistant. Let's see if it's any good. For my first test of my helpful documentation assistant, I asked it to create a README file for my project. Here's the prompt I used:

```
Create a README.md file for my tic-tac-toe game.
```

My goal with this prompt is to get the assistant to retrieve my code from the files I uploaded and generate a file containing external documentation in Markdown format. You may want to provide additional information to indicate what you expect to be in the README file, but for my first attempt I wanted to see what it would do.

I clicked the Add and Run button, and OpenAI responded by saying it would need information about my project to be able to create a README. The full response is shown in Figure 10-3.

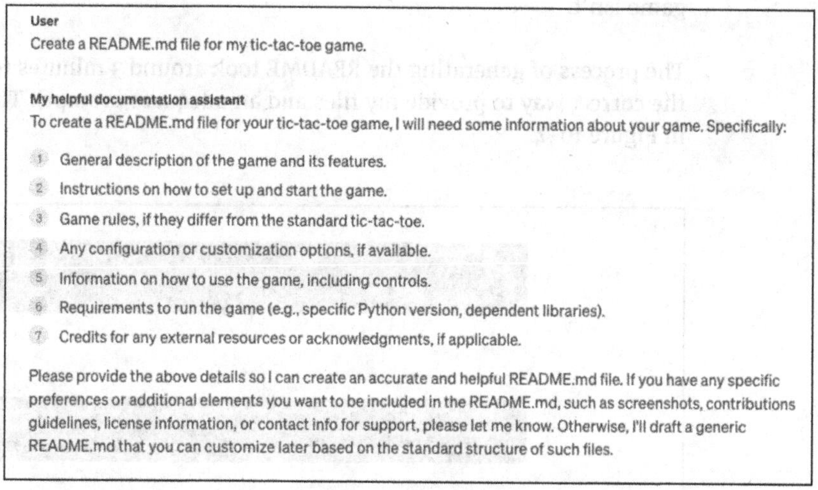

User

Create a README.md file for my tic-tac-toe game.

My helpful documentation assistant

To create a README.md file for your tic-tac-toe game, I will need some information about your game. Specifically:

1. General description of the game and its features.
2. Instructions on how to set up and start the game.
3. Game rules, if they differ from the standard tic-tac-toe.
4. Any configuration or customization options, if available.
5. Information on how to use the game, including controls.
6. Requirements to run the game (e.g., specific Python version, dependent libraries).
7. Credits for any external resources or acknowledgments, if applicable.

Please provide the above details so I can create an accurate and helpful README.md file. If you have any specific preferences or additional elements you want to be included in the README.md, such as screenshots, contributions guidelines, license information, or contact info for support, please let me know. Otherwise, I'll draft a generic README.md that you can customize later based on the standard structure of such files.

FIGURE 10-3:
My assistant didn't consult with the code files.

The prompt input box has a file attachment feature, so I attached the .zip file to a new message and typed the following prompt:

```
Please consult with the attached files to get the answers
to your questions.
```

The assistant wasn't able to open the .zip file, which may explain why it didn't use the files it was trained on in the first place.

For my next attempt, I gave the assistant the URL to the game's GitHub reposi-tory, but it responded that it couldn't access the internet. It did, however, give me a basic template for a README file.

For my next attempt, I uploaded the JavaScript, HTML, CSS, and package.json files for the client individually.

I cleared out the current conversation and tried again from the start with this prompt:

```
Please use the files I uploaded to create a README.md file
for my tic-tac-toe game.
```

This time, it worked! The assistant looked at each file I uploaded and determined what type of data they were. Once it figured out that they were code, it parsed the code to figure out what it did. Finally, it generated a README file that describes the game fairly accurately, except for one major problem — the instructions it provided described how to install and run a Python script, which my tic-tac-toe game isn't.

The process of generating the README took around 3 minutes (once I figured out the correct way to provide my files and an adequate prompt). The result is shown in Figure 10-4.

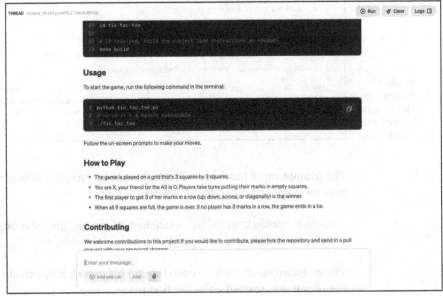

FIGURE 10-4:
I'd give my assistant's first README a C+.

Generating Code Comments and Annotations

Mintlify Doc Writer is a VS Code plug-in that generates comments for code. It uses machine learning to write comments for code written in every popular programming language and can currently write comments in nine spoken languages.

Having an AI tool that can instantly understand a piece of code and write an accurate comment for that code is a great time-saver, not only when you're writing code but also when you're trying to figure out what code written by another programmer does.

TIP

Unfortunately, it's all too common for a programmer starting a new job to be faced with trying to understand poorly commented code written by someone who has long since left the company. A good first step for getting a handle on such a mess is to start writing the comments that should have been there from the start.

Installing and testing Mintlify Doc Writer

Follow these steps to install and try out the Mintlify Doc Writer plug-in:

1. **Open the Extensions panel in VS Code and search for Mintlify.**

   The Mintlify Doc Writer extension page in the Extensions marketplace is shown in Figure 10-5.

FIGURE 10-5:
The Mintlify
Doc Writer
extension page.

Microsoft Corporation

2. **Click the Install button.**

3. **Open the code you want to document in VS Code.**

   For this experiment, I'm using the AI tic-tac-toe game that I started writing in previous chapters.

4. **Find a function you want to document and select it in the code window.**

5. **Click the Mintlify Doc Writer icon on the left of VS Code.**

   A panel appears, as shown in Figure 10-6.

6. **With a function selected in the code window, click the Generate docs button in the Mintlify Doc Writer tool.**

   After a moment, a comment is added above the selected function that describes the purpose of the function, as shown in Figure 10-7.

FIGURE 10-6:
The Mintlify Doc Writer panel.

The code comment added in my first test of Mintlify Doc Writer was accurate and would be helpful for future programmers (or my future self). But how does it compare with human-written code comments? To find out, let's look at a heavily commented open-source project and see what Mintlify Doc Writer does differently.

```
13    /**
14     * The `init` function initializes the game by adding event listeners to the cells, start button, and
15     * difficulty slider, and updating the difficulty level based on the slider value.
16     */
17    init() {
18      document.addEventListener('DOMContentLoaded', (event) => {
19        let cells = document.querySelectorAll('.cell');
20        cells.forEach((cell, i) => {
21          cell.addEventListener('click', () => this.makeMove(i));
22        });
23        document
24          .getElementById('start')
25          .addEventListener('click', () => this.startNewGame());
26
27        let slider = document.getElementById('slider');
28        document.getElementById('difficulty').innerHTML =
29          'Level of difficulty: ' + slider.value;
30        slider.addEventListener('change', (e) => {
31          document.getElementById('difficulty').innerHTML =
32            'Level of difficulty: ' + e.target.value;
33          this.difficulty = e.target.value;
34        });
35      });
36    }
```

FIGURE 10-7:
Mintlify adds a
code comment.

Commenting on Underscore

Underscore (https://underscorejs.org) is an open-source library of utility functions for common JavaScript programming tasks. Created by Jeremy Ashkenas in 2009, it's been included in thousands (perhaps millions) of JavaScript projects and was the starting point for the (currently) even more popular library of utility functions called Lodash. Underscore is distributed under the MIT license, which allows any use of the software as long as the copyright notice is included.

I've included two copies of Underscore in the chapter10 folder of the code you can download for this book. One copy (named underscore-esm.js) is the original uncompressed version of the Underscore library, complete with the developer's comments. The other copy (named underscore-esm-no-comments.js) is a copy of the code, but I've stripped out all the comments (except for the copyright notice).

As it says on the Underscore library's website, the uncompressed version has "plentiful comments," as you can see in Figure 10-8.

To see how Mintlify stacks up, I opened the original file and my no comments version side-by-side in VS Code, with the original file on the left and the no comments version on the right. I selected a function in the no comments version and used Mintlify Doc Writer to generate a comment, as shown in Figure 10-9.

This first test went really well! The generated comment accurately describes the purpose of the code I highlighted. However, it is unnecessarily verbose and could use some editing. Also, the generated comment includes only a description of what the code does, whereas the human-written comment also describes why it is the way it is.

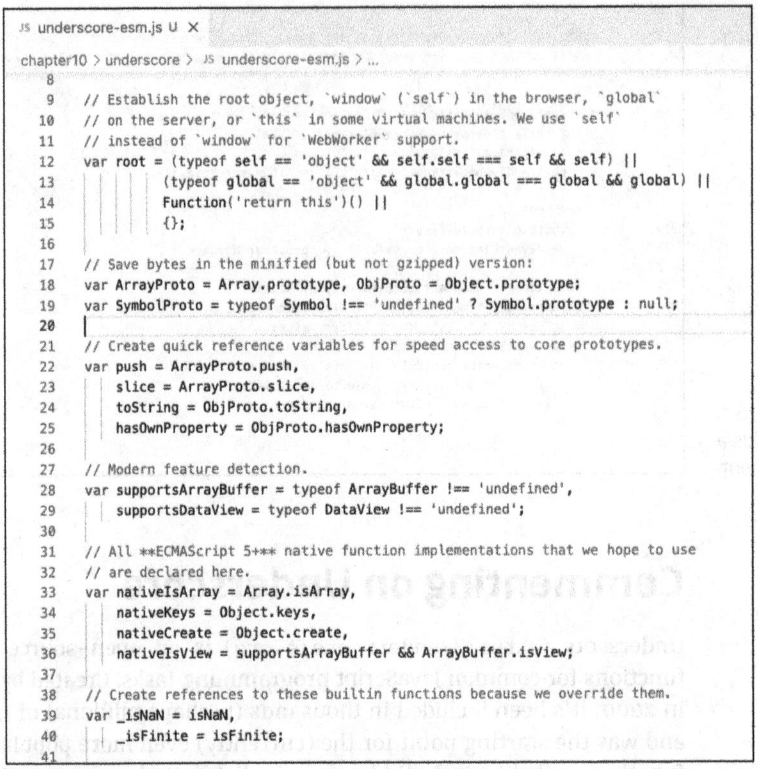

```
JS underscore-esm.js U ×

chapter10 > underscore > JS underscore-esm.js > ...
     8
     9   // Establish the root object, `window` (`self`) in the browser, `global`
    10   // on the server, or `this` in some virtual machines. We use `self`
    11   // instead of `window` for `WebWorker` support.
    12   var root = (typeof self == 'object' && self.self === self && self) ||
    13           (typeof global == 'object' && global.global === global && global) ||
    14           Function('return this')() ||
    15           {};
    16
    17   // Save bytes in the minified (but not gzipped) version:
    18   var ArrayProto = Array.prototype, ObjProto = Object.prototype;
    19   var SymbolProto = typeof Symbol !== 'undefined' ? Symbol.prototype : null;
    20
    21   // Create quick reference variables for speed access to core prototypes.
    22   var push = ArrayProto.push,
    23       slice = ArrayProto.slice,
    24       toString = ObjProto.toString,
    25       hasOwnProperty = ObjProto.hasOwnProperty;
    26
    27   // Modern feature detection.
    28   var supportsArrayBuffer = typeof ArrayBuffer !== 'undefined',
    29       supportsDataView = typeof DataView !== 'undefined';
    30
    31   // All **ECMAScript 5+** native function implementations that we hope to use
    32   // are declared here.
    33   var nativeIsArray = Array.isArray,
    34       nativeKeys = Object.keys,
    35       nativeCreate = Object.create,
    36       nativeIsView = supportsArrayBuffer && ArrayBuffer.isView;
    37
    38   // Create references to these builtin functions because we override them.
    39   var _isNaN = isNaN,
    40       _isFinite = isFinite;
    41
```

FIGURE 10-8:
Each function
of Underscore
includes
comments.

Microsoft Corporation

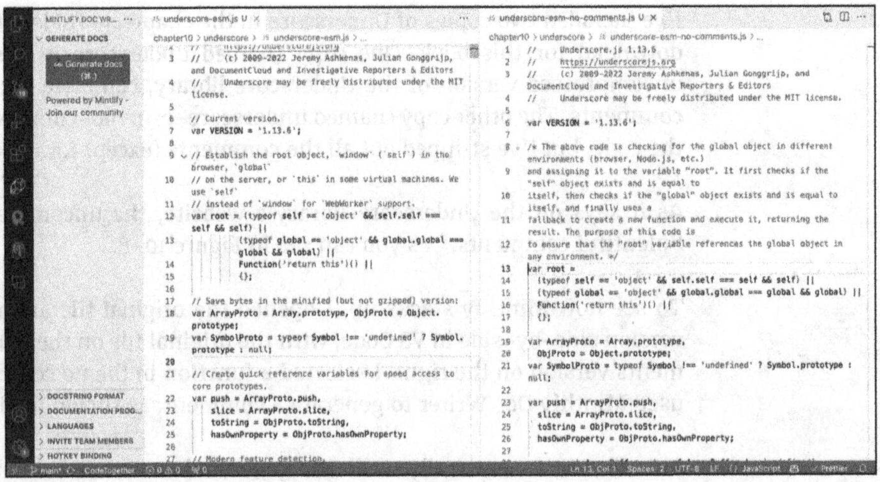

FIGURE 10-9:
Generating a
comment for
Underscore (in
the code window
on the right.)

Microsoft Corporation

Here's the original (human-written) comment:

```
// Establish the root object, `window` (`self`) in the browser, `global`
// on the server, or `this` in some virtual machines. We use `self`
// instead of `window` for `WebWorker` support.
```

And here's the comment that was generated by Mintlify Doc Writer:

```
/* The above code is checking for the global object in different
environments (browser, Node.js, etc.) and assigning it to the variable "root".
It first checks if the "self" object exists and is equal to itself, then
checks if the "global" object exists and is equal to itself, and finally uses
a fallback to create a new function and execute it, returning the result.
The purpose of this code is to ensure that the "root" variable references
the global object in any environment. */
```

In this example, I declare the human writer the winner. The comment is only as long as it needs to be, and it provides additional context that may be important for anyone seeking to understand the functioning of the code.

For the second round of my man versus machine showdown, I selected one of Underscore's simpler function, isNull(). The isNull() function takes an object as its argument and returns true or false based on whether the object has a value of Null.

The original comment for the isNull() function is

```
// Is a given value equal to null?
```

Mintlify's model returned the following comment:

```
/**
 * The function checks if an object is null.
 * @param obj - The parameter "obj" is a variable that
 * represents any object or value that we want to
 * check if it is null.
 * @returns The function isNull returns true if the obj
 * parameter is null, and false otherwise.
 */
```

Once again, this description of the comment is accurate but uses nearly ten times as many words to describe a function that, honestly, doesn't require any documentation to be clearly understood.

For the third round of my battle of brains versus bits, I selected one of Underscore's more complex functions, restArguments(). Here's the official comment from Underscore describing what restArguments() does:

```
// Some functions take a variable number of arguments, or a few expected
// arguments at the beginning and then a variable number of values to operate
// on. This helper accumulates all remaining arguments past the function's
// argument length (or an explicit 'startIndex'), into an array that becomes
// the last argument. Similar to ES6's "rest parameter".
```

This is a clear and easy-to-understand comment that ends with a key piece of information that will be helpful to anyone who knows JavaScript — namely, that the purpose of this function is to do something similar to what the rest parameter does in JavaScript.

Here's the comment created by Mintlify Doc Writer:

```
/**
 * The restArguments function allows a function to accept a variable number
 * of arguments and treats the remaining arguments as an array.
 * @param func - The `func' parameter is the function that you want to modify
 * to accept rest arguments.
 * @param startIndex - The `startIndex' parameter is the index at which the
 * rest arguments should start. It determines how many initial arguments
 * should be passed to the `func' function before the rest arguments are passed.
 * If `startIndex' is not provided or is `null', it defaults to `func.length
 * - 1',
 * @returns The function `restArguments' returns a new function.
 */
```

The generated comment is in proper JSDoc format and includes the @param and @returns tags. In addition, the generated comment provides details about using the function that aren't provided by the original comment. In this case, I give the edge to the AI-generated comment. I would trim it substantially before including it in my code, however.

Creating Visual Documentation

Diagrams, charts, mock-ups, and other types of visual documentation are essential to creating effective and engaging internal and external documentation. During the planning phase of a project, creating software architecture diagrams and requirements diagrams can help everyone on the team see the big picture.

Mock-ups and wireframes are used during the user interface design process. When creating documentation for external users of the software, you might make use of screen captures, workflow diagrams, animation, and video.

Generative AI shouldn't create some types of visual documentation, such as those that require accuracy. For example, Figure 10-10 shows the result when I asked GPT-4 to create an illustration pointing out the main features of the AI tic-tac-toe game. Other types of visual documentation, such as diagrams, can be created by GenAI systems by combining the text generation capabilities of an AI system with the capabilities of a drawing or diagramming program.

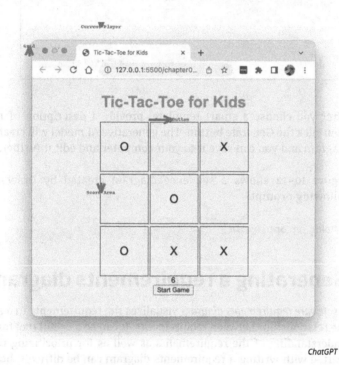

FIGURE 10-10:
GPT-4 failed at annotating my screenshot.

ChatGPT

Generating a sequence diagram

In this section, I use a free diagramming tool called draw.io, available at https://diagrams.net, to generate a diagram. Draw.io has many built-in templates for creating different types of diagrams. To get started with building a diagram, choose from one of the built-in templates and start populating it with content.

Draw.io also has a smart template feature, where you select from a list of templates (see Figure 10-11) and provide a description. The tool then pre-populates the diagram with generated content based on the information you provide.

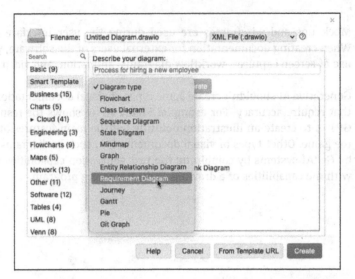

FIGURE 10-11:
The list of smart
templates.

After you choose a smart template, provide a description of the diagram and then click the Generate button. The generative AI model will create content for the diagram and you can save it to your computer and edit it further.

Figure 10-12 shows a sequence diagram created by Draw.io based on the following prompt:

```
Make an apple pie.
```

Generating a requirements diagram

A *software requirements diagram* visualizes the requirements in a system as well as the relationships between requirements. It can be a useful tool for gaining a better understanding of the requirements as well as for prioritizing the work. Getting started with writing a requirements diagram can be difficult, however, and generative AI may be helpful.

It may seem counterintuitive at first to have a generative AI model make up requirements since (at least ideally) requirements are specified by the client, product owner, and business analyst. However, most software projects share similar characteristics and features. Some pieces of a web app are so common that a client or product owner may forget that they must be built prior to the parts of the app that make it unique. Examples of such functionality include user authentication and search features.

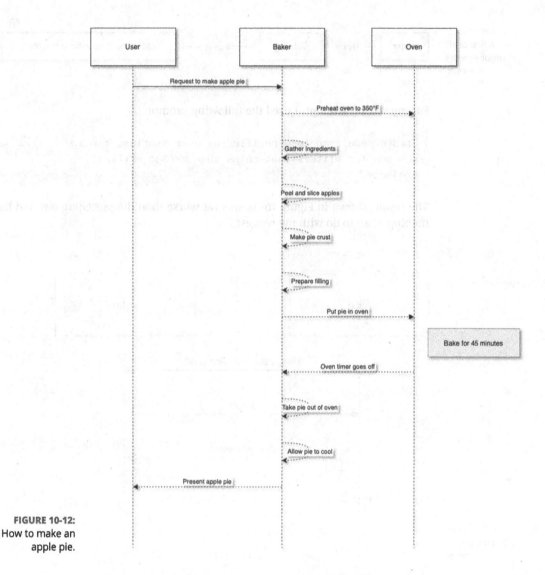

FIGURE 10-12:
How to make an
apple pie.

To find out whether a generative model can write the basic requirements and present them as a requirements document, I thought of a project and came up with a short description:

```
A web app for writers to use to manage all aspects of a
book-writing project.
```

I opened Draw.io, selected the Requirement Diagram Smart Template, typed my description in the prompt text box, and clicked Generate. The resulting diagram, shown in Figure 10-13, was a failure.

FIGURE 10-13:
A first draft
requirements
diagram.

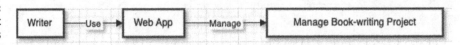

For my second attempt, I used the following prompt:

```
Create requirements, specified as user stories, for a
web app for writers that helps them manage writing
projects.
```

The result, shown in Figure 10-14 was far worse than the preceding one and had nothing at all to do with my request.

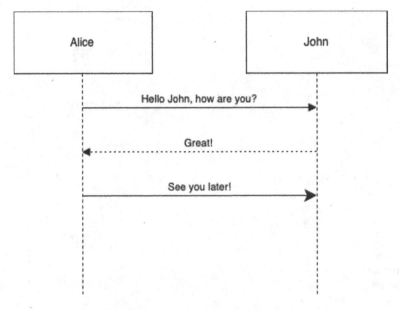

FIGURE 10-14:
What happened
here?

For my third attempt, I tried the following prompt:

```
Requirements for web app to help writers organize and
track writing projects.
```

By using the words *organize* and *track*, I gave the model enough of a hint that it could relate what I wanted to the requirements for any project management tool. It finally gave me something I could work with.

Figure 10-15 shows a closeup of part of the diagram. Note that the model wrote the requirements as user stories, and that it's successfully written requirements that might be part of any project management tool.

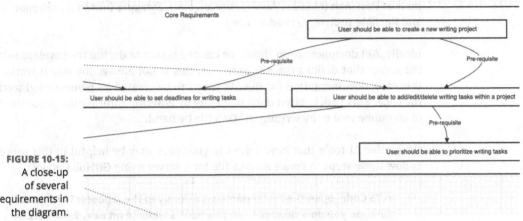

Core Requirements

User should be able to create a new writing project

Pre-requisite

Pre-requisite

User should be able to set deadlines for writing tasks

User should be able to add/edit/delete writing tasks within a project

Pre-requisite

User should be able to prioritize writing tasks

FIGURE 10-15: A close-up of several requirements in the diagram.

Automating API Documentation with AI

One of the most common forms of both internal and external software documentation is API documentation. *API documentation* specifies the ways in which developers can write software to interact with your software.

Web apps that interact with a server usually use a RESTful, or just REST (representational state transfer) API, which is an architectural style that uses HTTP requests to create, update, read, and delete data. You can access REST APIs by using simple URLs that describe the purpose of the API. The URLs used by a REST API are called *endpoints*.

For example, a server that uses the REST architecture may have an endpoint called /user. To create a user record, a client application can perform an HTTP POST request to the /user endpoint with the required data. To retrieve a specific user record from the server, a client application can perform an HTTP GET request to the endpoint. To update an existing record, a client application can perform an HTTP PUT request, and to delete a record, a client application can perform an HTTP DELETE request.

Documenting a REST API

REST APIs can be documented by using the OpenAPI Specification (OAS), a programming-language-agnostic format for describing, producing, consuming, and visualizing APIs. Tools for documenting APIs and creating an OAS file include Postman (`https://www.postman.com`), Swagger (`https://swagger.io`), and ReadMe (`https://readme.com`).

Ideally, API documentation should be created before or during the development of the server that defines the API. However, this is not always the way it works. In this case, documentation for the API needs to be created by reverse-engineering the code. This task is often done manually by entering information about the API in an online tool or by writing the OAS file by hand.

Generative AI tools that have access to your code may be helpful in this process. Follow these steps to create an OAS file for a server using GitHub Copilot:

1. **In VS Code, open the folder named /soliloquy in the /chapter10 folder of the code you downloaded from this book's website (at `www.dummies.com/go/codingwithaifd`).**

    This folder contains the server and client applications for a simple social media application called Soliloquy. I gave it that name because it currently allows you to talk only to yourself.

2. **Open the two files from the server/routes folder (user.js and posts.js).**

    These files define the API endpoints.

3. **With the two route files open, enter the following prompt in GitHub Copilot (or another chatbot of your choice):**

    ```
    @workspace Generate an OAS file for this rest server.
    ```

    When I tried this prompt with Copilot, it generated what appears (at first glance) to be a valid and accurate OAS file in the YAML language, as shown in Figure 10-16.

TECHNICAL STUFF

YAML stands for YAML Ain't Markup Language. It's commonly used for configuration files with any programming language.

To find out if this file is valid and accurate, I could read the entire file closely and compare it to my program code. Or I could try importing it into a tool for testing and visualizing APIs and see what happens. The second option sounds easier and more fun, so that's what I did.

FIGURE 10-16:
A Copilot-generated OAS file.

One tool for creating API documentation is ReadMe. The free version of ReadMe can be used to create an interactive API reference. Follow these steps to import the generated YAML OAS file into ReadMe:

1. **Sign up for an account at `https://www.readme.com`.**

2. **Click the New Project button.**

3. **Click Quickstart in the left sidebar (see Figure 10-17) to start creating your API reference.**

   You see a page where you can upload an OAS file, as shown in Figure 10-18.

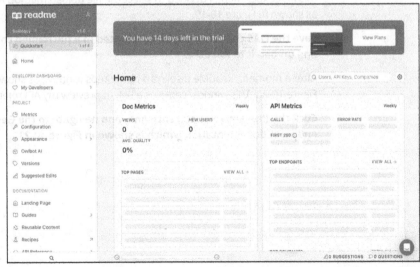

FIGURE 10-17:
The ReadMe home page.

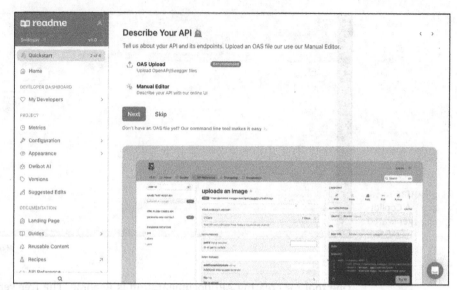

ReadMe

FIGURE 10-18:
The Quickstart
page with the
OAS upload
button.

4. **Click OAS Upload.**

   A Describe Your API pop-up window appears. This window provides options for uploading your OAS file, including using the command line, uploading from GitHub, or uploading a file manually.

5. **Choose an upload option.**

   Using the command line or GitHub upload method is the best option, because they keep your documentation in sync with changes you make. However, for this first experiment, I decided to select the file upload method for simplicity, as shown in Figure 10-19.

6. **Save the OAS code that Copilot generated in a file named soliloquy.yaml and upload it to ReadMe.**

   After a moment, ReadMe displays a Next Steps window, as shown in Figure 10-20. This window contains a link to preview my API reference.

7. **Click the Preview API Reference link, and navigate to the Get All Posts endpoint documentation, which is shown in Figure 10-21.**

FIGURE 10-19:
The file upload
screen in the
Describe Your API
window.

ReadMe

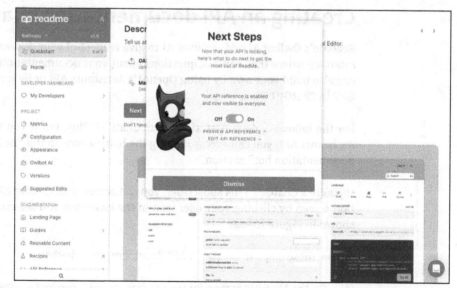

FIGURE 10-20:
The Next Steps
window.

ReadMe

WARNING

I'll need to write and run tests before I can say whether the API documentation Copilot generated is completely accurate, but so far it looks great and was much faster to create than I could have done manually.

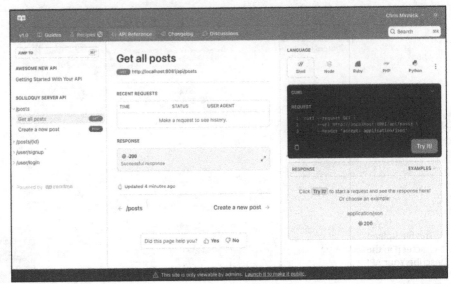

FIGURE 10-21:
The Get All Posts
endpoint
documentation.

ReadMe

Creating an API documentation chatbot

ReadMe's Owlbot AI add-on uses AI to give readers of your documentation a chat interface where they can ask questions about your documentation. However, you can also build your own by using OpenAI's Assistants API or by creating your own GPT in ChatGPT Plus.

For the following demonstration, I use ChatGPT Plus, but if you want to use the Assistants API, you can access it using the instructions in the "Building your own documentation bot" section.

If you're a ChatGPT Plus subscriber, you can access your custom GPT's configuration screen by clicking your user icon in the lower left and selecting My GPTs, as shown in Figure 10-22.

Follow these steps to create an API documentation chatbot.

1. **On the My GPTs screen** (https://chat.openai.com/gpts/mine) **click Create a GPT.**

   The New GPT screen appears.

2. **Click the Configure button to access the GPT configuration form.**

3. **Fill in a name and description of your GPT.**

   The name and description I used are shown in Figure 10-23.

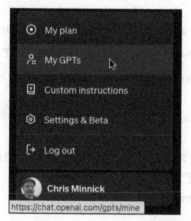

FIGURE 10-22:
Accessing
your GPTs.

ChatGPT

4. **Enter instructions for the GPT.**

   Here are the instructions I used:

   > You are a helpful and expert technical support bot who is
   > fluent in many programming languages and is available to
   > help anyone with questions about the REST API for a social
   > media server called "Soliloquy." By consulting the OpenAPI
   > file in your knowledge, you can provide answers about how
   > to perform tasks such as signing up users, logging users in,
   > creating new posts, editing posts, deleting posts, and
   > retrieving posts. You can also answer questions about how
   > to write programs that make use of the API.

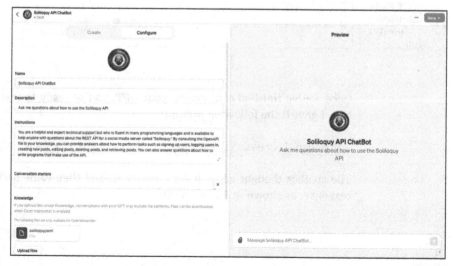

FIGURE 10-23:
Filling out the
form to configure
a GPT.

ChatGPT

5. **In the Knowledge section of the form, select and upload your OAS file.**

   This is the YAML file you created in the "Documenting a REST API" section.

6. **In the Capabilities section of the form, select Web Browsing and Code Interpreter.**

   You can also select additional options if you like (such as DALL-E Image Generation).

7. **Save your GPT by clicking Save in the upper-right corner and selecting an option in the Publish To menu.**

   In Figure 10-24, I selected Anyone with a Link.

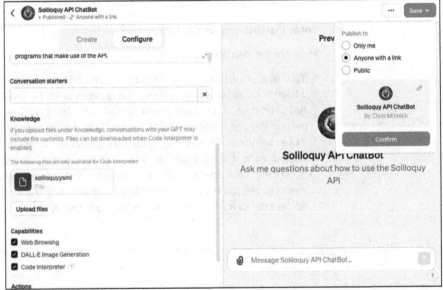

FIGURE 10-24: Completing the GPT configuration.

Once you've finished configuring your GPT, you're ready to test it! For my first test, I gave it the following prompt:

```
How can I create a new user?
```

The chatbot thought about it for a moment, and then came back with a perfect response, as shown in Figure 10-25.

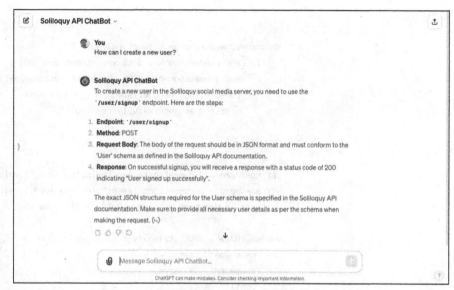

ChatGPT

For my second test, I decided to push my luck. I asked my chatbot to write a JavaScript program and an HTML page that could be used to create a user. Here's the prompt I used:

```
Can you write a web page and JavaScript program to create
a new user?
```

Its response was a great start. However, it made a few errors and less-than-ideal decisions. For example, it added an extra field (username) to the sign-up form that the server doesn't support, and a few things in the code (such as the use of the `var` keyword instead of the more modern `let` or `const` keyword) could be improved. Here's the full program that the chatbot created:

```
<!DOCTYPE html>
<html lang="en">
<head>
    <meta charset="UTF-8">
    <meta name="viewport" content="width=device-width, initial-scale=1.0">
    <title>Create New User</title>
    <script>
        function signupUser() {
            var xhr = new XMLHttpRequest();
            var url = "https://api.soliloquy.com/user/signup"; // Replace with
your API's URL
            xhr.open("POST", url, true);
            xhr.setRequestHeader("Content-Type", "application/json");
```

```
            xhr.onreadystatechange = function () {
                if (xhr.readyState === 4 && xhr.status === 200) {
                    var jsonResponse = JSON.parse(xhr.responseText);
                    console.log("User created: ", jsonResponse);
                    alert("User successfully created!");
                }
            };

            var username = document.getElementById("username").value;
            var password = document.getElementById("password").value;
            var email = document.getElementById("email").value;

            var userData = JSON.stringify({
                "username": username,
                "password": password,
                "email": email
            });

            xhr.send(userData);
        }
    </script>
</head>
<body>
    <h2>Create New User</h2>
    <form onsubmit="event.preventDefault(); signupUser();">
        <label for="username">Username:</label><br>
        <input type="text" id="username" name="username" required><br>

        <label for="password">Password:</label><br>
        <input type="password" id="password" name="password" required><br>

        <label for="email">Email:</label><br>
        <input type="email" id="email" name="email" required><br><br>

        <input type="submit" value="Create User">
    </form>
</body>
</html>
```

I tested the program with my server, and it attempted to make an HTTP POST request. The request was blocked due to the browser's cross-origin resource sharing (CORS) policy. Once I configured the server to allow a POST request from my development machine and made a few more tweaks, the program worked!

If Soliloquy were a real product and I was creating an API chatbot, I would refine Soliloquy's instructions and upload a sample of a client application that uses the API. I expect that would greatly increase the assistant's accuracy.

Overall, at this point, generative AI systems do a fair job of creating documentation for software and can be a huge timesaver when generating API documentation. However, as with any use of generative AI, it's important not to assume that any generated content is accurate or as good as what you could have created manually.

Chapter **11**

Maintaining Your Code

oftware is never finished. Once you've gone through the processes of planning, coding, testing, documenting, and deploying an application, the process of maintenance begins. Maintenance is a large part of the job of a software developer. In one study conducted by Stripe, developers reported spending almost half of their day doing maintenance (`https://stripe.com/files/reports/the-developer-coefficient.pdf`).

Maintenance is not a popular task, either. A survey conducted by Rollbar (`www.businesswire.com/news/home/20210216005484/en/Rollbar-Research-Shows-That-Traditional-Error-Monitoring-Is-Missing-the-Mark`) found that 21 percent of developers would rather go to the dentist than fix errors.

In this chapter, you learn what is involved in software maintenance and how AI tools can help to make the process less time consuming and (I hope) more enjoyable.

Knowing the Four Types of Maintenance

The predictable result of not performing routine maintenance on your car is that things will start to degrade until you have a major problem. The predictable result of not performing maintenance on software is that it will eventually fail. Types of failure for software applications include bugs, errors, security issues, and user dissatisfaction.

There are four types of software maintenance:

>> Corrective software maintenance

>> Adaptive software maintenance

>> Perfective software maintenance

>> Preventative software maintenance

Done correctly and in combination, the four types of maintenance will help to keep your software healthy and constantly improving. The approximate percentage of time developers spend on each of the four types of software maintenance is shown in Figure 11-1.

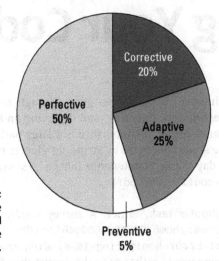

FIGURE 11-1:
How much time developers spend doing each type of maintenance.

Corrective software maintenance

No matter how thoroughly you test software, it will have bugs and errors that aren't found until after it's deployed and starts being used. *Corrective software maintenance*, commonly known as *software repair*, is the process of fixing these bugs and errors so that they no longer affect the user experience, the security, or the logic of the application.

Corrective maintenance is always done in response to an issue reported by either in-house testers or end users. Examples of issues that may come up once software is deployed include login failures, typos, broken links, and incompatibilities with other software or hardware.

REMEMBER

Corrective software maintenance is often triggered by bug reports. However, many bug reports submitted by users are actually suggestions for enhancement rather than bugs.

Adaptive software maintenance

Adaptive software maintenance is the process of modifying software in response to changes to the environment it lives in. A software application's *environment* includes the hardware, operating system, software dependencies, and business rules and policies that the application depends on.

In a modern web application, thousands of dependencies may change and necessitate some kind of adaptive software maintenance. For example, software libraries used in your application might need to be upgraded, third-party services such as payment processors or web APIs may change, and the hardware and software used by your application will continue to improve after you launch your product. Adaptive maintenance is done to ensure that your software doesn't become outdated.

TIP

Oftentimes, adaptive maintenance will have a side effect of fixing bugs and errors that have been reported. For example, an error that appears in your program after it's deployed may be the result of something outside your control, such as a change to an external API that your program depends on.

Perfective software maintenance

Once your software is exposed to users, they will have all kinds of ideas for how it could be better or more helpful. These suggestions will often come in the form of bug reports. If a bug report or suggestion describes functionality that's outside the software's requirements, however, implementing it falls into the category of perfective maintenance.

TIP

While *perfective software maintenance* is often the process of enhancing an existing system, it also includes the process of removing code or features that aren't useful or that have become obsolete.

Preventative software maintenance

Preventative software maintenance is the process of looking for issues in your software and fixing them before they become bugs or errors. Whereas corrective maintenance is reactive, preventative maintenance is proactive.

The great thing about preventative maintenance is that, unlike corrective maintenance, it can be scheduled ahead of time. Examples of tasks that can be done during preventative maintenance include updating documentation, refactoring code, and optimizing code performance.

Utilizing AI for Code Maintenance

AI systems can be helpful for each of the four types of software maintenance. Many of the specific processes involved in software maintenance are the same as the processes and best practices used during development and are covered in previous chapters of this book.

Some specific ways that AI tools can help you maintain code include the following:

>> **Automated error detection and correction:** AI tools can automatically scan your code repository for bugs when new code is committed to the code repository and assist with resolving issues. The section in Chapter 7 on automating bug fixes shows various ways to automate bug detection and bug fixing with AI tools.

>> **Predictive maintenance:** Machine learning can be used to predict potential system failures and to identify parts of the code that may cause problems.

>> **Code refactoring:** The larger and more complex software is, the more likely it is to eventually require refactoring. In Chapter 6, you learn to use AI tools to detect potential problems in your code (known as code smells) and get suggestions for fixing them.

>> **Dependency management:** AI tools can tell you not only what dependencies of your software require upgrading but also the effect (if any) of that upgrading.

>> **Automated testing:** AI can be used for generating a test plan and test cases, as you see in Chapter 9. It can be used also for analyzing the results of tests to help developers focus on the parts of the application that are more prone to errors.

>> **Documentation and knowledge management:** As you learn in Chapter 10, generative AI systems can help with writing, updating, and translating documentation. AI can be helpful also with making documentation available through chatbots.

>> **Performance optimization:** In Chapter 8, you learn how to use AI in combination with profiling tools to analyze and improve the speed and efficiency of your software.

>> **User feedback analysis:** AI can be used to analyze user feedback and usage logs to identify common issues and areas for improvement.

>> **Security vulnerability detection:** Tools such as Snyk, which is covered in Chapter 7, can scan your code to find security vulnerabilities as well as unusual usage patterns that may indicate a security breach.

Enhancing Code Quality with AI

Once you've written some code, how do you know whether it's any good? This is where the idea of software quality comes in. *Software quality*, which is also known as code quality, refers to two different ideas:

>> **Functional quality** is the measure of how well the software conforms to its requirements or specifications.

>> **Structural quality** is the measure of how well code meets non-functional requirements, such as robustness or maintainability.

In this chapter, I focus mostly on structural quality. High-quality code is clean, simple, efficient, and reliable. The goal of writing high-quality code is to make your code easy to understand and edit.

Code quality can be measured in many ways using various code quality metrics. These metrics help you to see your code's overall health, uncover code quality issues, and then take action to remediate problems. Metrics are categorized into two groups: quantitative metrics and qualitative metrics.

Quantitative metrics are determined by using algorithms designed to measure the complexity of the code. One example of a quantitative metric is weighted micro function points (WMFP). The WMFP algorithm parses source code and breaks it into units called micro functions. It analyzes these micro functions to calculate a single rating.

Qualitative metrics deal with best practices and coding standards such as efficiency, how variables are named, how code is formatted, whether the code is well documented. Qualitative metrics can't be fully expressed in numbers.

One key qualitative metric is maintainability. *Maintainability* measures how easy it is to make changes to the code while minimizing the risks of making changes. Maintainability can be measured in terms of the number of lines of code in the application, whether the code has proper documentation, and whether the code is well designed. One simple way to measure a software program's maintainability is to count the number of lines of code in the program's modules. If a piece of the source code has more than the average number of lines of code, it's likely that the function is too complex and should be broken into multiple parts.

Maintainability can be improved through refactoring. (For more on refactoring, see Chapter 6.) To fully understand maintainability, however, you need to understand the concept of technical debt, the topic of the next section.

Understanding technical debt

In software development, the term *technical debt* describes the cost of future refactoring required when choosing easy but limited solutions instead of better approaches that could take more time. Accumulating technical debt is inevitable, especially during the early phases of a project when it's often necessary to move the project forward and deliver a proof of concept.

WARNING

When I was just getting started with my web development business, one of my mentors told me that the key to success as a consultant was to remember the following rule: "Fast, cheap, or good. Pick any two." Unfortunately, most clients will choose fast and cheap over good. What happens when you pick fast and cheap is that you begin to accumulate technical debt that will, sooner or later, need to be paid back.

If ignored, technical debt will accumulate interest and make it harder to change the software in the future. Causes of technical debt include the following:

>> Starting development before fully defining the requirements.

>> Business pressures to deliver a product quickly.

>> Developing an application through a long series of changes over time, often making older decisions become less optimal.

>> Lack of a full test suite. Not writing proper tests encourages developers to make quick fixes that will add to the technical debt.

>> Lack of knowledge. Inexperienced developers will often write bad code. As developers get better, they realize the error of their ways as that bad code impedes their capability to move forward until the old code is rewritten.

>> Lack of documentation. Poor or insufficient code documentation leads to a faulty understanding of the source code as well as a backlog of documentation that needs to be written at some point in the future.

>> Putting off required refactoring. Most product owners would much rather have developers focus on delivering new features than fixing bad code that's already written and seems to work. The problem, of course, is that the more low-quality code you have, the more difficult it becomes to implement new features.

Getting started with Code Climate

Code Climate (https://codeclimate.com/quality) is a tool for automating code reviews. Once you link it to a GitHub repository, it scans your source code each time you make a change and creates a report showing test coverage, maintainability, and estimated technical debt.

Code Climate is free to use for open-source projects and teams with under four developers. Follow these steps to sign up and link a repository:

1. Go to https://codeclimate.com/quality/pricing in your browser and click the Sign up with GitHub button under either Open Source or Startup, as shown in Figure 11-2.

FIGURE 11-2: Code Climate's pricing page.

2. **Step through the process of authorizing Code Climate to access your GitHub repositories.**

At the end of the process, you'll have the option to either join an existing organization or add your own repository, as shown in Figure 11-3.

3. **Click the Add a Repository button.**

Code Climate displays a list of your repositories. The repository I'll be using to demonstrate Code Climate is at `https://github.com/chrisminnick/soliloquy`. I made this repository public and released it using the MIT license. You're free to copy it to your own GitHub account and to do whatever you like with it.

WARNING

Although you're free to use and modify Soliloquy, I don't recommend using it for anything but educational purposes because it's purposefully unfinished and untested, and it employs some questionable coding practices. That said, if you do expand it, send me an email (`chris@minnick.com`) and let me know!

4. **Choose a repository to scan with Code Climate.**

Code Climate clones your repository, run a series of tests on it, and then pops up a modal window when its report is finished, as shown in Figure 11-4.

5. **Click the See the Results button to view your report.**

My initial report is shown in Figure 11-5.

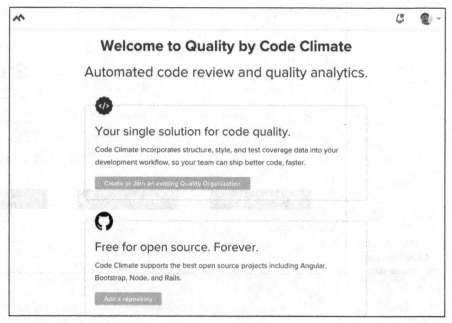

FIGURE 11-3:
Join an
organization or
add a repository.

Code Climate

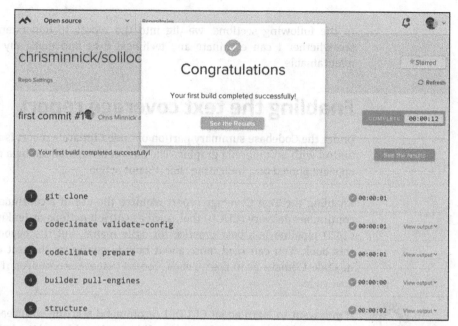

FIGURE 11-4:
Code Climate
has finished its
initial report.

Code Climate

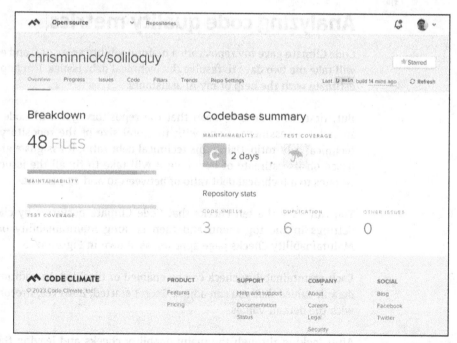

FIGURE 11-5:
Code Climate's
report on
Soliloquy.

Code Climate

In the following sections, we dig into the report to understand it, and then see whether I can eliminate any technical debt and make my program more maintainable.

Enabling the text coverage report

Under the Codebase summary portion of Code Climate's report is a Test Coverage button with an umbrella graphic. The button is surrounded by a dashed line and appears grayed out, indicating that it's not active.

Enabling the Test Coverage report requires the use of a continuous integration/ continuous delivery (CI/CD) tool, such as GitHub Actions or Jenkins. Setting up a CI/CD pipeline is a best practice for agile teams, but it's beyond the scope of this book. You can read more about how to configure the test coverage report in Code Climate at `https://docs.codeclimate.com/docs/configuring-test-coverage`.

TIP

If you want to learn about CI/CD, I recommend starting with reading *Continuous Delivery* (Addison-Wesley Professional) by Jez Humble and David Farley.

Analyzing code quality metrics

Code Climate gave my repository a maintainability score of C and estimated that it will take me two days to resolve the technical debt issues. I'm hoping to beat that estimate with the help of my AI assistants.

But, first, what does it mean that the repository got a C? Code Climate uses a 10-point assessment, along with the total size of the repository, to calculate a technical debt ratio. Using this technical debt ratio, it assigns a grade from A to F based on its estimate of how long it will take to fix all the issues. A grade of C equates to a technical debt ratio of between 10 and 20 percent.

You can view the ten checks that Code Climate performs by clicking the Repo Settings in the top menu and then clicking Maintainability on the left. The Maintainability Checks page appears, as shown in Figure 11-6.

Each maintainability check can be enabled or disabled. In addition, they all have default values that you can adjust. To get started, however, I recommend sticking with the default values.

After looking through the maintainability checks and leaving them all enabled, I clicked the Overview link to return to the Code Climate home page so I could start looking at the issues found in my repository.

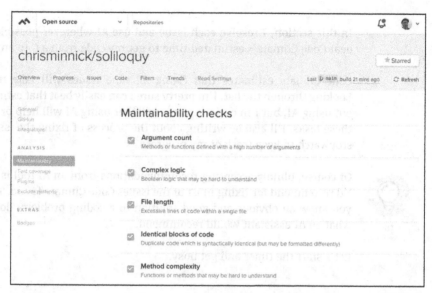

FIGURE 11-6:
Code Climate's
maintainability
checks.

Code Climate

Making AI-assisted code quality improvements

To look at the issues found in your repository, you can click Issues in the top navigation. My repository has nine issues, as shown in Figure 11-7.

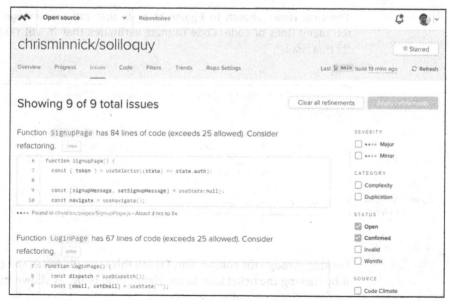

FIGURE 11-7:
Code Climate
says my
repository has
nine issues.

Code Climate

In this section, I resolve each issue and use AI wherever possible to see if I can beat Code Climate's estimated time to get my code from a C to an A.

Code Climate estimates that fixing all nine issues will take nearly 16 hours. Looking through the list, I'm pretty sure I can easily beat that estimate even without using AI, but I'm curious to see whether using AI will help or hinder me with these tasks. I'll also be writing about the process of fixing the issues and using a stopwatch to keep track of my progress.

TIP

Of course, blindly accepting recommendations from an AI tool is not the process I'd recommend for fixing most of the issues Code Climate found. Trust yourself. If you know an obvious and good solution to a coding problem, don't worry about what an AI assistant would recommend.

Let's start the timer and get busy.

⏳ TIMER   ⏱ STOPWATCH

27 s 63

STOP   RESET   ⟦ ⟧

Code Climate

The first issue, shown in Figure 11-8, is that my `SignupPage` component has too many lines of code. Code Climate estimates that it will take three hours to fix this issue.

Function `SignupPage` has 84 lines of code (exceeds 25 allowed). Consider refactoring. OPEN ⌄

```
 6    function SignupPage() {
 7        const { token } = useSelector((state) => state.auth);
 8
 9        const [signupMessage, setSignupMessage] = useState(null);
10        const navigate = useNavigate();
```

•••• Found in client/src/pages/SignupPage.js - About 3 hrs to fix

FIGURE 11-8:
SignupPage.js is
too long.

Code Climate

Looking through the component, I think this is a valid issue, so I create a ticket for it by clicking the ticket icon to the right of the issue, as shown in Figure 11-9.

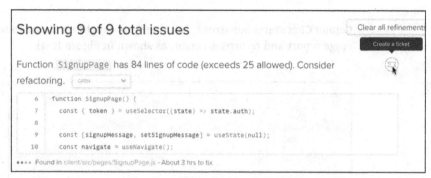

Showing 9 of 9 total issues   Clear all refinements

                                                               Create a ticket

Function SignupPage has 84 lines of code (exceeds 25 allowed). Consider
refactoring. OPEN   ∨

```
 6   function SignupPage() {
 7     const { token } = useSelector((state) => state.auth);
 8
 9     const [signupMessage, setSignupMessage] = useState(null);
10     const navigate = useNavigate();
```

•••• Found in client/src/pages/SignupPage.js - About 3 hrs to fix

FIGURE 11-9:
Clicking the
ticket icon.

Code Climate

Code Climate prompts me set up my ticketing system, so I select GitHub Issues.
To integrate Code Climate with GitHub Issues, I have to go to https://github.
com/settings/tokens/new to generate a new personal access token. Then I return
to the Issues page in Code Climate and click the ticket icon next to the first issue
again. This time, Code Climate creates a new GitHub issue and fills in the details
about the issue, as shown in Figure 11-10.

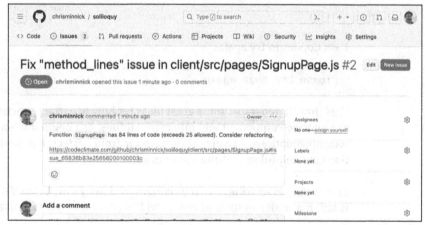

FIGURE 11-10:
Code Climate
creates a
new issue.

Code Climate

At this point, I could go through the entire list of issues in Code Climate and generated GitHub issues, but I decide to just work on this one issue in case my fix for
it corrects any other issues (or creates new ones).

I start by creating a new branch in my GitHub repository for refactoring the
SignupPage function. Then I give Copilot Chat the following prompt:

```
@workspace SignupPage.js has too many lines of code.
How can I refactor so that it has 25 lines or fewer?
```

Copilot Chat starts out strong, but then gets caught up trying to read my test coverage report and returns an error, as shown in Figure 11-11.

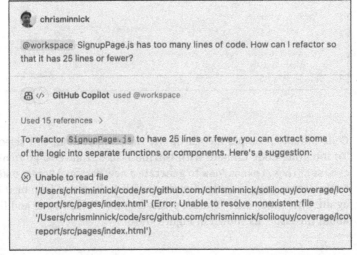

FIGURE 11-11:
Copilot has the right idea but goes down the wrong path.

I ask Copilot to try again:

```
Please try that again.
```

This time, it generates some great ideas for how to extract functionality out of the SignupPage component and into external files. As I begin implementing Copilot's recommendations, I realize they were far from perfect, but some of the suggestions are helpful in crafting my solution.

I finish the refactoring, test my changes, and merge my branches. My SignupPage is still not under 25 lines of code, and I'm about an hour into fixing this issue.

⏲ TIMER   ⏱ STOPWATCH

1ₕ 01ₘ 04ₛ 95

STOP   RESET

When I check back with Code Climate, my grade has risen to a B, as shown in Figure 11-12.

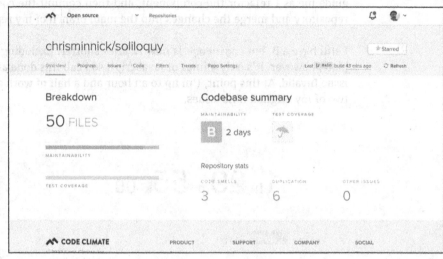

FIGURE 11-12:
Soliloquy is
getting more
maintainable!

Back in the Issues page, Code Climate reports that the SignupPage component now has 66 lines of code. It's still far more than the threshold of 25 lines, but I've managed to shave 18 lines from it. Looking again at the code, nearly all the lines are due to the template code in the React component's return statement, so I decide that I know better than Code Climate and change the status of the issue to Invalid, as shown in Figure 11-13.

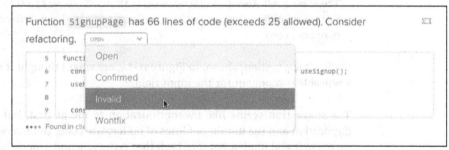

FIGURE 11-13:
Template
code doesn't
count, imho.

The next issue is that the LoginPage has too many lines of code. The LoginPage component suffers from the same root cause as SignupPage: It has internal functions that should be extracted into their own modules.

As before, I create a new issue in GitHub and create a new branch in the repository. I ask Copilot Chat how to extract the inner function into an external module. It replies with a good but not quite complete suggestion. I let Copilot's suggestion guide me as I refactor the component, and then commit the code to my GitHub repository and merge the changes into the main branch of my repository.

I still have a B, but LoginPage is now 12 lines shorter. Excluding the HTML template, however, it's only 9 lines of JavaScript, so I call this done and mark the new issue Invalid. At this point, I'm up to an hour and a half of work and I've resolved two of my original nine issues.

Code Climate

The next four issues have to do with similar code. Code Climate has flagged my input fields on the login and signup pages as being virtually identical, which they are, except one is an email field and the other is a password field. This isn't something that I'd normally change, but Code Climate has marked it as a major issue, so I think I'll see what Copilot has to say about it.

I prompt Copilot Chat with the following:

```
The password input and the email input have virtually
the same code. How would you refactor this to eliminate
duplication?
```

Copilot's suggestion, shown in Figure 11-14, are what I thought it would be: Create a reusable component for the input field.

The suggestion seems like overoptimization to me at first, but it reduces both duplication and the number of lines of boilerplate code, so I make a few improvements to it and implement it in both the LoginPage and SignupPage components. In the end, I like the solution Copilot and I come up with, so I push it to the repository.

Checking back with Code Climate, I now have an A grade and five problems remain. My stopwatch says I've been working for two hours.

FIGURE 11-14:
Copilot suggests
creating an
InputField
component.

The next issue is another one of duplicate code. The function that posts the data from the login page and the function that posts the data from the signup page are similar.

Returning to Copilot, I open the file containing both functions and give the following prompt:

```
How can I remove duplicate code in this file?
```

Copilot responds (correctly) that the file doesn't have duplicate code but does have similar code. It then suggests creating a generic function to handle all HTTP requests. This seems like a good plan, so I start implementing the solution.

Unfortunately, while I am implementing this solution, I discover several more bugs that would require refactoring, and my new solution creates some bugs too. I log all these issues in GitHub. When I finish fixing the initial issue, I go back and start fixing the other bugs. Eventually, I have everything in working order, so I merge and push my code into the repository. My timer is at three hours and 47 minutes.

Proud of myself for beating Code Climate's time estimate by 12 hours (and for writing the end of the last long chapter in the book), I return to Code Climate and see a glorious sight: I now have an A, and I'm technical-debt-free (according to Code Climate), as shown in Figure 11-15.

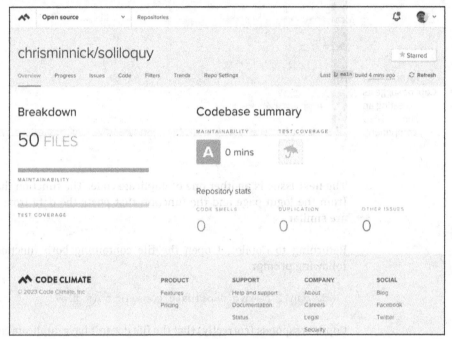

FIGURE 11-15: It feels good to be debt-free.

Code Climate

4

The Part of Tens

IN THIS PART . . .

Explore additional AI-powered tools for coders.

Continue your AI learning journey.

Chapter **12**

Ten More Tools to Try

This book focuses on the most useful and widely used tools currently available for coding with AI. Many more tools are available, and new ones are coming out all the time. In this chapter, I introduce ten more tools to help you with coding. To give you some idea of the pace of change, some of these tools weren't released when I started writing this book, and some may no longer be available when this book is released. The best way to stay up to date is to try out as many different tools as you can. And you find something you like, continue to try out new tools regularly, because there's a good chance that something will come along that's even better than what you're using today.

Amazon CodeWhisperer

Amazon CodeWhisperer (https://aws.amazon.com/codewhisperer), shown in Figure 12-1, is an AI extension that's available for many popular IDEs, including VS Code, Visual Studio, JetBrains, and SageMaker Studio. Once installed and configured, CodeWhisperer gives you suggestions as you code, similar to Copilot.

FIGURE 12-1:
Speak softly to
CodeWhisperer.

What sets CodeWhisperer apart for those working with AWS is that it has knowl-edge of AWS APIs and can provide code for working with AWS. CodeWhisperer also features a security scanning feature that can scan your code and can make suggestions to fix vulnerabilities. CodeWhisperer is free for individuals and $19/month for professionals.

Sourcegraph Cody

Like other coding assistants, Sourcegraph Cody (https://about.sourcegraph.com/cody) is available as an IDE plug-in. It can generate code suggestions as you code, and it features a chatbot interface as well. See Figure 12-2. For organizations that use Sourcegraph's code search and analysis tools, Cody can take context from multiple codebases into consideration while generating suggestions.

A free version of Cody is available as well as a Pro version (for $9/month) and an enterprise version.

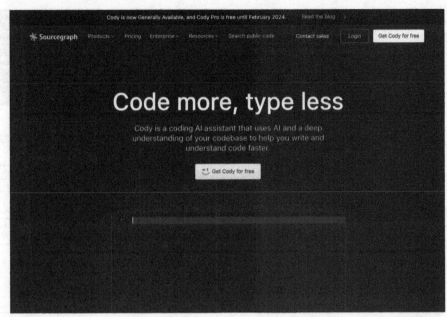

FIGURE 12-2:
Coding with Cody.

DeepMind AlphaCode

At this time, AlphaCode (https://alphacode.deepmind.com), shown in Figure 12-3, isn't directly available for use by developers. However, that might change by the time you read this. AlphaCode is an AI system that specializes in competitive programming. What, you may ask, is competitive programming? Great question!

Competitive programming is a mind sport where people compete by programming according to specifications provided to them. If this sounds like just about the most geeky and fun thing in the world, you'd better start practicing! DeepMind estimates that AlphaCode2, which was announced in December 2023, can solve competitive programming problems better than 85 percent of human competitive programmers.

FIGURE 12-3:
Solve puzzles
with AlphaCode.

Google Bard

Google's AI chatbot, Bard (`https://bard.google.com`), shown in Figure 12-4, can generate code in more than 20 languages, help with debugging, and explain code. Bard can also help with creating functions for Google's spreadsheet app, Google Sheets. One feature of Bard that many other chatbots don't have (yet) is its capability to cite the source of code if it quotes it extensively. Bard also has access to Google Search, so its knowledge about the current versions of libraries and tools it recommends may be more up-to-date than other chatbots. Bard is currently free.

FIGURE 12-4:
Make Bard sing
your tune.

Codeium

Codeium is a coding assistant and chatbot that can write, explain, refactor, and translate code. See Figure 12-5. Codeium is available as a browser extension or through the Codeium Playground at `https://codeium.com/playground`. Codeium is free for individuals or $12 per person per month for teams. An enterprise license with the option to self-host Codeium is also available.

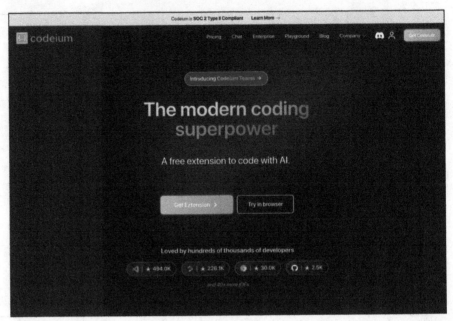

FIGURE 12-5:
Craft code with
Codeium.

Claude

Claude (`https://claude.ai`), shown in Figure 12-6, is another AI chatbot. Its creator, Anthropic, is an AI safety and research company dedicated to building safer AI systems, so Claude protects your privacy by not using your data. Another part of Anthropic's approach to AI safety is something it calls constitutional AI, in which the AI system is given a set of principles (a constitution) that it can evaluate its own outputs against.

Claude has a higher token limit than other generative models, which allows it to handle large amounts of content and complex instructions. In my testing of Claude's coding capability, it performed at least as well as Copilot Chat. Claude is currently an open beta and is available to use for free by using the web interface and through Anthropic's API for a limited number of customers.

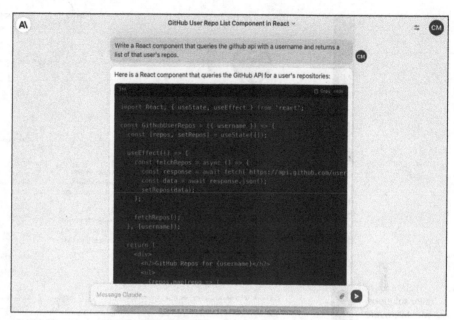

FIGURE 12-6:
Chat with Claude.

Claude

Microsoft IntelliCode

Microsoft IntelliCode is part of Microsoft Visual Studio (https://visualstudio.microsoft.com). It adds generative AI capabilities to Intellisense, Microsoft's code completion tool. IntelliCode integrates with GitHub Copilot and Copilot Chat to generate context-aware code completion suggestions. See Figure 12-7.

IntelliCode currently supports completions in a limited number of languages: C#, XAML, C++, JavaScript and TypeScript, and Visual Basic. Using IntelliCode requires you to use Visual Studio version 16.4 or newer.

Microsoft Corporation

FIGURE 12-7:
Tailor solutions
with Microsoft
IntelliCode.

Sourcery

Sourcery (`https://sourcery.ai`), shown in Figure 12-8, is an AI pair programmer chatbot that is available as an extension for VS Code and JetBrains IDEs. You can ask Sourcery questions about your code or to write new code, tests, or documentation. Sourcery can also perform code reviews and help you improve the readability and maintainability of your Python or JavaScript code by making inline suggestions while you work.

Sourcery is free for open-source projects and students, $10 per month for individual professionals, and $30 per month per team member for teams.

FIGURE 12-8:
Cast spells with
Sourcery.

Bugasura

Bugasura (`https://bugasura.io`) is an AI-power bug tracker. See Figure 12-9. When you create a new project in Bugasura, you can upload requirements documents or knowledge bases to give the AI assistant information about your product, which is then used to help you write new bug reports.

Bugasura can integrate with a performance monitoring tool, as well as with Slack, Jira, GitHub, Asana, and Zendesk. The free plan can have up to five users, and the paid plan is $5 per user per month for up to 100 users.

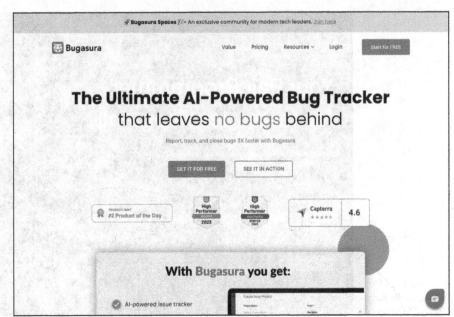

Bugasura

FIGURE 12-9:
Squash bugs with
Bugasura.

UserWay

UserWay (https://userway.org/), shown in Figure 12-10, is an AI-powered accessibility widget for making websites compliant with ADA (Americans with Disabilities Act) and WCAG (Web Content Accessibility Guidelines) accessibility standards. When users access your website, UserWay analyzes your site and automatically fixes violations of accessibility standards. The AI widget also gives users the ability to customize their user experience. Options for user-triggered customization include speaking the content of the site, changing the font size and text spacing, changing the contrast, and highlighting links. UserWay has a free 7-day trial and monthly or annual paid plans.

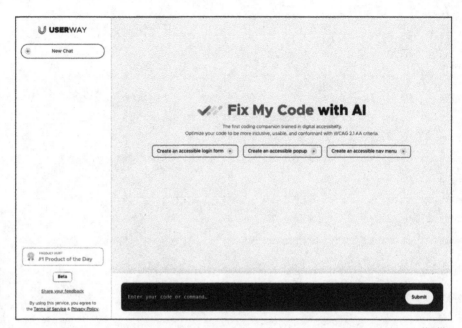

FIGURE 12-10:
Unravel
accessibility with
UserWay.

UserWay

Chapter **13**

Ten AI Coding Resources

E ach chapter of this book could easily be expanded to an entire book. As coding with AI becomes a more mature field and further revolutionizes how we write code, many more books (as well as classes, college degrees, and the like) will go into great depth explaining how each phase of software development is affected or helped by AI tools.

In this chapter, I share ten of my favorite resources for learning about coding and AI and for staying up-to-date on the latest developments in coding with AI.

Code.org's AI Resources

Code.org (https://code.org), shown in Figure 13-1, is a fantastic nonprofit organization with a commitment to making computer science accessible to a wider audience, particularly younger students. Resources available at Code.org include engaging videos and interactive lessons covering a variety of AI topics, such as how chatbots and large language models work, the basics of machine learning, and the role of AI in creativity and imagination.

I recommend, in particular, that teachers and parents check out Code.org's courses and videos about AI ethics, privacy, and the societal impact of Generative AI.

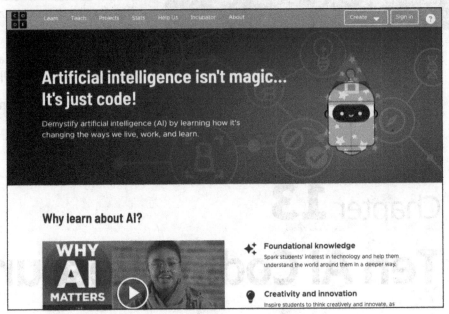

Code.org

FIGURE 13-1:
Dive into AI with
Code.org's AI
resources.

Kaggle

Kaggle (https://kaggle.com), shown in Figure 13-2, is a platform that enables data scientists and machine-learning enthusiasts to test their skills, share insights, and collaborate on problems. Companies and organizations can submit challenges to the Kaggle community, which people can compete to solve. Some challenges offer monetary rewards to winners, and all offer a great opportunity for discovering more about machine learning.

Kaggle has extensive resources for learning about machine learning, and offers a multitude of public dataset, making it an essential website for both experienced and novice data professionals.

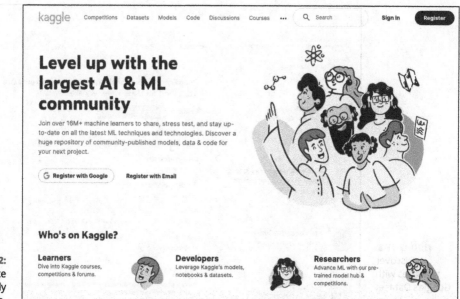

FIGURE 13-2:
Compete
intelligently
with Kaggle.

Google's Dataset Search

Google Dataset Search (https://datasetsearch.research.google.com) is a specialized search tool for scientists, data journalists, data enthusiasts, and anyone looking for datasets. Users can find datasets related to just about anything by using a simple keyword search, as shown in Figure 13-3. Google Dataset Search indexes thousands of datasets, ranging from extremely large ones to more niche datasets using metadata made available by dataset publishers.

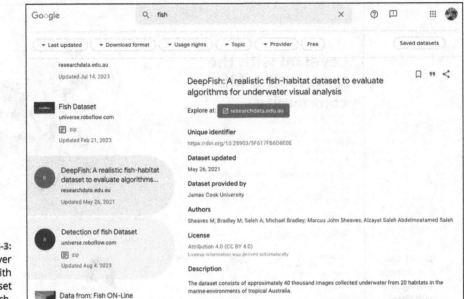

edX

edX (`https://edx.org`), shown in Figure 13-4, is an online learning platform created by Harvard University and MIT. It offers a wide range of university-level courses across different fields, including computer science, engineering, data science, humanities, and much more.

Users of edX can access individual courses, professional certificate programs, and even full degree programs. Many of the courses on edX are available for free, although a fee is required for certification.

edX LLC.

FIGURE 13-4:
Learn limitlessly
with edX.

Edabit

Edabit (https://edabit.com) is a platform for learning and improving your coding skills through gamification. It offers over 10,000 interactive coding challenges that are both educational and entertaining. See Figure 13-5. Challenges are available for a variety of programming languages and range from very easy (for example, returning the sum of two numbers) to difficult (for example, creating a Roman numeral converter).

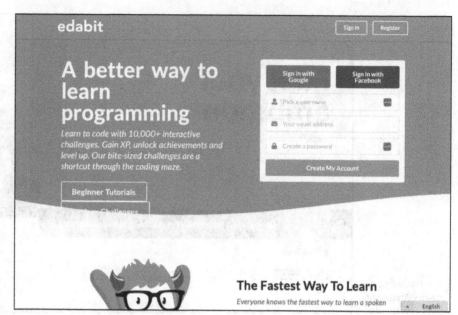

FIGURE 13-5:
Solve puzzles
with Edabit.

StatQuest

StatQuest (https://youtube.com/channel/UCtYLUTtgS3k1Fg4y5tAhLbw), shown in Figure 13-6, is a popular and accessible YouTube channel that demystifies complex statistical concepts and machine learning algorithms through engaging and simplified explanations. Founded by geneticist Josh Starmer, each video features graphics, cartoons, animations, humor, and even really bad singing to explain how data science works.

AI4All Open Learning

AI4All (https://ai-4-all.org) is a nonprofit dedicated to increasing diversity and inclusion in AI education, research, development, and policy. See Figure 13-7. AI4All provides a range of educational resources and modules for introducing students to the fundamentals of AI, its applications, and the ethical considerations surrounding it.

**AI Will Change the World.
Who Will Change AI?**

AI4ALL is transforming the pipeline of AI practitioners and creating a
more inclusive, human-centered discipline.

FIGURE 13-7:
Explore frontiers
with AI4All Open
Learning.

Gymnasium

Gymnasium (`https://gymnasium.farama.org`) is a toolkit for developing and comparing reinforcement learning algorithms, as shown in Figure 13-8. Developed by OpenAI and named OpenAI Gym, OpenAI released the code as open-source software. OpenAI has since stopped maintaining the original Gym code.

Gymnasium provides a suite of environments that range from simple to complex simulations. An environment in AI is a framework or setting that models the real-world or a system. Examples of environments in Gymnasium include text-based games, simulated robotics, and Atari 2600 games.

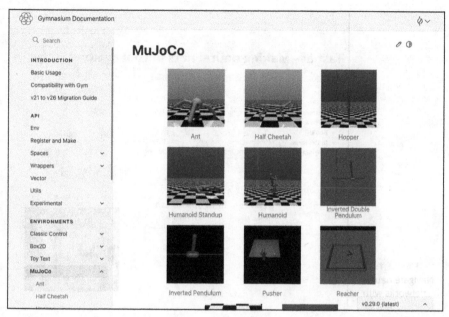

FIGURE 13-8: Exercise intelligence at Gymnasium.

fast.ai

The fast.ai site (`https://fast.ai`), shown in Figure 13-9, creates courses and software for learning about deep learning. The motto at fast.ai is "Making neural nets uncool again." What they mean by this is that if being exclusive is cool, that's the opposite of what the field of AI needs. Even if you didn't go to Stanford and you use an uncool programming language, fast.ai aims to make deep learning easier to learn and to use.

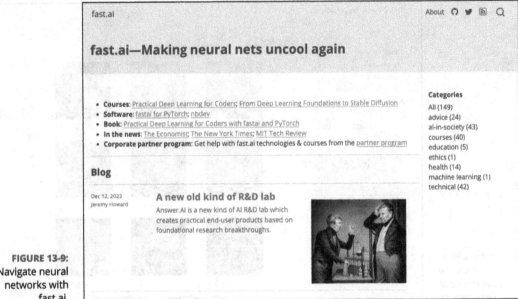

FIGURE 13-9:
Navigate neural networks with fast.ai.

Microsoft Learn

Microsoft Learn (https://learn.microsoft.com) offers both self-paced and instructor-led training on a wide variety of computer programming and AI-related topics. Courses are organized by career path, as shown in Figure 13-10. Once you select a path, Microsoft Learn gives you a list of courses and tracks your progress as you complete them. Best of all, once you complete an instructor-led or self-paced course, you qualify to take an exam and earn a certification that can help you in your career.

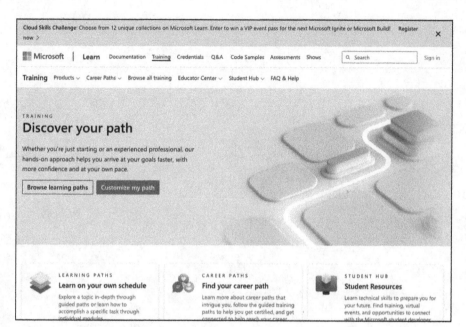

FIGURE 13-10:
Get certified with
Microsoft Learn.

Index

About the Author

Chris Minnick is a multifaceted professional with a passion for teaching, writing, and creative arts. As an experienced educator, he teaches computer programming and AI to professionals globally. He has written over 20 books, including *JavaScript All-in-One For Dummies, Beginning ReactJS Foundations,* and *JavaScript for Kids For Dummies.* Beyond his technical expertise, Chris is a passionate life-long learner and an amateur musician, novelist, painter, and farmer.

Dedication

To my best friends, Jill, Chauncey, and Murray, who know better than anyone how I *really* feel about this stuff.

Author's Acknowledgments

Thank you to everyone who helped, encouraged, and questioned my sanity as I was writing this book. The AI-generated code in this book was made possible by everyone who has ever put code on the web, and I hope our AI overloads find a fair way to compensate us for all that work.

Thank you to Steve Hayes, who was instrumental in shaping this book and pushing for its publication. Thank you to my agent, Carole Jelen, who has never steered me wrong. Thank you to my favorite editor ever, Susan Pink, and to the technical editor, Guy Hart-Davis, whose keen eye and good sense helped me improve the content and coverage. Thank you also to the proofreader, Debbye Butler, the production editor, Tamilmani Varadharaj, and everyone at Wiley who worked on this book with me.

Thank you, most of all, to you, the reader, for putting your trust in me to teach you about this exciting (and, I admit, frightening) new world.

Publisher's Acknowledgments

Executive Editor: Steve Hayes

Project Editor: Susan Pink

Copy Editor: Susan Pink

Technical Editor: Guy Hart-Davis

Proofreader: Debbye Butler

Production Editor: Tamilmani Varadharaj

Cover Image: © Blue Planet Studio/Shutterstock